TOP 10
BERLIN

JÜRGEN SCHEUNEMANN

Left **Berlin Reichstag** Right **A café in the Hackesche Höfe**

LONDON, NEW YORK,
MELBOURNE, MUNICH AND DELHI
www.dk.com

Produced by DK Verlag, Munich
Reproduced by Connecting People,
Starnberg & Colourscan, Singapore
Printed and bound in China by Leo
Paper Products Ltd

First published in Great Britain in 2002
by Dorling Kindersley Limited
80 Strand, London WC2R 0RL
A Penguin Company

**Reprinted with revisions 2006,
2007, 2008**
**Copyright 2002, 2008 © Dorling
Kindersley Limited, London**

ISBN: 978 1 40532 115 0

Contents

Berlin's Top 10

Left **"East Side Gallery" on the Berlin Wall** Right **Façade of a house in Prenzlauer Berg**

Left **The *Berlin* memorial on Tauentzienstraße** Right **The park of Schloss Sanssouci**

BERLIN'S
TOP 10

BERLIN'S TOP 10

TOP 10 Berlin Highlights

Berlin is Germany's liveliest city and one of the most fascinating capitals in the world. You'll find no other place where art and culture, museums and theatres, entertainment and nightlife are more diverse and exciting than on the banks of the Spree River. Once reunited, Berlin quickly developed into a cosmopolitan city, and today there is an air of energy and vibrancy about it.

1 Brandenburger Tor and Pariser Platz

The Brandenburger Tor, Berlin's most famous sight, is located in Pariser Platz, where the famous Hotel Adlon and the embassies breathe a modern, stylish elegance *(see pp8–9)*.

2 Reichstag

No other building is a more potent symbol of Germany's history than the Reichstag *(below)*. Since its redesign by Sir Norman Foster in 1997–9, the structure has become one of the most popular sights in Berlin. Visitors are attracted by its vast egg-shaped dome, affording fantastic views across the city *(see pp10–11)*.

3 Unter den Linden

The magnificent, tree-lined boulevard *(below)* in the eastern part of the city has always been a central axis. Berlin's most important historic buildings are assembled here *(see pp12–15)*.

4 Potsdamer Platz

The new heart of the old metropolis beats on Potsdamer Platz, where exciting new structures, such as the Sony Center, have been erected. With its restaurants, film museum, cinemas, shops and musical theatre it is a unique world of entertainment *(see pp16–9)*.

5 Pergamon-museum

Berlin's most impressive museum, a mecca for those interested in culture, houses the famous Pergamon Altar from ancient Greece (see pp20–23).

6 Kurfürsten-damm

Berlin's much visited strolling and shopping avenue is the main thoroughfare in the heart of the western city. New restaurants and stylish boutiques have increased the hustle and bustle along this grand boulevard (see pp24–5).

7 Kaiser-Wilhelm-Gedächtnis-Kirche

The tower ruins of the memorial church, built to commemorate Kaiser Wilhelm I, still stand today as a silent reminder of the horrors of war (see pp26–7).

9 Kulturforum

This complex of museums, which includes the famous Gemäldegalerie (gallery of paintings), the Kunstgewerbemuseum (museum of arts and crafts) and the Neue Nationalgalerie, as well as concert halls such as the Philharmonie, guarantees a unique cultural experience for visitors to Berlin (see pp32–5).

8 Schloss Charlottenburg

The historic rooms of the former Hohenzollern summer residence invite visitors to experience a slice of Prussian history, while the Baroque-style gardens, among the most beautiful in Germany, are perfect for strolling and sunbathing (see pp28–31).

10 Zoologischer Garten

Germany's oldest zoo and aquarium, in the centre of the city, is the largest animal park in the world, boasting some 14,000 animals and over 1,800 different species (see pp36–7).

Brandenburger Tor & Pariser Platz

The best known of Berlin's symbols, the Brandenburg Gate stands proudly in the middle of Pariser Platz, asserting itself against the hyper-modern embassy buildings that now surround it. Crowned by its triumphant Quadriga sculpture, the famous Gate has long been a focal point in Berlin's history: rulers and statesmen, military parades and demonstrations – all have felt compelled to march through the Brandenburger Tor.

The Brandenburg Gate seen from the east

○ One of the best spots for a coffee break in Pariser Platz is Café Meyerbeer, in the Palais am Pariser Platz. Don't miss its great cake display.

✔ A small exhibition, housed in the northern side wing of the Brandenburger Tor, tells the history of the Gate.

• Pariser Platz
• Map F3, K3

• Tourist information, Brandenburger Tor
• Map F3, K3
• Apr–Nov: 9:30am–6pm daily; Nov–Mar: 10am–6pm daily
• (030) 25 00 25

Top 10 Sights

1. Brandenburger Tor
2. Quadriga
3. Hotel Adlon Berlin
4. DG Bank
5. Akademie der Künste
6. French Embassy
7. Palais am Pariser Platz
8. Eugen-Gutmann-Haus
9. Haus Liebermann
10. American Embassy

Brandenburger Tor

Since its restoration in 2002, Berlin's symbol is now lit up more brightly than ever before. Built by Carl G Langhans in 1789–91 and modelled on the temple porticos of ancient Athens, the Gate has, since the 19th century, been the backdrop for many events in the city's turbulent history.

Quadriga

The sculpture, 6 m (20 ft) high above the Gate, was created in 1794 by Johann Gottfried Schadow as a symbol of peace. As a model for the laurel-crowned goddess of peace in the chariot, Schadow used his niece, who subsequently became famous throughout Berlin.

Hotel Adlon Berlin

Completed in 1997 and now favoured by visiting dignitaries, Berlin's most elegant hotel is a reconstruction of the original Hotel Adlon. This legendary hotel, destroyed in World War II, was host to the rich and famous, including Greta Garbo, Thomas Mann and Charlie Chaplin *(see p72)*.

DG Bank

This modern building, designed by the American architect Frank Owen Gehry, combines the clean lines of Prussian architecture with some daring elements.

Akademie der Künste
The new building, erected between 2000 and 2005 by Günter Behnisch and Manfred Sabatke, incorporates behind a vast expanse of windows the ruins of the old art academy, which was destroyed in World War II. Today it is the home of the Academy of the Arts of the Province of Berlin-Brandenburg.

French Embassy
In 1999–2001, an elegant new building was constructed by Christian de Portzamparc, on the site of the old embassy, which was destroyed in World War II. Its colonnades and tall windows, a homage to the former French Embassy palace, are particularly remarkable and worth seeing.

Palais am Pariser Platz
This complex by Bernhard Winking, a successful modern interpretation of Neo-Classical architecture, is slightly hidden to the north of the Brandenburger Tor. It is worth venturing inside where you will find a café, a restaurant and a souvenir shop around a pleasantly shaded courtyard.

Eugen-Gutmann-Haus
With its clean lines, the Dresdner Bank, built in the round by the Hamburg architects' team gmp in 1996–7, recalls the style of the New Sobriety movement of the 1920s. In front of the building, which serves as the Berlin headquarters of the Dresdner Bank, stands the famous original street sign for the Pariser Platz.

Haus Liebermann
Josef Paul Kleihues erected this building at the north end of the Brandenburger Tor in 1996–8, faithfully recreating an earlier building on the same site. The house is named after the artist Max Liebermann *(right)*, who lived here. In 1933, watching Nazi SA troops march through the Gate, he famously said: "I cannot possibly eat as much as I would want to puke out."

American Embassy
The last gap in the line of buildings around Pariser Platz was finally closed in late 2007. A dispute between the embassy and the Berlin Senate delayed building for several years: an entire street was to be moved to satisfy the USA's security requirements. But in the end, the historical street stayed where it was.

For more on historical architecture in Berlin **see pp38–9**

🔟 Reichstag

Of all the buildings in Berlin, the Parliamentary Building is probably one of the most symbolic. The mighty structure, erected in 1884–94 by Paul Wallot as the proud manifestation of the power of the German Reich, was destroyed by arson in 1933 and bombed during World War II. In 1996, the artist Christo wrapped up the Reichstag and, in 1994–9, the British architect Sir Norman Foster transformed it into one of the most modern parliamentary buildings in the world. Today it is the official seat of the Bundestag, the German parliament.

Main entrance of the Reichstag

🍴 If a meal at the Käfer restaurant exceeds your budget, many stalls in the vicinity of the Reichstag sell hot dogs.

⌚ Large numbers of visitors come to see the Reichstag cupola. It is best to avoid weekends or to start queuing half an hour before the opening time. Tuesday is the quietest day.

- Platz der Republik 1
- Map F3, K2
- Open 8am–midnight (last admission 10pm)
- (030) 22 73 21 52
- www.bundestag.de

Top 10 Sights

1. The Cupola
2. Plenary Hall
3. Portico "Dem deutschen Volke"
4. Restored Façade
5. Restaurant Käfer
6. Installation "Der Bevölkerung"
7. Memorial for Delegates to the Reichstag
8. German Flag
9. Platz der Republik
10. Memorial for Victims of the Wall

The Cupola
The new Reichstag cupola by Sir Norman Foster affords breathtaking views of Berlin. It is open at the top to air the building and – a touch of irony here – to allow for the dissemination of debates throughout the country. A ramp winds its way up to the top.

Plenary Hall
The newly designed plenary hall is the seat of the Deutscher Bundestag, the German parliament, which has convened here again since 20 April 1999. Technologically, the hall is one of the most advanced in the world. The federal eagle caused a row: considered too "fat", it had to be slimmed down.

Portico "Dem deutschen Volke"
The dedication "To the German People" was designed in 1916, against the will of Wilhelm II.

Restored Façade
Despite extensive renovations, small bullet holes from World War II are still visible in the building's façade.

Restaurant Käfer
This luxury restaurant next to the cupola on the Reichstag's roof offers an excellent view of the historical centre of Unter den Linden. It is very popular and you may well have to wait for a seat *(see p101)*.

Installation "Der Bevölkerung"
Hans Haacke's work of art "To the People" is a counterpoint to the portico inscription opposite.

Memorial by Dieter Appett
Unveiled in 1992, the memorial commemorates 97 Social Democratic and Communist Reichstag delegates who were murdered under the Third Reich.

The German Flag
The giant German flag was first raised on the occasion of the official national celebrations of German reunification on 3 October 1990.

Platz der Republik
Celebrations often take place on the lawn in front of the Reichstag, most recently in 1996, when the building was wrapped up by Christo.

Memorial for Victims of the Wall
Opposite the southern side of the Reichstag, a memorial recalls the Berlin Wall, which ran only a few steps away from this spot. One of the crosses commemorates Chris Gueffroy: shot in February 1989 when trying to escape, he was one of more than 100 people who died at the Wall.

The Reichstag Fire

When the Reichstag went up in flames on 27 February 1933, the Dutch Communist van der Lubbe was arrested and charged with arson. It is, however, much more likely that the Nazis had started the fire themselves. Adolf Hitler used the Reichstag fire as a pretext to get the "Enabling Act" passed by parliament. This allowed him to dispose of all his opponents, marking the beginning of a 12-year reign of terror.

Berlin governmental buildings **see pp40–1**

Unter den Linden

"As long as the lime trees still blossom in Unter den Linden, Berlin will always be Berlin," Marlene Dietrich once sang about this magnificent avenue. Today the lime trees blossom more beautifully than ever in the historical centre of Berlin, because the old buildings along the street have been extensively restored and modern architecture has created new highlights. The "Linden" – originally a royal bridle-path linking the Stadtschloss (the king's town residence) and Tiergarten – became Berlin's most fashionable street in the 18th century, and was synonymous with the city that was then the capital of Prussia.

Deutsches Historisches Museum in the Zeughaus

The largest selection of cakes in Berlin tempts visitors in the Café im Opernpalais. In summer, you can enjoy them outside.

- Map F/G3, K3/4

- Deutsches Historisches Museum, Unter den Linden 2 • 10am–6pm daily • (030) 20 30 40 • www.dhm.de • Admission charge

- St Hedwigskathedrale, Bebelplatz • 10am–5pm Mon–Sat, 1–5pm Sun • (030) 203 48 10 • www.hedwigs-kathedrale.de

- Staatsoper, Unter den Linden 7 • Box Office 10am–8pm Mon–Fri, 2–8pm Sun • (030) 20 35 45 55 • www.staatsoper-berlin.de • Admission charge

Top 10 Sights

1. Deutsches Historisches Museum in the Zeughaus
2. Staatsoper Unter den Linden
3. St Hedwigskathedrale
4. Humboldt-Universität
5. Neue Wache
6. Kronprinzenpalais
7. Bebelplatz
8. Opernpalais
9. Russian Embassy
10. Frederick the Great's Statue

St Hedwigs-kathedrale

Designed by Georg W von Knobelsdorff in 1740–2 and modelled on the Pantheon in Rome, this is the seat of the Catholic archdiocese in Berlin. Frederick the Great commissioned the cathedral to appease Catholics in Berlin after conquering Silesia *(see p44)*.

Deutsches Historisches Museum

Germany's largest history museum, reopened in 2003, provides an overview of more than 1,000 years of German history. Housed in the Zeughaus – the royal arsenal built in 1706 – it is the oldest and, architecturally, the most interesting building in the avenue Unter den Linden *(see p14)*.

Staatsoper Unter den Linden

The richly ornamented State Opera House is one of Germany's most attractive. Neo-Classical in style, it was built by von Knobelsdorff in 1741–3 as Europe's first free-standing opera house, to plans devised by Frederick the Great himself *(see p56)*.

Buses No. 100 and No. 200 run along the entire length of Unter den Linden, with bus stops at nearly all the famous sights.

Humboldt-Universität
Berlin's oldest and most highly regarded university was founded in 1890, on the initiative of Wilhelm von Humboldt. Twenty-nine Nobel Prize winners were educated here, including Albert Einstein.

Neue Wache
The central German memorial for all victims of war was created in the years 1816–8 and designed by Karl Friedrich Schinkel. An enlarged reproduction of the moving *Pietà* sculpture by Käthe Kollwitz stands in the centre of the room.

Kronprinzenpalais
The Neo-Classical Palais, built in 1732–3 by Philipp Gerlach, was originally a residence for the heirs to the Hohenzollern throne. After World War I it became an art museum, and after 1948 the East German government housed state visitors there. Until 2003 it was used for exhibitions of the Deutsches Historisches Museum opposite.

Bebelplatz
Originally named Opernplatz, this wide, open space was designed by Georg W von Knobelsdorff as the focal point of his Forum Fridericianum. The elegant square was meant to introduce some of the splendour and glory of ancient Rome to the Prussian capital. In May 1933, it became the scene of the infamous Nazi book burning.

Opernpalais
The charming building next to the Staatsoper, built in 1733–7, served as a palace for the princesses

Russische Botschaft
The gigantic Russian Embassy, built in Stalinist "wedding-cake style", was the first building to be constructed in Unter den Linden after World War II *(see also p118)*.

Frederick the Great's Statue
One of Christian Daniel Rauch's grandest sculptures, this statue shows the "Old Fritz" (13.5 m/ 45 ft high) on horseback, wearing a uniform and tricorn hat *(see also p113)*.

Old print roll from 1821 with views of the avenue Unter den Linden

Deutsches Historisches Museum

1 The Dying Warriors
The 22 reliefs by Andreas Schlüter, displayed on the walls of the courtyard rather than in one of the museum's exhibitions, portray the horrors of war in an unusually immediate way.

2 Martin Luther
Luther's portrait, by Lucas Cranach the Elder, is the focal point of exhibition rooms devoted to Martin Luther and the Reformation.

3 Europe and Asia
This group of Meissen porcelain figures reflects the fascinating relationship between the two continents.

4 Steam Engine
A full-sized steam engine from the year 1847 marks the entrance to the exhibition on the Industrial Revolution.

5 Clothes from the Camps
Among the many exhibits illustrating the years under Nazi rule is the jacket of a concentration camp inmate –a chilling reminder of the Third Reich.

6 Gloria Victis
The moving allegorical figure of Gloria Victis, created by the French sculptor Antonin Mercié, bears witness to the death of a friend during the final days of the Franco-Prussian War of 1870–1.

Gloria Victis Statue

7 Soldiers Plundering a House
This painting by Sebastian Vrancx, dating from around 1600, depicts a scene from the wars of religion that tore the Netherlands apart during the 16th century.

8 Saddle
A valuable saddle, dating from the middle of the 15th century, is decorated with elaborately carved plaques made of ivory.

9 The Berlin Wall
An original section of the Wall, together with the banners of a peaceful pro-unification demonstration in 1989, commemorates the fall of the Berlin Wall.

10 V2 Rocket
In the section on Nazi Germany is a V2 rocket engine – next to an 88-mm flak gun. The V2 was one of the *Wunderwaffen* ("wonder weapons") used at the end of World War II.

Portrait of Martin Luther in the Zeughaus

Top 10 Events

Zeughaus Unter den Linden

Schlüter's "Dying Warrior"

Originally the royal arsenal, the Zeughaus was built in 1706 in the Baroque style according to plans by Johann Arnold Nering. It is an impressive structure, with its main and side wings surrounding an historical central courtyard that is protected by a modern glass cupola roof. Especially memorable are Andreas Schlüter's figures of 22 dying warriors, lined up along the arcades in the courtyard. They portray vividly the horrors of war.

A cone-shaped glass annex, erected by the Chinese-born architect Ieoh Ming Pei in 2001 for special exhibitions and temporary shows, stands behind the museum.

The permanent exhibition in the main historical building includes a collection entitled "Images and Testimonials of German History". Highlighting the most important periods and events in the history of the country, the displays include a surprising variety of exhibits dating back to the days of the early Medieval German Empire through the period of the Reformation and the Thirty Years' War as well as the wars of Liberation and the failed Revolution of 1848, right up to the two World Wars and more recent events of the 20th century up to 1994.

The opening of the Reichstag in the White Salon of Berlin Schloss on 25 June 1888

Potsdamer Platz

The heart of the new metropolis of Berlin beats on Potsdamer Platz. This square, where Berliners and tourists alike now flock to cinemas, restaurants and shops, was already a hub of urban life in the 1920s. After World War II, it became a desolate wasteland, but since the fall of the Berlin Wall, Potsdamer Platz – for a long time Europe's largest building site – has become a city within the city, surrounded by imposing buildings erected in the last ten years, and still being added to today.

Reconstruction of the first traffic lights in Europe

Apart from visiting the famous Café Josty, make sure you do not miss Diekmann in the Weinhaus Huth.

- Potsdamer Platz
- Map F4, L2/3

- Deutsche Kinemathek
- Potsdamer Str. 2
- 10am–6pm Tue–Sun, 10am–8pm Thu
- (030) 300 90 30
- Admission charge

- Theater am Postdamer Platz
- Marlene-Dietrich-Platz 1
- 8pm daily
- Admission charge

- Spielbank Berlin
- Marlene-Dietrich-Platz 1
- 11:30–3am daily
- (030) 25 59 90
- Admission charge

- Cinemaxx
- Voxstr. 2
- 12:30pm–1:30am daily
- (01805) 246 36 299
- Admission charge

Top 10 Sights

1. Sony Center
2. Deutsche Kinemathek
3. Café Josty
4. Weinhaus Huth
5. Marlene-Dietrich-Platz
6. Potsdamer Platz Arkaden
7. Spielbank Berlin
8. Cinemaxx
9. DaimlerChrysler Quartier
10. Theater am Potsdamer Platz

Sony Center

The Sony Center *(right)* is the most ambitious, successful and architecturally interesting building in the new Berlin. The cupola structure, designed by Helmut Jahn and opened in 2000, is the European headquarters of the Sony company, and with its cinemas and restaurants it is also a social magnet.

Deutsche Kinemathek

This museum takes you backstage in the Hollywood and Babelsberg film studios. Exhibits include Marlene Dietrich's costumes *(see p18)*.

Café Josty

Café Josty harkens back to its legendary predecessor, a regular haunt for artists and intellectuals in the 19th century. The new Café Josty is partially housed in the historic Kaisersaal (Emperor's Hall) of the former Grand Hotel Esplanade.

Weinhaus Huth

The only building on Potsdamer Platz to have survived World War II, the Weinhaus today accommodates restaurants and the fascinating art gallery of the DaimlerChrysler company.

The best time to visit the Sony Center is in the early evening, when the inside of the Plaza is lit up.

Marlene-Dietrich-Platz

This square in front of the Stella-Musical-Theater is dedicated to the great actress. A brash *Flower Balloon* (left), by the artist Jeff Koons, enlivens the centre of the square.

Locator Map

Potsdamer Platz Arkaden

The arcades draw visitors with over 130 shops, exclusive boutiques and popular restaurants on three storeys. The lower ground floor is a food court, serving dishes from around the world.

Spielbank Berlin

Berlin's casino *(below)* invites visitors to *faites vos jeux*. Apart from roulette, Black Jack is also played, and an entire floor is given over to gambling machines.

Cinemaxx

The Cinemaxx on Potsdamer Platz with its 17 screens is one of Berlin's largest cinemas. The bigger screens of the multiplex cinema show current Hollywood blockbusters, while the three smallest screens are for viewings of low-budget and German films. There is also a small bar serving drinks.

DaimlerChrysler Quartier

The Berlin headquarters of the famous car manufacturer was designed by Hans Kollhoff and Renzo Piano. Daimler's former software company, debis, was based in the building shown *left*.

Theater am Potsdamer Platz

Berlin's largest show stage, this venue has shown hits such as *The Hunchback of Notre Dame* and *The Blue Man Group*. The 1,300-seat theatre is often sold out.

For more on the Filmmuseum see pp18–9

17

Left **S-Bahn sign** Centre **Café Josty sign** Right **Arty bears on Potsdamer Platz**

🔟 Exhibitions in the Kinemathek

Film poster

1 Marlene Dietrich
This exhibition of the film star's estate includes costumes, touring luggage, photographs, letters and notes, posters and film clips.

2 Metropolis
This film, directed by Fritz Lang in 1927, has an alarming vision of a future world as its subject. Models and props from the film are on display.

3 Caligari
The best known German film of the 1920s, *The Cabinet of Dr Caligari* (1920), was a masterpiece of Expressionist filmmaking by Robert Wiene.

4 Leni Riefenstahl
This exhibition reveals the technical tricks used in the Nazi propaganda film *Olympia,* made by Leni Riefenstahl in 1936–8.

5 Film and National Socialism
This exhibition features documents relating to the propaganda uses of film, everyday cinema and the industry's victims: some film stars allowed themselves to be used by the Nazis, others refused to cooperate. The life and work of the actor Kurt Gerron, who was persecuted and murdered, is documented as an exemplary case.

6 Post-War Cinema
The story of films and filmmaking in East and West Germany, with props and costumes of popular stars of post-war German cinema such as Hanna Schygulla, Romy Schneider, Heinz Rühmann and Mario Adorf.

7 Artificial Worlds
The tricks employed by special effects studios, ranging from the first effects of the 1930s to computer animation.

8 Transatlantic
This exhibition of documents, letters, keepsakes and souvenirs retraces the careers of German film stars in Hollywood.

9 Pioneers and Divas
The infant days of cinema are featured here – as well as stars of the silent era such as Henny Porten and Asta Nielsen.

10 Exile
Documents relate the difficulties encountered by German filmmakers when making a new start in the USA in 1933–45.

Façade of the Kinemathek

For more on Berlin museums see pp46–7

Europe's largest building site

In the 1920s, Potsdamer Platz was Europe's busiest square, boasting the first automatic traffic lights in the world. During World War II this social hub was razed to the ground. Untouched for almost 50 years, the empty square shifted back into the centre of Berlin when the Wall came down. During the 1990s, Potsdamer Platz became Europe's largest building site – millions of curious onlookers from around the world came to watch progress from the famous red info box. Altogether, around 17 billion euros were invested to create the present square.

DaimlerChrysler House

Moving the Esplanade

The Senate of Berlin stipulated that Sony should preserve the "Breakfast Room" and the "Emperors' Hall" of the Grand Hotel Esplanade, both protected following destruction in World War II. Accordingly, in 1996, the rooms were moved – 1,300 tons were loaded onto wheels and shifted by 75 m (246 ft) during the course of a week.

The historic Emperors' Hall is today incorporated into the modern Sony Center

🔟 Pergamonmuseum

The Pergamonmuseum is one of the most important museums of ancient art and architecture in the world. The museum was built in 1909–30 by Alfred Messel and Ludwig Hoffmann to house Berlin's collection of antiquities as well as vast temples and palace rooms in their original size. These works of art, excavated by German archaeologists in the Near East at the end of the 19th century, were shown here for the first time.

Main entrance of the Pergamonmuseum

🍴 On the Museumsinsel there is a café at the Bode-Museum (Antique Sculpture Collections) and also at the Altes Museum (Egyptian Museum), which is a little closer to the Karl-Liebknecht-Straße.

☑ Visitors wishing to explore all the museums on Museumsinsel on the same day, should buy a day ticket for €12. However, Sundays are generally best avoided because of the long queues and large groups of visitors.

• Museumsinsel, Bodestr. 1–3 (entrance Am Kupfergraben)
• Map G3, J5
• (030) 209 055 77
• www.smb.museum
• 10am–6pm Mon–Sun, 6–10pm Thu
• Admission charge

Top 10 Exhibits

1. Pergamon Altar
2. Market Gate of Miletus
3. Assyrian Palace
4. Ishtar Gate
5. Goddess Persephone
6. Goddess Athena
7. Aleppo Room
8. Roman Mosaic
9. Palace of Mshatta
10. Temple of Athena

1 Pergamon Altar

The colossal Pergamon Altar, dating from the year 160 BC, is the largest and most important treasure of the Berlin museums. The altar was part of a much larger temple complex in the Greek town of Pergamon (today the town of Bergama in Turkey), excavated in the 19th century by the German archaeologist Carl Humann *(see also pp22–3)*.

2 Market Gate of Miletus

This vast gate (AD 120) is over 16 m (52 ft) high. To the right of the entrance, a hairdresser has carved an advertisement for his shop into the stone.

3 Assyrian Palace

The interior of this palace from the days of the Assyrian kings (12th century BC) has been completely restored and boasts impressive statues of lions.

4 Ishtar Gate

The imposing Ishtar Gate and the Processional Way that led to it are fully preserved. The original avenue in ancient Babylon was 180 m (590 ft) long. The gate was built in the 6th century BC, during the reign of Nebuchadnezar II. Original faïence wall tiles depict the sacred lions.

For more on Berlin museums see pp46–7

Goddess Persephone
The 5th-century BC Greek statue *(left)* of the goddess of the underworld sports a mysterious smile, the expressive symbol of her divinity.

Goddess Athena
The beauty ideal prevalent in Greek antiquity is perfectly reflected in this statue's features. It is one of many valuable and impressive sculptures worth exploring in the collection of antiquities.

Key to plan

	Antiquities (ground floor)
	Islamic Art (first floor)

Aleppo Room
Dating from the early 17th century, this small room features magnificent wooden cladding taken from the house of a Christian merchant's family in Syria. A beautiful example of Ottoman architecture, the room originally served as a reception hall.

Roman mosaic
This magnificently executed Roman floor mosaic dates back to the 3rd or 4th century AD. It was excavated in Gerasa in Jordan.

Palace of Mshatta
A gift from Sultan Hamid I to Kaiser Wilhelm II, this desert palace, built in AD 744 in Jordan, has an elaborately decorated southern façade.

Temple of Athena
Dedicated to Athena of Nikephoros, this full-scale temple from the 2nd century BC has a simple yet elegant design.

A Roman sarcophagus from the 2nd century AD, showing scenes from the story of Medea

🔟 Figures on the Pergamon Altar

1 Eastern Altar Frieze
The eastern side of the altar frieze – the side first lit up by the rising sun – depicts the battle between the gods and the giants.

2 The God Apollo on the Eastern Frieze
Like no other deity on the altar, the god Apollo is depicted as a noble man of ideal beauty, thus bearing witness to the artistic mastery of Classical sculpture in Greece.

3 The Titaness Phoebe
An impressive figure depicted on the southern frieze, Phoebe is shown, with her daughter Asteria, fighting an enormous giant with a torch, sword and lance.

4 Zeus in Battle
On the eastern frieze, the father of all the gods on Mount Olympus fights three giants at the same time. Zeus is armed for this battle with his most dangerous weapons – thunder and lightning.

The goddess Athena in the altar frieze

5 The Goddess Athena
The goddess Athena is also shown on the eastern frieze, as a powerful figure of light who drags her opponents to their deaths by their hair.

Athena

6 The Gods of the Sea
Three pairs of sea gods are depicted on the staircase frieze (on the northern staircase): Doris and Nereus, Oceanus and Tethys as well as Triton and Amphitrite.

7 The Goddess Aphrodite
Victorious, the fighting goddess rises proudly above two dead giants.

8 Statues of Women
Larger-than-life figures of women, found near the altar in the excavations, are displayed in front of the Pergamon Altar.

9 The Beisser Group
The so-called Beisser Group on the northern frieze is a group of unknown deities. One god, almost defeated, desperately tries to fight off a giant who has clamped his teeth into his arm.

10 Telephos Frieze
The frieze in the upper altar courtyard depicts Telephos, son of Hercules. The kings of Pergamon thought themselves to be descended from Telephos and worshipped him accordingly.

For more on Berlin museums see pp46–7

Saving the Museumsinsel

The "island of museums" is a treasury of antique architecture – yet it was slowly decaying. Since 1992 a total of 1.6 billion euros has been spent on the renovation and modernization of Museumsinsel. A "master plan" was hatched by renowned

The Palace of Mshatta

architects, such as David Chipperfield and O M Ungers, which would transform the complex into a unique museum landscape – just as it had first been conceived in the 19th century by Friedrich Wilhelm IV, when he established the "free instutition for art and the sciences". By 2014, all museums will be linked by an "architectural promenade", creating a conceptual as well as a structural link between the various parts. This promenade will consist of a variety of light rooms, courtyards and vaults as well as new exhibition halls. The core of the complex will be a new central entrance building. Once renovated, the museums will gradually reopen – the Alte Nationalgalerie opened in 2001 and the Egyptian collection returned to the Altes Museum in 2005. The Museumsinsel is now a UNESCO World Heritage Site.

Pergamon and Asia Minor

From 241 until 133 BC, the antique city of Pergamon was the capital of the Hellenistic Pergamenian Empire, ruling the northwestern region of Asia Minor. Apart from many temples, the town, which is now known as Bergama, and is in Turkey, also boasted a famous library.

A 17th-century carpet with floral motifs from western Anatolia

🔟 Kurfürstendamm

After years of decline, the Kurfürstendamm, or Ku'damm for short, has once again become a fashionable hot spot. Breathtaking architecture, elegant boutiques and a lively scene with street artists around Breitscheidplatz have made this shopping boulevard Berlin's most attractive and – at 3.8 km (2.5 miles) – also its longest avenue for strolling.

Corner of Kurfürstendamm and Joachimsthaler Straße

🔵 Only a few cafés in the Ku'damm have survived: the most charming is Café Wintergarten in the Literaturhaus at the southern end of Fasanenstraße.

🕐 It is best to avoid Ku'damm on Saturday mornings when the boulevard is teeming with locals and tourists out on shopping trips.

• Map B/C5, P3/4

• Tourist information
• Neues Kranzler-Eck, Kurfürstendamm 21
• Mon–Sat 10am–8pm Sun 10am–6pm daily
• (030) 25 00 25

• Story of Berlin, Kurfürstendamm 207–8
• 10am–8pm daily (last admission at 6pm)
• (030) 88 72 01 00
• www.story-of-berlin.de

• Europa-Center, Tauentzienstr. 9
• 24 hours (shops: 10am–8pm)
• (030) 348 00 88
• www.24EC.de

Top 10 Sights

1. Breitscheidplatz
2. Kaiser-Wilhelm-Gedächtnis-Kirche
3. Europa-Center
4. Neues Kranzler-Eck
5. Fasanenstraße
6. Ku'damm-Eck
7. Lehniner Platz
8. The Story of Berlin
9. Galerie Brusberg
10. Iduna-Haus

Breitscheidplatz
Here, in the heart of the city, artists, Berliners and visitors swarm around J Schmettan's globe fountain, known by locals as "Wasserklops" (water meatball).

Kaiser-Wilhelm-Gedächtnis-Kirche
One of Berlin's most haunting symbols, the tower of the original church – destroyed during World War II – stands in the centre of Breitscheidplatz, serving as both memorial and reminder of the terrors of war *(see p26)*.

Europa-Center
The oldest shopping centre in West Berlin, originally opened in 1962, is still worth a visit. You will find a variety of shops, including a grocery store, a cinema and fashion boutiques.

Ku'damm: www.kurfuerstendamm.de

Neues Kranzler-Eck
4 This glass and steel skyscraper was built in 2000 by the architect Helmut Jahn. The legendary Café Kranzler was retained as a bar in front of the office block *(see pp86–7)*. You will also find the tourist information centre here *(see p163)*.

Fasanenstraße
5 A small street off Ku'damm, Fasanenstraße with its galleries, expensive shops and restaurants is one of Charlottenburg's most elegant areas *(see pp80–1)*.

Ku'damm-Eck
6 This hotel and business complex (2001) has endowed the boulevard with new splendour *(right)*.

Lehniner Platz
7 The square is home to the Schaubühne, built as Universum cinema in 1928 by Erich Mendelsohn, converted in 1978.

The Story of Berlin
8 This interesting multi-media show takes visitors on a tour of 800 years of Berlin's history – from the Great Elector to the capital of Prussia, from Willy Brandt to the Fall of the Wall. Underneath the museum a nuclear bunker can be visited.

Galerie Brusberg
9 This Neo-Classical building *(right)* provides a glimpse of Ku'damm's erstwhile splendour.

Iduna-Haus
10 The remarkable turreted house at this street corner *(left)* is one of few bourgeois houses preserved from the late 19th century. The richly ornamented, gleaming white Art Nouveau façade has been lavishly restored.

When Ku'damm was no more than a log road

In 1542, today's magnificent boulevard was just a humble "Knüppeldamm," or log road. It served the Electors as a bridle path, linking the town residence (Stadtschloss) and their hunting lodge (Jagdschloss). It was not until 1871 that the area around the Ku'damm developed into a fashionable "new west end". Chancellor Otto von Bismarck had the boulevard modelled on the Champs Elysées in Paris, and requested that his statue be erected in the street as a thank you. So far, however, the Berliners have failed to oblige him.

TOP 10 Kaiser-Wilhelm-Gedächtnis-Kirche

One of the most haunting symbols of Berlin, the ruins of the memorial church in the heart of the city's West End, have been irreverently nicknamed "the hollow tooth". The Neo-Romanesque church was given the name of Kaiser Wilhelm Memorial Church in 1895, to honour Wilhelm I. Following damage by severe bombing raids in 1943, the ruins of the tower were left standing as a memorial. Next to it, Egon Eiermann erected a new church in 1957–63. Religious services are now conducted here.

The "hollow tooth" – the Tower Ruins

There are fantastic views of the church from the Mövenpick Café in the Europa-Center opposite.

If possible, visit the interior of the new church on a sunny day around lunchtime, when the blue glass window is at its most impressive.

- Breitscheidplatz
- Map D4, N4 • www.gedaechtniskirche.com
- (030) 218 50 23
- Church 9am–7pm, memorial hall 10am–6:30pm Mon–Sat
- Services 10am and 6pm Sun
- Admission free

Top 10 Sights

1. Tower Ruins
2. Kaiser's Mosaic
3. Mosaic of the Hohenzollerns
4. Coventry Crucifix
5. New Bell Tower
6. Main Altar
7. Tower Clock
8. The Orthodox Cross
9. Original Mosaics
10. Figure of Christ

Kaiser's Mosaic

One of the mosaics that have been preserved depicts Emperor Heinrich I on his throne, with imperial orb and sceptre *(below)*. Originally decorated throughout with scenes from German imperial history, the church interior was meant to place the Hohenzollerns within this tradition.

Tower Ruins

Only the tower of the memorial church survived the destruction of World War II that razed much of the city to the ground. Today only 63 m (206 ft) high, it once rose to 113 m (370 ft). The hole in the tower's roof has a sharply ragged edge which is why the tower was nicknamed "hollow tooth" by the Berliners.

Mosaic of the Hohenzollerns

The surprisingly coloured mosaic of the Hohenzollerns adorns the vestibule of the church ruins. It depicts Emperor Wilhelm I together with Queen Luise of Prussia and her entourage.

Coventry Crucifix

This small crucifix was forged from old nails that were found in the ruins of Coventry Cathedral. It commemorates the bombing of Coventry, England, by the German Luftwaffe in 1940.

New Bell Tower

The new hexagonal bell tower rises 53 m (174 ft) high next to the tower ruins, on the site of the old church's main nave.

Main Altar

The golden figure of Christ created by Karl Hemmeter is suspended above the modern main altar in the new church. In the evening light, the windows behind the altar glow an overwhelming dark blue.

Tower Clock

The tower bears a clock based on a Classical design, with Roman numerals. At night, it is lit in blue by modern light-emitting diodes to match the lighting inside the new church.

The Orthodox Cross

A gift from the Russian Orthodox bishops of Volokolomsk and Yuruyev, this cross was given in memory of the victims of Nazism.

A Church with Two Lives

The Kaiser-Wilhelm-Gedächtnis-Kirche has the Berliners to thank for its preservation: in 1947, the Senate had planned to demolish the Tower Ruins for safety reasons. In a referendum only about ten years later, however, one in two Berliners voted for its preservation. And so the idea came about to build a new church next to the ruin and to preserve the vestibule of the old church as a striking memorial hall to the horrors of war.

Original Mosaics

Mosaics showing Prussian dukes are preserved on the walls and ceilings all along the stairways.

Figure of Christ

Miraculously, the vast, plain sculpture of Christ, which is suspended from the ceiling, survived the bombing of the church.

For more on Berlin churches see pp44–5

Schloss Charlottenburg

The construction of Schloss Charlottenburg, designed as a summer residence for Sophie Charlotte, wife of the Elector Friedrich III, began in 1695. Between 1701 and 1713 Johann Friedrich Eosander added a cupola and the Orangerie was extended. Today, it has been extensively renovated.

Schloss Charlottenburg

🍴 The Orangery Café (left of the main entrance) has an attractive garden.

⭐ At weekends, the palace park is overcrowded, but a midweek early-evening stroll can be very romantic (open till 8pm).

• Spandauer Damm
• Map A/B3 • Admission charge in all museums
• Two-day ticket for all museums: €12
• Altes Schloss • 9am–5pm Tue–Sun • Neuer Flügel • Apr–Oct: 10am–5pm Tue–Sun; Nov–Mar: 11am–5pm Tue–Sun
• (030) 32 09 451

• Belvedere • Apr–Oct: noon–5pm Tue–Fri, 10am–5pm Sat & Sun; Nov–Mar: noon–4pm Tue–Sun

• Neuer Pavillon
• 10am–5pm Tue–Sun
• (030) 32 09 451

• Mausoleum • Apr–Oct: 10am–5pm Tue–Sun
• (030) 32 09 14 46

• Museum für Vor- und Frühgeschichte
• 9am– 5pm Tue–Fri, 10am–5pm Sat, Sun
• (030) 326 74 80

Top 10 Sights

1. Altes Schloss
2. Porzellankabinett
3. Schlosskapelle
4. Monument to the Great Elector
5. Neuer Flügel
6. Schlossgarten
7. Belvedere
8. Neuer Pavillon
9. Mausoleum
10. Museum für Vor- und Frühgeschichte

Altes Schloss
The Baroque tower of the oldest part of the palace (1695) by Johann Arnold Nering is crowned by Richard Scheibe's golden statue of Fortuna.

Porzellankabinett
The small, exquisite mirrored gallery has been faithfully restored to its original glory. Valuable porcelain items from China and Japan are on display.

Schlosskapelle
The luxurious splendour of the palace chapel recalls the once magnificent interior design of the palace, before it was destroyed in World War II. But appearances can be deceptive: apart from the altar which is preserved in its original form, the entire chapel – including the king's box – is a costly reconstruction.

Monument to the Great Elector 4

The equestrian monument of Friedrich Wilhelm I is considered to be one of his most dignified portraits. Made in 1696–1703 by Andreas Schlüter, it originally stood on the Rathausbrücke, near the destroyed Stadtschloss.

Palace Layout

Neuer Flügel 5

Built between 1740 and 1747 by Georg Wenzeslaus von Knobelsdorff, the new wing contains Frederick the Great's private quarters.

Schlosspark 6

The palace park, originally Baroque in style, was redesigned by Peter Joseph Lenné between 1818 and 1828 as an English-style landscape garden.

Belvedere 7

Friedrich Wilhelm II liked to escape to the romantic Belvedere, a summer residence built in 1788 by Carl Gotthard Langhans, which served as a tea pavilion. Today it houses a collection of precious Berlin porcelain objects.

Neuer Pavillon 8

This Italianate villa behind the palace, designed by Schinkel for Friedrich Wilhelm III in 1825, was inspired by the Villa Reale del Chiatamone in Naples. The pavilion clearly shows the Hohenzollern's love of the Italian style.

Mausoleum 9

Slightly hidden, this Neo-Classical building (above) by Schinkel, is the final resting place for Queen Luise and other Hohenzollerns.

Museum für Vor- und Frühgeschichte 10

The museum displays archaeological finds from prehistory right up to the Middle Ages, including tools, ceramics and textiles. Also on display is part of the famous Priamus treasure excavated by Heinrich Schliemann in Troy, which comprises precious golden jewellery from antiquity.

For more on Charlottenburg see pp78–83

Left **The new wing** Centre **Frederick the Great's Watteau painting** Right **Neuer Pavillon**

Palace Rooms

1 Goldene Galerie
The festival salon in the Neuer Flügel, 42 m (138 ft) long, was designed, in the Rococo style, by G W von Knobelsdorff for Frederick the Great. The richly ornamented room has a cheerful appearance.

2 Ahnengalerie
The wooden panelling of the so-called oak gallery is carved with preciously gilded portraits of the Hohenzollern ancestors.

3 Gris-de-Lin-Kammer
This small chamber in Friedrich's second palace apartment is decorated with paintings, including some by his favourite artist, Antoine Watteau. The room was named after its violet-coloured damask (gris-de-lin in French) wall coverings.

4 Schlafzimmer Königin Luise
Queen Luise's bedchamber, designed in 1810 by Karl Friedrich Schinkel, features the clear lines typical of the Neo-classical style. The walls are clad silk fabrics and wallpaper.

5 Winterkammern
Friedrich Wilhelm II's early classical rooms contain paintings, wall carpets and furniture of the time.

Ahnengalerie

6 Bibliothek
Frederick the Great's small library has outstanding elegant bookcases and an unusual, light green colour scheme.

7 Konzertkammer
Furniture and gilded panelling in the concert hall have been faithfully recreated as during Frederick the Great's time. Here hangs Gersaint's Shop Sign, which the king bought directly from the artist Watteau and is considered to be one of the artist's most important works.

8 Grünes Zimmer
The green room in Queen Elisabeth's quarters gives an excellent impression of royal chambers furnished in the 19th-century Biedermeier style.

9 Rote Kammer
The elegant chamber, decorated entirely in red and gold, is adorned by portraits of King Friedrich I and Sophie Charlotte.

10 Friedrich I's Audienzkammer
The ceiling paintings and Belgian tapestries in Friedrich I's reception chamber depict allegorical figures symbolizing the fine arts and the sciences. There are also magnificent lacquered cabinets, modelled on Asian originals.

The Hohenzollern and Berlin

In 1412, the Hohenzollern dynasty, not originally resident in the Berlin area, was asked by the Luxemburg King Sigismund to liberate the province of Brandenburg from the menace of robber barons. Burggraf Friedrich of Hohenzollern from

Prussia's first king: Friedrich I

Nuremberg was so successful in this enterprise that he was made an Elector in 1415 – this is where the histories of the Hohenzollerns and Berlin first became entwined, a relationship that was to last for 500 years. Right from the start, the family attempted to limit the powers of the town. Culture flourished under its rulers, especially under the Great Elector, who brought 20,000 Huguenot craftsmen to Berlin, as well as founding an art gallery and several schools. Friedrich Wilhelm I, father of Frederick the Great, transformed Berlin into a military camp, with parade grounds and garrisons, and scoured the town for tall men to join his body guard. In the 19th century, however, relations between Berlin and the Hohenzollerns became decidedly less cordial.

Frederick the Great

Frederick the Great in Charlottenburg

Frederick II had two apartments furnished for himself in the palace, and he took a strong personal interest in the design of the Neuer Flügel in 1740–7. From 1745, after the end of the Second Silesian War, he stayed at the palace less and less often, preferring his palace at Sanssouci, although larger festivities in the presence of the King still took place at Charlottenburg.

The Altes Schloss, designed in 1695 by Johann Arnold Nering

 For more on historical architecture in Berlin see pp38–9

🔟 Kulturforum

The Kulturforum is a unique complex of museums, concert halls and libraries, based at the south-eastern end of the Tiergarten. Every year, some of the most outstanding European art museums, as well as the famous concert hall of the Berlin Philharmonic Orchestra, attract millions of visitors who are interested in culture and music. The Kulturforum, based in the former West Berlin, has been growing since 1956, as a counterpoint to the Museumsinsel in the former East Berlin. Here visitors can admire some of the best examples of modern architecture in the capital.

Neue Nationalgalerie in the Kulturforum

🔵 Enjoy a break around the quiet back of the Nationalgalerie.

⭐ A day ticket (€8) gives admission to all museums.

Top 10 Sights

1. Gemäldegalerie
2. Neue Nationalgalerie
3. Philharmonie
4. Kunstgewerbemuseum
5. Musikinstrumentenmuseum
6. Kammermusiksaal
7. Kupferstichkabinett
8. St Matthäuskirche
9. Staatsbibliothek
10. Kunstbibliothek

• Map E4, L1/2

• Gemäldegalerie, Matthäikirchplatz 8 • 10am–6pm Tue–Wed, 10am–10pm Thu, 10am–6pm Fri–Sun • (030) 266 29 51 • Adm. charge

• Neue Nationalgalerie, Potsdamer Str. 50 • 10am–6pm Tue–Wed, 10am–10pm Thu, 10am–6pm Fri–Sun • (030) 266 29 51 • Adm. charge

• Kunstgewerbemuseum, Matthäikirchplatz • 10am–6pm Tue–Wed, 10am–10pm Thu, 10am–6pm Fri–Sun • (030) 266 29 51 • Adm. charge

• Musikinstrumentenmuseum, Tiergartenstr. 1 • 9am–5pm Tue–Wed & 9am–10pm Thu, 9am–5pm Sat & Sun • (030) 254 810 • Adm. free Thu eve.

Gemäldegalerie
1 Berlin's largest art museum boasts some of the finest masterpieces of European art. They are displayed in the modern Neubau, built in 1998 by the architects Heinz Hilmer and Christoph Sattler. The superb collection includes paintings by Holbein, Dürer, Gossaert, Bosch, Brueghel the Elder, Vermeer, Titian, Caravaggio, Rubens, Rembrandt and many others.

Neue Nationalgalerie
2 Based in a building by Mies van der Rohe, the gallery exhibits mainly 20th-century art, with an emphasis on German Expressionism, such as Karl Schmitt-Rottluff's Farm in Daugart (1910) (see also p48).

Philharmonie
3 This tent-like building, designed by Hans Scharoun in 1960–3, was the first new structure in the Kulturforum. Considered one of the best concert halls in the world, it is the seat of the Berlin Philharmonic Orchestra. It is also known, jokingly, as "Circus Karajani", after Herbert von Karajan (1908–89) who conducted the Philharmonic Orchestra for many years. Sir Simon Rattle has been the conductor since 2002.

For more on Berlin museums see pp46–7

4 Kunstgewerbe-museum

Craft objects from the Middle Ages to the present day and from around Europe are on show here, including valuable items like this Baroque clock and the Guelphs' treasure *(see also p47)*.

5 Musikinstrumen-tenmuseum

Concealed behind the Philharmonie is this fascinating little museum of musical instruments. More than 750 exhibits, particularly of early instruments such as harpsichords, are on show *(see also p47)*, as well as a 1929 Wurlitzer.

6 Kammer-musiksaal

The smaller relative of the larger Philharmonie, this concert hall is one of Germany's most highly regarded venues for chamber music. It was built in 1984–8, to a design by Hans Scharoun, carried through by his pupil Edgar Wisniewski.

7 Kupferstich-kabinett

The Gallery of Prints and Drawings holds more than 520,000 prints and 110,000 drawings from all periods and countries, including this portrait of Dürer's mother *(see also p49)*.

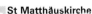

8 St Matthäuskirche

This church is the only historical building to have been preserved in the Kulturforum. Built by F A Stüler in 1844–6, it is also a venue for art installations as well as a hall for classical concerts.

9 Staatsbibliothek

Built in 1967–78 according to plans by Hans Scharoun, the National Library has a collection of five million books, manuscripts and journals, making it one of the largest German-language libraries in the world.

10 Kunstbibliothek

The unassuming Art Library holds, among other items, a vast collection of art and advertising posters. It also hosts temporary exhibitions on architecture and art as well as design shows.

Left **Merchant Georg Gisze** Centre **Venus and the Organ Player** Right **Portrait of Holzschuher**

Gemäldegalerie

1 Portrait of Hieronymus Holzschuher
Albrecht Dürer painted this portrait of the mayor of Nuremburg in 1529.

2 Portrait of the Merchant Georg Gisze
This painting by Hans Holbein (1532), showing the merchant counting his money, reflects the rise of the wealthy citizen during the Renaissance.

3 Madonna with Child and Singing Angels
A 1477 painting by Sandro Botticelli depicts the Madonna and Child, surrounded by angels carrying lilies.

4 The Birth of Christ
Martin Schongauer's altar painting (c.1480) is one of only a few religious paintings by the artist that have been preserved.

Botticelli's Madonna

5 Victorious Eros
Caravaggio's painting (1602), after Vergil's model, shows Eros, the god of love, trampling underfoot the symbols of culture, glory, science and power.

Victorious Eros

Key

Exhibition area

6 Portrait of Hendrickje Stoffels
In a 1656–7 portrait of his lover Hendrickje Stoffels, Rembrandt's focus is entirely on the subject.

7 The French Comedy
This painting by Antoine Watteau belonged to Frederick the Great's collection.

8 The Glass of Wine
Skilfully composed by Vermeer (1658–61), this scene shows a couple drinking wine.

9 Venus and the Organ Player
This Titian (1550–2) reflects the playful sensuality typical of the Italian Renaissance.

10 Dutch Proverbs
More than 100 proverbs were incorporated into this painting by Pieter Brueghel (1559).

For more on Berlin's art galleries see pp48–9

Top 10 Architects

Architecture in the Kulturforum

The Kulturforum was planned to fill the large area between Potsdamer Straße and Leipziger Platz that had been destroyed during World War II. The original idea for a varied townscape of museums and parks is credited to the Berlin architect Hans

Sculpture by Henry Moore

Scharoun, who had designed plans for this in the years 1946 and 1957. It was also Scharoun who, with the construction of the Philharmonie in 1963, set the character of the Kulturforum: the tent-like, golden roofs of the music hall, the Kammermusiksaal and the Staatsbibliothek, all designed by Scharoun and – after his death – realized by his pupil Edgar Wisniewski, are today among Berlin's best-known landmarks. All the buildings are characterized by the generous proportions of their rooms. In their day, the Scharoun buildings were highly controversial but today they are considered to be classics of modern architecture.

Mies van der Rohe's Nationalgalerie

The Neue Nationalgalerie, built to plans by Mies van der Rohe in 1965–8, is the only museum in the world designed by this Bauhaus architect. Having emigrated to the USA in 1937, van der Rohe returned to Berlin for its construction.

The Philharmonie, designed by Hans Scharoun – famed for its superb acoustics

Gemäldegalerie: **www.smb.museum/gg**

🔟 Zoologischer Garten

Berlin's Zoological Garden is Germany's oldest zoo and, with over 1,400 different species, it is one of the best-stocked in the world. Animals have been kept and bred here, in the northwest of the Tiergarten district, since 1844. A total of about 13,000 animals live in the zoo, ranging from saucer jellyfish to the Indian elephant. Some enclosures are interesting buildings in their own right. In summer, a visit to the zoo is a favourite day out for Berliners, and many animals, such as the panda and baby gorillas, have become celebrities.

The Elephant Gate – the Zoo's main entrance

🅾 There is a café with terrace inside the zoo, to the right of the Elephant Gate.

✔ A day at the zoo is not complete without a visit to the aquarium. The basins and terraria teem with life, as do the zoo enclosures. A combined ticket for €16.50 entitles you to visit both zoo and aquarium.

Hardenbergplatz 8 and Budapester Str. 34 • (030) 25 40 10 • Map D4, N5 • www.zoo-berlin.de • mid-Oct–mid-Mar: 9am–5pm daily; mid-Mar–mid-Oct: 9am–6:30pm daily • Aquarium: 9am–6pm daily • Admission charge

Top 10 Zoo Sights

1. Panda Bears
2. Monkey House
3. Lions' Outdoor Enclosure
4. Giraffe House
5. Nocturnal Animal House
6. Elephant House
7. Aviaries
8. Crocodile Hall
9. Aquarium
10. Amphibians' Section

Monkey House
Monkeys and apes are at home in this house, and here you can watch gorillas, orang-utangs and chimpanzees swinging from tree to tree and playing in the straw. The venerable Eastern Lowland Gorillas, who raise several young in a group, are always a popular attraction. Sangha, one of several gorillas born in the zoo, is now a full member of the family. The zoo's most famous gorilla was Bobby, who died in 1935.

Panda Bears
Bao-Bao the Giant Panda (one of the most endangered species in the world) is the greatest star of the Berlin Zoo. He was presented to Germany by China as an official gift in 1980. His female partner Yan Yan is on loan from China for breeding purposes.

Lions' Outdoor Enclosure
The kings of the desert usually sit aloft the high rocks. The lions are fed at 2:30pm in summer and at 3:30pm in winter.

Giraffe House

The African-style Giraffe House is the oldest house (1871–2). Visitors enjoy watching the giraffes as they nibble the leaves of a tree or bend down, in slow motion, to take a drink.

Nocturnal Animal House

This house, in the cellar of the Predatory Animal House, houses the creatures of the night, including nocturnal reptiles and birds. Here you can admire striped bandicoots, fruit bats and slender loris. Asleep during the day, their hearing is outstanding and their eyes may light up uncannily in the dark.

Elephant House

These good-natured pachyderms have a healthy appetite: fully-grown male Indian elephants devour up to 50 kg (110 lb) of hay a day! Two elephants have been born in captivity.

Aviaries

Nowhere else in the city can you hear such singing, tweeting and whistling – cockatiels, parrots, hornbills and humming-birds sound off in the Bird House aviaries.

Crocodile Hall

Not for the timid: in the crocodile hall visitors cross a small wooden footbridge, only 2 m (6 ft) above the dozing creatures. Opened in 1913, it was the first zoo enclosure accessible to the public.

Aquarium

The greatest draw in the aquarium, where Caribbean and Amazonian habitats have been recreated, are the blacktip reef sharks and green morays. The electric eel, able to generate up to 800 volts, and the sting-rays are also popular.

Amphibians' Section

Poisonous snakes, bird spiders and reptiles as well as other amphibians crawl and slither around behind glass on the second floor of the aquarium. A particularly spectacular event is the feeding of the spiders.

 Aquarium: **www.aquarium-berlin.de**

Left **Statues at Altes Museum** Centre **Schloss Bellevue** Right **Portico of the Konzerthaus**

Historic Buildings

Brandenburger Tor
More than a mere symbol, the Brandenburg Gate is synonymous with Berlin *(see pp8–9)*.

Schloss Charlottenburg
This palace boasts Baroque and Rococo splendours and a beautiful park, making it one of the most attractive in Germany *(see pp28–31)*.

Schloss Bellevue
Built according to plans by Philipp Daniel Boumann in 1785–90, this palace was the residence of the Hohenzollerns until 1861. Since 1994 the stately building with its Neo-Classical façade has been the official residence of the President of the Federal Republic. The modern, egg-shaped Presidential Offices stand immediately next to the old palace. ✆ *Spreeweg 1 • Map E4 • Not open to the public*

Reichstag
The seat of the Deutscher Bundestag, the German parliament, with its spectacular cupola, is a magnet for visitors *(see pp10–1)*.

Berliner Rathaus
Berlin's Town Hall, also known as "Red Town Hall" because of the red bricks from Brandenburg Province

with which it is built, harks back to the proud days when Berlin became the capital of the new Empire. Built in 1861–9 according to designs by Hermann Friedrich Waesemann, the town hall was one of Germany's largest and most magnificent buildings, built to promote the splendour of Berlin. The structure was modelled on Italian Renaissance palaces, and the tower is reminiscent of Laon cathedral in France. The exterior was decorated with *Die steinerne Chronik* (the stone chronicle) in 1879, depicting scenes from the city's history *(see p131)*. ✆ *Rathausstraße 15 • Map G3, K6 • 8am–8pm daily*

Konzerthaus
The Concert Hall, one of Karl Friedrich Schinkel's masterpieces, was until recently known as *Schauspielhaus* (theatre). The building has a portico with Ionic columns, and a large number of statues of allegorical and historical personages, some riding lions and panthers, as well as deities, muses and bacchants.
✆ *Gendarmenmarkt 2 • Map L4*
• 10am–8pm daily
• (030) 203 09 21 01

Hackesche Höfe
This complex of 19th-century warehouses consists of nine interlinked courtyards, some of

Southern façade of the Berliner Rathaus

which are decorated in Art-Nouveau style, originally by August Endell. In the early 1990s the complex was completely renovated. The first courtyard is particularly attractive: coloured glazed tiles with geometric patterns decorate the house from the foundations up to the guttering. In the last courtyard, trees are

Victoria, the goddess of victory, on the Siegessäule

grouped around an idyllic well. The Hackesche Höfe is one of Berlin's most popular hotspots; restaurants, cafés, a cinema and the Chamäleon variety show attract visitors from afar.

Ⓢ *Rosenthaler Str. 40–41 • Map G3, J5 • 9am–2am daily*

Hackesche Höfe

Siegessäule

The Victory Column in Tiergarten, 62 m (203 ft) high, decorated with the statue of Victoria, offers great views *(see p97)*.

Altes Museum and Gardens

The façade of the Old Museum, possibly one of the most attractive Neo-Classical museums in Europe, is remarkable for the shiny red marble used in its construction, which is visible behind 18 Ionic columns. Built in 1830 according to plans by Karl Friedrich Schinkel, it was at the time one of the first buildings to be created specifically as a museum. Originally it was to house the royal collection of paintings; today it is home to a collection of antiquities and the Egyptian Museum. In front of the museum, on Museumsinsel, are the gardens designed by Peter Joseph Lenné. Conceived as the king's herb garden, it is today decorated with a granite bowl by Gottlieb Christian Cantian, weighing 70 tons *(see p114)*.

Zeughaus

Designed by J A Nering as the first Berlin Baroque building, the former Royal Prussian Arsenal is now the Deutsches Historisches Museum *(see pp12–15)*, with a modern addition by L M Pei.

Left **Neue Nationalgalerie in the Kulturforum** Right **Nordic Embassies**

Modern Buildings

Sony Center
One of Berlin's largest new structures is the spectacular Sony Center (see p16).

Neue Nationalgalerie
This impressive low building with its huge windows was built in 1965–8 according to plans by Mies van der Rohe. It was the first building to be designed by the pioneering Bauhaus architect after his emigration to the USA. He was able to make use of his earlier designs for the Havana headquarters of the Bacardi company, which had been abandoned following the Cuban Revolution (see pp32, 48). ⓢ Potsdamer Str. 50 • Map E4 • 10am–6pm Tue–Wed, until 10pm Thu, 10am–6pm Fri–Sun

Bundeskanzleramt
Berliners are not too fond of the Chancellor's new offices, although this is the only new government building to have been designed by a Berlin architect. Axel Schultes developed a vast, elongated office complex, which extends north of the Reichstag, in a bend of the Spree, even stretching across the river. In the centre of the

The new Bundeskanzleramt

hyper-modern building stands a gleaming white cube with round windows, which Berliners quickly nicknamed "washing machine". Critics describe the design as pompous, while civil servants dislike their small offices. The interior of the building is decorated with valuable modern paintings. The Chancellor's office on the 7th floor has a view of the Reichstag. d Willy-Brandt-Str. 1 • Map J/K2 • Not open to the public

Ludwig-Erhard-Haus

Ludwig-Erhard-Haus
The seat of the Berlin Stock Exchange, Ludwig-Erhard-Haus was designed by the British architect Nicholas Grimshaw in 1994–8. Locals call it the "armadillo", because the 15 giant metal arches of the domed building recall the giant animal's armour. ⓢ Fasanenstr. 85 • Map N4 • 8am–6pm Mon–Fri

The Kant-Dreieck in Charlottenburg

Philharmonie and Kammermusiksaal

Two modern concert halls in the Kulturforum were designed by Hans Scharoun in 1961 and 1987 respectively – the Chamber Music Hall was completed according to Scharoun's plans by his pupil Edgar Wisniewski. Both buildings are renowned for their excellent acoustics as well as for their tent-like roof structures *(see also pp32–5 and 56–7)*.

Philip-Johnson-Haus

This retail and office complex, built in 1994–7 by US star architect Philip Johnson, reflects in its design the clear lines of the Bauhaus style.
 Friedrichstr. 200 • Map L4

Quartiere 205–207 Friedrichstraße

The Galeries Lafayettes and the Friedrichstadtpassagen are based within these three office blocks by architects Nouvel, Pei and Ungers *(see p119)*.

Nordische Botschaften

No other new embassy building has caused as much of a stir as the five embassies of the Scandinavian countries: the green shutters open and close depending on the amount of available light. Klingelhöferstr. • Map N6 • Not open to the public

DG Bank on Pariser Platz

This elegant building by Frank Owen Gehry combines Prussian and modern architecture. The giant dome inside is particularly remarkable *(see pp10–1)*. Pariser Platz 3 • Map K3 • 10am–6pm Mon–Fri

Kant-Dreieck

The aluminium sail on top the KapHag-Group's headquarters, built by Josef Paul Kleihues in 1992–5, has become a symbol of the new Berlin. Originally, the structure was to be built one-third higher than it is now, but the plans were vetoed by the Berlin Senate. Kantstr. 155 • Map N4 • 9am–6pm Mon–Fri

For more on architecture in Potsdamer Platz **see pp16–9**

Left **At Checkpoint Charlie** Centre **Grafitti on the Wall** Right **Marlene Dietrich in the "Blue Angel"**

🔟 Moments in History

1685: Edict of Potsdam

Berlin's history as a cultural capital began in 1685, when the far-sighted Great Elector announced in the Edict of Potsdam that around 20,000 Huguenots would be taken in by Berlin. Many were excellent craftsmen and scientists, who, having fled Catholic France because of their Protestant beliefs, brought a new age of cultural ascendancy to the provincial town.

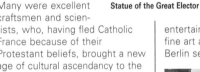

Statue of the Great Elector

1744: Frederick the Great

Although "Old Fritz", as Frederick the Great was nicknamed, preferred the isolation of Sanssouci to the bustle of Berlin, in 1740 he began to transform the city into a new metropolis. In particular, the "Forum Fridericianum" in Unter den Linden brought new splendours to the town, and masterpieces such as the national opera house helped transform Berlin into one of the most important European cities.

Frederick playing the flute in Sanssouci

1928: Golden Twenties

Between 1919 and 1933, Berlin flourished culturally and became an important metropolis. Film, theatre, cabaret shows and thousands of restaurants and bars transformed the town into an international centre of entertainment. In the realms of fine art and architecture, too, Berlin set new standards.

May 1945: Berlin in ruins

1945: Surrender

Signed in Berlin-Karlshorst on 8 May 1945, Germany's unconditional surrender marked more than the end of World War II. The previous Jewish population of 161,000 had virtually disappeared and Berliners called their city "the empire's fields of rubble".

1953: Workers' Uprising in East Germany

On 17 June 1953, construction workers in Frankfurter Allee demonstrated against an increase in the average rate of

Old Photos of Berlin: www.luise-berlin.de/Historie/indexhis.htm

1953: workers on a frieze in Frankfurter Allee

production. Soviet tanks suppressed the rebellion while, in West Berlin, the uprising was interpreted as a demonstration for German unification.

1961: Building of the Wall

The building of the Berlin Wall, which commenced during the night of 12 August 1961, was, after the surrender of 1945, the second most traumatic event for many Berliners. Many families were torn apart by the concrete wall and more than 100 people were to be killed over the following 30 years at the border dividing East and West.

1963: "I am a Berliner"

No other politician was as enthusiastically received in Berlin as the US President John F. Kennedy. On 17 July 1963, in front of Rathaus Schöneberg, he declared to the cheering crowd: "I am a Berliner". Berliners had forgiven the US for staying silent when the Wall was built. Kennedy confirmed once more that the Western Allies would stand by Berlin and support the town, just as they had done during the blockade of 1948–9, when the US and Britain air-lifted food to the "island" of West Berlin.

1968: The late Sixties

During the late 1960s, West Berlin students transformed Germany. Rudi

Dutschke and others propounded political change, free love and a reappraisal of Germany's Nazi past. The movement came to an untimely end when Dutschke was assassinated in April 1968.

1989: Fall of the Wall

The fall of the Berlin Wall in November 1989 heralded a new dawn. For the first time in 30 years, Berliners from both halves of the divided city were able to visit each other. The town celebrated all along Ku'damm and in front of the Brandenburg Gate.

Celebrations after the Fall of the Berlin Wall

When the Wall was built, Willy Brandt, then governing mayor of West Berlin, had promised: "Berlin will survive!" He was right.

1991: Berlin becomes the capital of Germany

In 1991, Berlin was officially declared the capital of the reunified Federal Republic of Germany. Allied Forces left the city during 1994, but it was only when the Bundestag, the German parliament, moved here from Bonn on 19 April 1999 that Berlin became the "real" capital. Today, all the main ministries, the Bundesrat (upper house), and the Chancellor's and the President's offices are based in Berlin.

1991: Berlin becomes the capital

For famous Berliners see pp50–1

Left **St Hedwigskathedrale** Centre **Berliner Dom interior** Right **Main altar in Marienkirche**

Churches & Synagogues

Berliner Dom

Berlin Cathedral, the largest and most lavish church in town, was reopened in 1993, after almost 40 years of restoration. Designed by Julius Raschdorf in 1894–1905, the building reflects the empire's aspirations to power. In particular, the imperial stairs, made from black marble, are a manifestation of the proximity of the Hohenzollern town residence opposite the cathedral. Members of this ruling dynasty are buried in the crypt. The main nave, topped by a 85-m (279-ft) high dome is remarkable. The church is dominated by a magnificent 20th-century Neo-Baroque pulpit and the giant Sauer organ. ✪ *Am Lustgarten • Map K5 • Apr–Sep: 9am–8pm daily; Oct–Mar: 9am–7pm daily • (030) 20 26 91 19*

The interior of Nikolaikirche

Gotthard Langhans. The font (1437) and the fresco *Dance of the Dead* (1485) are among the church's oldest treasures. The richly ornamented Baroque pulpit was created by Andreas Schlüter in 1703. ✪ *Karl-Liebknecht-Str. 8 • Map J6 • 10am–6pm Mon–Sat, noon–6pm Sun; Services 10:30am Sun • Admission charge*

St Hedwigs-kathedrale

Berlin's largest Catholic church was commissioned by Frederick the Great in 1747–73 after his conquest of Silesia *(see pp 12–15)*. ✪ *Bebelplatz • Map K4 • 10am–5pm Mon–Sat, 1–5pm Sun*

Font in Marienkirche

Marienkirche

Work started in 1270 on the Church of St Mary, which nestles at the foot of the Fernsehturm. Gothic and Baroque in style, it has an impressive Neo-Gothic tower, added in 1790 by Carl

Nikolaikirche

Berlin's oldest sacred building, the Church of St Nicholas was built in 1230, in the Nikolaiviertel. The present church, with its red-brick twin towers, dates from around 1300. It is particularly famous for the portal on the west wall of the main nave, created by Andreas Schlüter. It is adorned with a gilded relief depicting a goldsmith and his wife. The church was rebuilt in 1987 and today houses parts of the municipal museum. ✪ *Nikolaikirchplatz • Map K6 • 10am–6pm Tue–Sun • Admission charge*

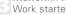

Neue Synagoge – Centrum Judaicum: **www.cjudaicum.de**

Kaiser-Wilhelm-Gedächtnis-Kirche

A landmark in West Berlin, the Kaiser Wilhelm Memorial Church successfully combines modern architecture with the ruins of the church tower *(see pp26–7)*.

Neue Synagoge

Berlin's largest synagogue, built originally in 1859–66, was demolished in World War II but completely reconstructed in 1988–95. Its magnificent dome is visible from afar *(see p123)*.

🕙 *Oranienburger Str. 29–30*
• *Map G3, J4*
• *(030) 88 02 83 00*
• *Admission charge*

Friedrichswerdersche Kirche

This small brick church was built by Karl Friedrich Schinkel in 1824–30, in the Neo-Gothic style. Originally it was meant to serve the German and French communities of the Friedrichswerder district. Today, the Schinkel Museum is based here.

🕙 *Werderscher Markt*

Synagoge Rykestrasse

The small synagogue looks the same today as when it was originally built 100 years ago *(see p140)*.

Christi-Auferstehungs-Kirche

The only Russian-Orthodox church in Berlin, the Church of Christ's Ascension is known for its green

Dome of the Neue Synagoge

onion domes. Services are still held in Russian, following Ortho-dox rituals. 🕙 *Hohenzollerndamm 166*
• *Map B6 • Only during service 10am & 6pm Sat, 10am Sun*

Französischer Dom

At 66 m (216 ft) high, this Baroque tower, which dates back to 1701–5, is a magnificent ornamental structure for the church serving Berlin's Huguenot community.

🕙 *Gendarmenmarkt 5 • Map L4 • (030) 206 499 22 • noon–5pm Tue–Sat, 11am–5pm Sun*

The nave of Friedrichswerdersche Kirche

Berlin's Top 10

For more on Berlin's historic architecture see pp38–9

45

Left **Detail from the Pergamon Altar frieze** Right **Tapestry in the Kunstgewerbemuseum**

🔟 Museums

1 Pergamonmuseum
Berlin's most impressive museum is a vast treasure trove of antiquities *(see pp20–3)*.

2 Ägyptisches Museum
The star exhibit in the Egyptian Museum, currently in the Altes Museum, is the beautiful bust of Nefertiti, wife of Akhenaton. The long-necked limestone bust, discovered in 1912, probably served as a model. Also worth seeing is the "Berlin Green Head", a small bust from the 4th century BC. The museum also holds numerous mummies, sarcophagi, murals and sculptures.

Bust of Nefertiti

🚇 *Bodestr. 1–3, Am Lustgarten • Map K5*
• 10am–6pm Mon–Sun, until 10pm Thu
• (030) 266 3660 • Admission charge

3 Deutsches Historisches Museum
Germany's largest History Museum uses unique exhibits, documents and films to take the

The Jewish Museum

visitor on a journey through German history, from the Middle Ages to the present day. Special exhibitions are devoted to particular themes *(see pp12–5)*.

4 Dahlem Museums
The five museums based in southern Berlin are a fantastic resource of exotic cultures. Four museums are devoted to Far Eastern, Indian, North American and African art, from prehistory to the present day. Among the star exhibits are bronzes from Benin and Japanese woodcuts. The Ethnologisches Museum (Museum of Ethnology), devoted to the cultures of the Pacific area, is equally impressive. Among its exhibits are gold treasures of the Inca *(see p89)*.

5 Jüdisches Museum
The new Jewish Museum, housed in a spectacular building designed by Daniel Libeskind, documents the German–Jewish relationship through the centuries. There are special exhibitions on the influence of Berlin Jews on the town's cultural life, and on the life of the Enlightenment philosopher Moses Mendelssohn. An empty room commemorates the loss of Jewish culture. There is also an exciting programme of special events *(see p103)*.

6 Deutsches Technikmuseum

The fascinating Museum of Technology, on the site of a former station, has fascinating hands-on displays on the history of technology *(see p103)*.

7 Kunstgewerbemuseum

European crafts from over five centuries are on display at this museum. Its most valuable exhibits are the treasure of the Guelphs from Braunschweig and the silver treasure of the town council in Lüneburg. The museum also holds valuable Italian tin-glazed earthenware, Renaissance faïence and German Baroque glass and ceramics. Popular displays show Neo-Classical porcelain and furniture, Jugendstil art and Tiffany vases, as well as 20th-century Art-Deco and modern designs. ◈ *Matthäikirch-platz • Map L1/2*
• *10am–6pm Tue-Fri, 11am–6pm Sat, Sun*
• *(030) 266 2951*
• *Admission charge*

8 Museum für Naturkunde

With over 60 million exhibits, the Natural History Museum is one of the largest of its kind. A star feature is the world's largest dinosaur skeleton, a brachiosaurus found in Tanzania In 1909. Six further dinosaur skeletons as well as many fossils of mussels, birds and mammals take the visitor back to prehistoric times. It is also worth making a visit to the glittering exhibition of meteorites and minerals. ◈ *Invalidenstr. 43 • Map F2 • 9:30am–5pm Tue–Fri, 10am–6pm Sat & Sun*
• *Admission charge*

Brachiosaurus in the Natural History Museum

9 Haus am Checkpoint Charlie

The museum at the former Allied checkpoint documents events at the Berlin Wall *(see p103)*.

10 Musikinstrumentenmuseum

Some 750 musical instruments can be heard in this museum, including such famous ones as Frederick the Great's harpsichord. Don't miss the silent-film organ which still works (first Sat in the month, noon). ◈ *Tiergartenstr. 1*
• *Map L2 • 9am–5pm Tue–Fri, until 10pm Thu, 10am–5pm Sat, Sun • Admission charge*

Harlequin Group, c.1740, in the Kunstgewerbemuseum

Left *The Adoration of the Shepherds* Centre *Cupid Victorious* Right *Hamburger Bahnhof*

🔟 Art Galleries

1 Gemäldegalerie
Berlin's best art museum, the Gemäldegalerie focuses on European art of the 13th to 19th centuries, such as Caravaggio's *Cupid Victorious (above)*, and works by Dürer, Rembrandt and Rubens *(see pp34–5)*.

2 Neue Nationalgalerie
The National Gallery's collection includes modern German art and classics of the 20th century. It often holds spectacular temporary exhibitions. ◈ *Potsdamer Str. 50 • Map E4 • 10am–6pm Tue–Wed, 10am–10pm Thu, 10am–6pm Fri–Sun • Admission charge*

3 Alte Nationalgalerie
The Old National Gallery, built by Friedrich August Stüler in 1866–76 on the Museumsinsel, has been completely restored. Today it holds a collection of 19th-century (and mainly German) paintings, including works by Adolf von Menzel, Wilhelm

Mao by Warhol, in the Hamburger Bahnhof

Leibl, Max Liebermann and Arnold Böcklin. The gallery also has sculptures by Schadow, Rauch and Reinhold Begas. ◈ *Bodestr. 1–3 • Map J5 • 10am–6pm Tue–Sun, until 10pm Thu • (030) 20 90 55 77 • Admission charge*

4 Hamburger Bahnhof
A "museum of the present day", the historic Hamburg Station houses modern paintings, installations and multi-media art. One of its highlights is the Erich Marx Collection, with works by Joseph Beuys. Apart from famous artists like Andy Warhol, Jeff Koons and Robert Rauschenberg, it also owns works by Anselm Kiefer, Sandro Chiao and others. ◈ *Invalidenstr. 50–51 • Map F2 • 10am–6pm Tue–Fri, 11am–8pm Sat, 11am–6pm Sun • Admission charge*

The Glass of Wine by Jan Vermeer, in Gemäldegalerie

Head of a Faun by Picasso (Berggruen)

Deutsches Guggenheim
Sponsored by the Deutsche Bank, the museum hosts temporary exhibitions, often showing modern art from the US *(see p113)*. ◎ *Unter den Linden 13–15 • Map K4 • 11am–8pm daily, till 10pm Thu • Admission charge (free Mon)*

Museum Berggruen
Heinz Berggruen, born in Berlin in 1914, emigrated but returned to Berlin in 1996. His collection, including works from Picasso's "blue period", is based in a historic building by Stüler. ◎ *Schlossstr. 1 • Map B3 • 10am–6pm Tue–Sun • Admission charge (free 1st Sun of the month)*

Bauhaus-Archiv
Few schools have exercised as much influence on 20th-century architecture and design as the Bauhaus, founded in 1919 by Walter Gropius. On show in the museum are furniture, sketches, everyday objects and paintings. ◎ *Klingelhöferstr. 14 • Map N3 • 10am–5pm Wed–Mon • Admission charge*

Berlinische Galerie
Huge collections of mostly German, east European and Russian painters, photographers, graphic designers and architects from the 20th century, such as Baselitz, Grosz and Kirchner. ◎ *Alte Jakobstr. 124 128 • Map G4 • (030) 78 90 26 00 • 10am–6pm Wed–Mon • Admission charge*

Bröhan-Museum
A unique collection of Art-Nouveau and Art-Deco objects from around Europe is on display at this small museum. Also an exhibition of paintings by Berlin artists. ◎ *Schlossstr. 1a • Map B3 • 10am–6pm Tue–Sun • Adm. charge*

Art Deco vase in the Bröhan-Museum

Kupferstichkabinett
Five centuries of prints and calligraphies, including works by Botticelli, Dürer, Rembrandt, Goya, Daumier and the Dutch Old Masters. ◎ *Matthäikirchplatz 6 • Map L1 • 10am–6pm Tue–Fri, 11am–6pm Sat, Sun • Admission charge*

For more on art galleries in the Kulturforum see pp32–5

Left **Philosopher G W F Hegel** Centre **The brothers Grimm** Right **Conductor von Karajan**

Famous Berliners

Marlene Dietrich
The famous filmstar (1901–92), born in Schöneberg, began her career in Berlin in the 1920s. Her breakthrough came with the film *The Blue Angel* (1931). She lies buried in the Friedenau cemetery in Steglitz. Her personal possessions are exhibited in the Filmmuseum Berlin in the Sony Center on Potsdamer Platz.

Albert Einstein
In 1914, the physicist Albert Einstein (1879–1955) became the director of the Kaiser Wilhelm-Institute for Physics. He was awarded the Nobel Prize for Physics in 1921 for his Theory of Relativity, first developed in 1905. Einstein mostly lived and worked in Potsdam, but stayed closely connected with Berlin through his lectures and teaching activity. In 1933 Einstein, who was Jewish, had to emigrate from Germany to the USA where he stayed until his death.

Albert Einstein taught in Berlin

Bertolt Brecht
Born in Augsburg, Bavaria, Bertolt Brecht (1898–1956) wrote some of his greatest works,

Brecht's study

such as the *Threepenny Opera*, in a small apartment in Charlottenburg. In the Third Reich, the playwright emigrated to the US, but he returned to Germany after World War II and founded the Berliner Ensemble in East Berlin in 1949. Until his death, Brecht lived in Chausseestraße in Berlin Mitte, with his wife, Helene Weigel. His renovated apartment has been turned into a museum.

Herbert von Karajan
This famous Austrian conductor (1908–1989) was head of the Berlin Philharmonic Orchestra from 1954 until 1989. During this time he helped create the orchestra's unique sound, which remains legendary until this day. Herbert von Karajan was both revered and feared by his musicians because of his genius and his fiery temperament. Berliners still refer to the Philharmonie as "Circus Karajani".

Robert Koch

Robert Koch

Like few other physicians of his day, Robert Koch (1843–1910) laid the foundations and shaped the face of modern medicine with his pioneering discoveries. The Director of the Institute for Infectious Diseases, Koch also taught and researched at the Charité Hospital. In 1905 he received the Nobel Prize for Medicine for his discoveries in the field of microbiology.

Theodor Fontane

A Huguenot, Fontane (1819–98) was one of the most important 19th-century novelists in Germany. He also worked as a journalist for more than 20 years, penning many of his articles and essays in the Café Josty on Potsdamer Platz. Fontane is particularly well known for his *Walks in the Province of Brandenburg*, in which he describes the mentality of the people, historic places and the Brandenburg landscapes.

Käthe Kollwitz

The sculptor and painter Käthe Kollwitz (1867–1945) portrayed the social problems of the poor, and her work provides a powerful, haunting commentary on human suffering. Kollwitz spent a large part of her life in a modest abode in the square that is now named after her, in the Prenzlauer Berg district. A monument recalls how she captured the lives of poor Berlin families, burdened with large numbers of children, and of social outcasts. Her *Pieta* now adorns the Neue Wache (see p13).

Jacob and Wilhelm Grimm

The brothers Jacob (1785–1863) and Wilhelm (1786–1859) Grimm are well known around the world, thanks to their collection of classic fairy tales including *Little Red Riding Hood* and *Hansel and Gretel*. Equally important, however, was their linguistic output, the *German Grammar* and *German Dictionary* which are standard reference works even today.

Georg Wilhelm Hegel

The influential philosopher Hegel (1770–1831) taught at Humboldt University from 1818 until his death.

Sculpture by Kollwitz

Felix Mendelssohn Bartholdy

The composer (1809–47), a grandson of Moses Mendelssohn, was also the conductor of the Staatskapelle (state orchestra) at the opera house in Unter den Linden. His grave is found in one of the cemeteries in front of the Hallesches Tor in Kreuzberg.

Felix Mendelssohn Bartholdy

For moments in history in Berlin **see pp42–3**

Left **Ku'damm Kneipe** Centre**Strandbar Mitte** Right **Tables outside Zwiebelfisch**

Kneipen (Pubs)

Green Door

This Berlin classic never goes out of style. A young urban crowd enjoys some of the best drinks and cocktails money can buy in Germany (the *Mojito* is a particular delight), mingling at the minimalist retro-style bar and along the curved, green walls. At weekends, the place is packed to bursting. There's an outdoor bell, but the door policy is pretty liberal as long as you look sober. ◈ *Winterfeldstr. 50 • Map D4/5 • 6pm–3am Sun–Thu, 6pm–4am Fri, Sat • (030) 215 25 15*

Strandbar Mitte

One of Berlin's more unusual pubs. The Strandbar Mitte was the first of a new type of open-air pubs and cafés which are near canals or city beaches. In summer, sip your beer or cocktail and enjoy a magnificent view of Museum Island. ◈ *Monbijoustr. 3 • Map G3 • 10am–1am (in summer) • (030) 28 38 55 88*

Bellini Lounge

Bellini Lounge

Voted Berlin's best bar in 2005, this new and flashy venue serves some of the city's best cocktails, includ-

Berliner Weiße

ing rums from around the world. The crowd is a mix of artists, media people, students and a few tourists. In summer the Lounge spills onto the street, great for people-watching; whilst in winter you can enjoy the bar's colourful aquarium. ◈ *Oranienburger Str. 42 • Map J4 • 4pm–5am Fri–Sat, 4pm–3am Sun–Wed • (030) 970 056 18*

E & M Leydicke

This slightly dated winery is still a big hit with tourists as well as groups of pupils and students. Try the sweetish stra wberry and raspberry wines. ◈ *Mansteinstr. 4 • Map E6 • 6pm–midnight daily • (030) 216 29 73*

Morena-Bar

With its walls completely covered with Spanish tiles, this bar draws an upmarket Kreuzberg crowd as well as students who like to meet here for a beer. At weekends it is full to bursting and gets livelier by the hour. ◈ *Wiener Str. 60 • 9pm–9pm daily • (030) 611 47 16*

Zum Nußbaum

One of only a few traditional pubs in the historic Nikolaiviertel worth checking out, the Nußbaum serves draught beer and traditional Berlin food. ◈ *Am Nußbaum 3 • Map K6 • noon–midnight • (030) 242 30 95*

Diener, favoured by actors

Zwlebelfisch

7 A classic of the ageing Charlottenburg scene, this is where the last survivors of the 1968 generation prop up the bar and reminisce about the great days of the revolution in West Berlin. The artists in the photographs on the walls are all past clients, many of them from the 1968 generation. In the summer, there are tables outdoors on Savignyplatz – great for people-watching and taking in the scene. ⊗ *Savignyplatz 7–8 • Map N3 • noon–6am daily • (030) 312 73 63*

Diener-Tattersaal

8 An atmospheric pub popular with local actors, serving draught beers and traditional German and Austrian fare. The pub bears the name of Franz Diener, the legendary boxer who knocked out the erstwhile boxing world champion, Max Schmeling. ⊗ *Grolmanstr. 47 • Map P3 • 6pm–3am daily • (030) 881 53 29*

Café am Neuen See

9 The only Berlin Kneipe that is also a café. The "Italian breakfast" is opulent and delicious. In summer, crowds gather in the vast beer garden. Customers bring their own food to grill and sit at the long tables, chatting over a local beer. ⊗ *Tiergarten, Neuer See, Lichtensteinallee 2 • Map M5 • Mar–Oct: 10am–11pm; Nov–Feb: 10am–8pm daily • (030) 254 49 30*

Schülter 52

10 This bar and restaurant is popular for its superb cocktails and wines, plus its colourful clientele – mostly actors, film producers and aspiring writers. The dark wooden floors and naked walls are typical for Charlottenburg. ⊗ *Schlüterstr. 52 • Map N3 • from 6pm daily • (030) 364 106 15*

Outside at Café am Neuen See

For Berlin bars **see pp54–5**

Left **Lola-Lounge** Centre **The Bar am Lützowplatz** Right **The Reingold bar**

🔟 Bars & Lounges

1 Newton-Bar

The best cocktails in town are mixed at this elegant bar in Gendarmenmarkt. Service is charming and the fastest in town, and in summer there's even a fold-down bar on the pavement outside. Heavy leather armchairs make for comfortable sitting, and the walls are adorned with enlarged photographs of nudes by Helmut Newton, after whom the bar is named. Highly recommended: the Caribbean and Latin-American cocktails – chin-chin! ◈ *Charlottenstr. 57 • Map L4 • 10am–3am daily • (030) 20 29 54 21*

In the Newton-Bar

2 Lola-Lounge

The new Lola-Lounge is a minimalist designer's dream. It attracts a young, urban and suitably fashionable crowd who enjoy the computerized lighting system and the laidback lounge atmosphere of this bar in a restaurant. Choose from a long list of exotic and delicious cocktails. ◈ *Rosa-Luxemburg-Str. 17 • Map H2 • 8pm–2am Tue–Thu • (030) 27 59 44 30*

3 Le Bar du Paris Bar

Despite its name, the Paris Bar was until quite recently only a French restaurant. Now this trendy celebrity haunt has its own bar, and although the cocktails are not quite as good as those of the competition, it is easy to forget this when you are enjoying one of their wonderful French wines or champagnes. ◈ *Kantstr. 152 • Map N3 • from 6pm daily • (030) 31 01 50 94*

4 Harry's New York Bar

Sip your tropical concoctions and champagne cocktails while seated underneath the portraits of 43 US presidents in this bar, a sister venue of the famous bar in Venice. The clientele is more sedate than in other Berlin bars, but the ambience is upmarket, and evening entertainment (jazz singers and piano) is more stylish than elsewhere. ◈ *Grand Hotel Esplanade, Lützowufer 15 • Map N6 • from noon daily • (030) 25 47 88 33*

5 Trompete

This trendy bar, which belongs to the actor Ben Becker, has very quickly established itself as *the* place to be. The bar, with its soft leather armchairs and settees and completely black walls, is relaxed and comfortable. At weekends, Trompete hosts live concerts ranging from jazz and salsa to house. ◈ *Lützowplatz 9 • Map P6 • from 7pm Thu, from 10pm Fri, Sat, Sun • (030) 23 00 47 94*

6 Bar am Lützowplatz

For a long time, this was the favourite bar of the "beautiful people". It is now a little quieter than it used to be, but this venue still boasts the longest bar in Berlin.

Ice-cold Mojito cocktail

The interior is truly astounding, and the well-dressed barmen with their white dinner jackets, as well as the outstanding cocktails they mix make this a "must" for any visitor.
Ⓢ Lützowplatz 7 • Map M6 • from 2pm daily • (030) 262 68 07

7 Mister Hu

Thanks to its reputation for fine cocktails, the ocean-themed Mister Hu is one of the most popular bars in town. The relaxed ambience attracts students, artists and alternative nighthawks. There are outdoor tables in summer. Cock-

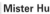

Expensive but good: the Paris Bar

tails with rum are particularly good. And don't ask for Mr Hu – there's no bartender with that name. Ⓢ Goltzstr. 39 • Map E5
• 5pm–4am Sun–Thu, 5pm–5am Fri
• (030) 217 21 11

8 Victoria Bar

This homely bar, with its understated 1960s-retro ambiance and subdued lighting, is a great place to relax. The cocktails are mixed by the renown barman Stefan Weber, and are served to a mainly 30-something Bohemian crowd, accompanied by sophisti-cated lounge music. Ⓢ Potsdamer Str. 102 • Map E5 • 6:30pm–4am Fri–Sat, 6:30pm–3am Sun–Thu • (030) 257 599 77

9 Reingold

Portraits of 1930s writers Erika and Klaus Mann adorn the walls of this bar, which is friend-lier and more intimate than most other bars in Berlin. The cocktails are excellent. Ⓢ Novalisstr. 11 • Map F2 • 7pm–4am daily • (030) 28 38 76 76

10 Café M

The (in)famous Café M Kneipe in Schöneberg is today even noisier than it used to be. If you find the rock music too loud, you can always escape to the tables out-side Ⓢ Goltzstr. 33 • Map E6 • 8am–2am Mon–Thu, from 9am Fri–Sun • (030) 216 70 92

For pubs see pp52–3

Left **Deutsches Theater** Centre **Friedrichstadtpalast** Right **Inside the Tanztheater in Berlin**

10 Performing Arts Venues

1 Staatsoper Unter den Linden
Both the theatre troupe and the orchestra of the venerable Berlin Opera – now ably directed by Daniel Barenboim – enjoy top reputations. Nowhere else can you see so many top stars of classical music *(see pp12–15)*.
🄯 *Unter den Linden 5–7 • Map K4*
• (030) 20 35 45 55

The Berlin Philharmonic Orchestra

2 Philharmonie
Germany's "temple" of classical music still presents the best performers in the world. Designed by Scharoun, the concert hall has unique acoustics, much appreciated by artists and audience alike. Concerts by the Berlin Philharmonic Orchestra are very popular and are often sold out for weeks ahead *(see pp32–5)*. 🄯 *Herbert-von-Karajan-Str. 1 • Map L2 • Box Office: 3–6pm Mon–Fri, 11am–2pm Sat–Sun • (030) 25 48 81 32*

3 Wintergarten Varieté
Berlin's largest variety show relates back to the traditions of its famous predecessor from the 1920s. Every evening, André Heller and

Wintergarten

Bernhard Paul direct a varied classical cabaret show in the former cinema, which has been transformed into an amazingly beautiful theatre. The shows change three or four times a year, but there is always a mix of acrobatics, comedy and song on offer. 🄯 *Potsdamer Str. 96 • Map E5 • Box Office: noon–6pm Mon–Fri, 2pm–6pm Sat • (030) 25 00 88 88*

4 Chamäleon-Varieté
The lack of technology is more than made up for with much wit and ingenuity by the small, alternative Chamäleon stage. If you are seated in the front row, you are likely to get pulled onto the stage.
🄯 *Rosenthaler Str. 40–1, Hackesche Höfe • Map J5 • 8pm Tue–Fri, 7pm, 10pm Sat, 7pm Sun • (030) 282 71 18*

5 Bar jeder Vernunft
This venue, whose name means "devoid of all reason", is Berlin's most popular comedy theatre. The cabaret offers a humorous and, at times, romantic programme of songs and *chansons*, reviews, cabaret, slapstick and comedy, all under the roof of an amazing mirror tent dating from the 1920s. Many stars of the international and German cabaret scene can be seen regularly among the performers here: for example Tim Fischer, Georgette Dee, the Pfister Sisters and Gayle Tufts, as well as older

stars such as Otto Sander.
🕿 Schaperstr. 24 (car park Freie Volksbühne) • Map C5 • Box office open noon–7pm daily • (030) 883 15 82

Inside the mirror tent: Bar jeder Vernunft

Deutsches Theater
Performances at the German Theatre, one of the best German-language venues, include mainly classic plays in the tradition of Max Reinhardt. Experimental theatre by young playwrights is performed at the DT Baracke. 🕿 Schumannstr. 13 • Map J3 • 7:30pm daily • (030) 28 44 12 25

Theater des Westens
For two decades, this theatre has been producing its own shows, such as La Cage aux Folles, and now shows guest productions such as Les Misérables and Hair. 🕿 Kantstr. 12 • Map N4 • 7:30pm Tue–Fri, 2:30pm & 7:30pm Sat & Sun • (01805) 44 44

Theater des Westens

Friedrichstadtpalast
The long-legged dancers in Friedrichstadtpalast are as popular today as they were in the 1920s in their legendary former venue, which was damaged during World War II. Long celebrated as the "world's greatest variety show", the performances have today become even more spirited and entertaining. 🕿 Friedrichstr. 107 • Map J4 • Box Office (030) 23 26 23 26

Hebbel-Theater
The Hebbel-Theater has attained cult status in Berlin, thanks to its modern and varied programme of concerts, dance and song. Top performers from around the world appear here. 🕿 Hallesches Ufer 32 • Map F5 • 7:30pm daily • (030) 25 90 04 27

Volksbühne
Frank Castorf has transformed this former Socialist stage into a theatre, which has become famous for its classy, and at times controversial performances. 🕿 Rosa-Luxemburg-Platz • Map H2 • (030) 240 657 77

Left **Tom's Bar** Centre **Façade of the Connection** Right **The Mann-o-Meter**

Gay & Lesbian Attractions

Christopher Street Day on Ku'damm

Christopher Street Day

Every summer, Germany's largest gay festival, Christopher Street Day, transforms Berlin into a giant street party, with thousands of gays and lesbians parading from Kurfürstendamm down the Straße des 17. Juni to Siegessäule. At night, the party continues in the city's many gay clubs and Kneipen.
🕏 *Kurfürstendamm, Straße des 17. Juni • Map P3/4 • 4th weekend in June*

Siegessäule

Berlin's oldest and best-selling gay newspaper is named after the Victory Column, Berlin's landmark. This colourful monthly magazine includes all sorts of useful information, a round-up of what's on, small ads and interviews from the city's gay scene. 🕏 *Free in gay cafés and shops*

Siegessäule front covers

Mann-o-Meter

Berlin's best-known advice centre for gays offers help and advice of all kinds. Apart from psychological support in relation to Aids, safe sex and coming out, its counsellors offer help in finding accommodation, give support to those in troubled relationships and provide legal advice. Mann-o-Meter is also a good starting point for gay visitors to Berlin who wish to find out abut the gay scene – and, last but not least, the café is also a good place to meet people. 🕏 *Bülowstr. 106 • Map E5 • 5–10pm Mon–Fri, 4–10pm Sat, Sun • (030) 216 80 08*

SchwuZ

"SchwuZ" in Kreuzberg is one of the best venues for gay parties in Berlin. At weekends, this is where a young crowd hangs out, dancing, chatting, drinking and enjoying the entertainment. The parties are often themed – details can be found in gay magazines such as *Siegessäule* or *Sergej*.
🕏 *Mehringdamm 61 • Map F5 • from 11pm Fri, Sat • (030) 629 088 20 • Admission charge*

Tom's Bar

One of the traditional pubs in Berlin, in the centre of the city's gay heart in Motzstraße, Tom's Bar is not for those who are

shy and timid; Tom's Bar is a well-known pick-up joint. Below the (rather dark and dingy) Kneipe is a darkroom.
🅢 *Motzstr. 19 • Map D5 • from 7pm daily • (030) 213 45 70*

Inside the Prinz-Eisenherz bookstore

⑥ Prinz-Eisenherz-Buchhandlung

Germany's oldest openly gay bookstore stocks the entire range of German and international gay and lesbian publications. Its knowledgeable bookshop assistants will track down rare or out-of-stock titles at your request. The bookshop also hosts frequent literary readings.
🅢 *Lietzenburger Str. 9A • Map N3 • 10am–8pm Mon–Sat • (030) 313 99 36*

⑦ Connection

Connection is perhaps not the best, but certainly one of the most popular gay discos in Berlin. Late at night, this is where gays mainly from the scene meet and dance to house and techno rhythms. In the base-ment under the club is a labyrinth of darkrooms. 🅢 *Fugger-str. 33 • Map D5 • from 11pm Fri, Sat • (030) 218 14 32 • Admission charge*

⑧ Café Berio

A long-time favourite among Berlin's scene, the Café Berio is an old-fashioned café that has been turned totally gay. In the summer its terrace is a great place to have breakfast while people watching.
🅢 *Maaßenstr. 7 • Map E5 • 8am–1am daily • (030) 216 19 46*

⑨ Schwules Museum

The small Gay Museum is situated in Kreuzberg. It docu-ments, through temporary exhi-bitions, the high and low points of gay and lesbian life since the 19th century. Next to the muse-um is an archive, a small library and a venue for cultural events.
🅢 *Mehringdamm 61 • Map F5 • 2–6pm Mon, Wed–Fri, Sun, 2–7pm Sat • (030) 69 59 90 50 • Admission charge*

⑩ SO 36

This famous – and infamous – dance venue for young gays has been extremely popular for many years. The Sunday night club "Café Fatal" is legendary, when old German chart hits and dance tunes are played. 🅢 *Oranienstr. 190 • Map H5 • for current programmes and opening hours check their website • www.so36.de • (030) 61 40 13 06*

Schwules Museum: **www.geocities.com/schwulesmuseum/**

Left **Inside Quartier 206** Centre **Food department Galeries Lafayette** Right **In Winterfeldtplatz**

🔟 Shops & Markets

1 Kaufhaus des Westens (KaDeWe)

The KaDeWe

Whatever you are looking for, you will find it here, in Europe's largest temple of consumption. On eight floors, the venerable KaDeWe (department store of the West) offers more than three million products. On its gourmet floor, West Berlin's former "shop window", you can choose from 1,800 cheeses, 1,400 breads and pastries and 2,000 cold meats. The window displays and inner courtyards are also worth a visit in themselves (see also p170).
🧭 Tauentzienstr. 21–24 • Map D4, P5
• (030) 21 21 20 51

2 Galeries Lafayette

This small French department store specializes in classic womens- and menswear on one level, and young fashion upstairs. The French delicacies on sale in the food department make many a heart beat faster (see also p119).

3 Antik- und Flohmarkt Straße des 17. Juni

Berlin's largest art and antiques market specializes in genuine antique furnishings and fittings, cutlery and porcelain, books, paintings, clothing and jewellery. The traders are professionals and demand high prices, but in return you are assured of buying something splendid. With its street artists and buskers, the market is an ideal weekend spot for a bit of browsing, dawdling and people-watching (see p85).
🧭 Straße des 17. Juni • Map M4
• 10am–5pm Sat, Sun

4 Department Store Quartier 206

Berlin's most recent fashion store is also the most expensive in town. Here, the man-about-town can purchase his Gucci or DKNY ties, while the lady tries on Versace or Calvin Klein gear on three floors in the Friedrichstadtpassagen (see p119).
🧭 Friedrichstr. 71 • Map L4
• (030) 20 94 62 40 • 11am–8pm Mon–Fri, 10am–6pm Sat

5 Stilwerk

Style is writ large in this trendy shop. Stilwerk is not a department store, however, but

The famous glass cone at Lafayette

Façade of the Stilwerk shopping centre

a shopping centre, specializing in designer furniture, lamps and fittings – basically anything good and expensive (see also p85). ® Kantstr. 17 • Map C4 • (030) 31 51 50 • 10am–8pm Mon–Fri, 10am–6pm Sat

Gipsformerei Staatliche Museen
If you fancy a Schinkel statue for your home or an elegant Prussian sculpture from the palace gardens, you'll find moulded plaster reproduction in all shapes and sizes here. ® Sophie-Charlotten-Str. 17–18 • Map A3 • (030) 326 76 90 • 9am–4pm Mon–Fri, till 6pm Wed

Königliche Porzellan-Manufaktur (KPM)
Prussia's glory and splendour to take away – traditional KPM porcelain for your dining table at home. Apart from elegant porcelain dinner services, figures and accessories made in the Berlin factory are also on sale. ® Unter den Linden 35 • Map F/G3, K3/4 • (030) 206 41 50 • 10am–7pm Mon–Fri, 10am–6pm Sat

Markt am Winterfeldtplatz
The trendiest and also the most attractive weekly food and clothing market in Berlin has developed into a hotspot of the Schöneberg crowd. This is the place for meeting up on Saturday mornings (see p107).

Türkenmarkt am Maybachufer
Berlin's largest weekday Turkish market lures visitors with its smells and dishes from A thousand-and-one-nights. Bartering is expected (see p107). ® Maybachufer • Map H5 • noon–6.30pm Tue–Fri

Berliner Antik- und Flohmarkt
Numerous antique and junk shops are hidden underneath the S-Bahn arches at Friedrichstraße Station. Much of it is overpriced, but occasionally you will find a bargain. ® Friedrichstr., S-Bahn arches • Map J4 • (030) 208 26 45 • 10am–6pm Wed–Mon

Left **Popkomm** Centre **Christopher Street Day Parade** Right **The Berlin Marathon**

Festivals & Fairs

Berliner Filmfestspiele

The Berlinale is the only top German film festival, and is attended by Hollywood stars and German starlets alike. Until 1999, the film festival took place all around the Zoo-Palast cinema; today the traditional festival draws thousands of cinema fans to the area around Potsdamer Platz. ◈ *Filmhaus Potsdamer Platz • Map L2 • (030) 25 92 00 • 2nd and 3rd week in February*

Zoo-Palast cinema during the Berlinale

Internationale Funkausstellung (IFA)

The latest in entertainment technology from around the world and high-tech toys for young and old are on show at the IFA (International Broadcasting Exhibition) in the ICC. ◈ *Messe Berlin, ICC • Map A5 • (030) 303 80 • every year in Aug or early Sep • Admission charge*

Popkomm

As one of Europe's biggest music festivals, the trendy Popkomm attracts top acts and thousands of music fans for its mix of concerts, talks and parties at the Messe and in clubs around the city. ◈ *Messe Berlin • Map A5 • (030) 303 830 09 • mid to late September*

Christopher-Street-Parade

This gay parade openly and brashly celebrates alternative lifestyles. At the end of June, up to 500,000 gays and lesbians from around the world boisterously dance, drink and celebrate in the streets of Central Berlin *(see also p58)*. ◈ *Kurfürstendamm and Straße des 17. Juni • Map P3/4 • (030) 23 62 86 32 • 4th weekend in June*

Berliner Festwochen

Classical concerts, exhibitions and events organized around a particular theme form the cultural highpoint of the year. ◈ *Various venues • September*

Lange Nacht der Museen

For one night, entrance to many of Berlin's museums is free. Many institutions also put on special events for that weekend, and the street artists and

IFA, ITB and Grüne Woche at the Messe

Internationale Filmfestspiele Berlin: **www.berlinale.de**

Karneval der Kulturen

sellers entertain the public, who normally wait in long queues.
🕔 *Berlin museums • (030) 902 69 93*
• *last weekend in January or August*

7 Grüne Woche
The largest gourmet feast in the world, Green Week is a tasty agricultural and gastronomical fair for everyone. Nowhere else can you enjoy a culinary journey around the world in such a condensed space.
🕔 *Messe Berlin, ICC • Map A5*
• *(030) 303 80 • 2nd half of January*
•*Admission charge*

8 Theatertreffen Berlin
Since 1963, the most interesting theatre productions from around Germany have been performed annually here in Berlin. 🕔 *Various venues • May*
• *Admission charge*

9 Karneval der Kulturen
Multicultural Berlin celebrates for three days in the colourful Kreuzberg district in a cheerful street carnival parade.
🕔 *Kreuzberg • Map G/H5/6 • Whitsun*

10 Internationale Tourismusbörse (ITB)
The world's largest tourism fair offers up-to-date information to the general public, often at elaborately designed stalls. The night-time shows put on by many of the exhibiting countries are especially popular.
🕔 *Messe Berlin • Map A5 • (030) 303 80*
• *March • Admission charge*

Sports Highlights

1 Berlin-Marathon
The most exuberant marathon in the world attracts thousands of runners.
🕔 *Straße des 17. Juni • 2nd or 3rd Sunday in September*

2 Berlin Parade
Inline-skaters from around the world meet for "blading".
🕔 *Straße des 17. Juni • June*

3 Sechstagerennen
The Six Day Race is one of Berlin's most venerable sports events. 🕔 *Velodrom*
• *1st half of January*

4 German Open
Top-quality ladies' tennis, usually sold out.
🕔 *Tennisclub Rot-Weiß • May*

5 Berliner Neujahrslauf
The New Year's Day Run is a race for those who are fit and not afraid of the cold.
🕔 *Brandenburger Tor • Map K3*
• *1st January*

6 Internationales Stadionfest (ISTAF)
Germany's biggest athletics festival.
🕔 *Olympiastadion*
• *1st week in September*

7 DFB-Pokalfinale
German's soccer Cup Final is played to a crowd of 76,000 fans every year.
🕔 *Olympiastadion*

8 Deutsches Traberderby
The derby for professional trotter races. 🕔 *Trabrennbahn Mariendorf • 1st week in August*

9 Internationales Reitturnier
German show-jumpers meet.
🕔 *Trabrennbahn Mariendorf*
• *3rd week in November*

10 Berliner Motorradtage
The international meeting of bikers is a noisy event.
🕔 *Kurfürstendamm • end March*

Left **Filmpark Babelsberg** Centre**Roller-skating in Berlin** Right **In Museumsdorf Düppel**

🔟 Children's Attractions

1 Deutsches Technikmuseum

The technology museum is a giant playground for children, excellent for learning through play. There are locomotives to clamber over, windmills to play with and the exhibition "Spektrum", where older children can conduct their own physics and chemistry experiments *(see p103)*.

2 Labyrinth Kindermuseum

Berlin's only Museum for Children is particularly suitable for children at the preschool stage and in the early school years. Three or four themed exhibitions each year deal with subjects in a child-friendly and entertaining way – for example "Snoops and Detectives". Every exhibition is interactive, allowing children to join in and experiment, becoming independent through their experiences in play. ✪ *Osloer Str. 12 • 1–6pm Tue–Fri; 1–6pm Sat; 11am–6pm Sun • (030) 49 30 89 01 • Admission charge*

3 Grips-Theater

This famous Berlin theatre for children and young people has been showing the hit musical *Linie 1* for over ten years. The play, which is best suited to older children and adolescents, tells of the exciting life in the big city, using a U-Bahn line running from East to West Berlin as a metaphor. ✪ *Altonaer Str. 22 • Map D3 • Phone for performance times • (030) 39 74 74 77 • Admission charge*

4 Museumsdorf Düppel

A visit to the historical museum village of Düppel is like time travel back to the Middle Ages. Children can watch activities such as sowing, harvesting and feeding *(see p91)*.

5 Zoologischer Garten

If you are visiting Berlin with children you should not miss out on the Zoo. Particular favourites are the Monkey House (with baby gorillas and chimpanzees) and the Baby Zoo, where children are allowed to touch and feed the young of various animal species *(see pp36–7)*.

Giraffe House in the Zoo

6 Filmpark Babelsberg

Exciting shoot-outs, a walk-on film set with a U-boat, a town on an island and a small town in the Wild West are the most popular attractions at the film park – and not just with the children. A tour of the former UFA-Film studios lets visitors look behind the scenes: children try out make-up and costumes and admire the "sandman", a TV figure popular with children in East Germany since 1959. Everywhere in the park you will encounter props and figures from well-known German films. "Special effects" are demonstrated on the visitors in an imaginative exhibition. The "World of Horror" chills more than just children's spines.

The Sandman in Filmpark Babelsberg

⊗ *Großbeerenstr., Potsdam* • *Apr–Oct: 10am–6pm daily; Jul–Aug: 10am–8pm daily. Closed Mon–Fri in Sep* • *(0331) 721 27 55* • *Admission charge*

ZEISS-Großraum-planetarium

Artificial stars, planets and nebulae take you to far-away galaxies under the silvery dome of the Planetarium (see p142).

Circus Cabuwazi

Europe's largest circus puts on shows and workshops, run by professionals, specifically for young children and teenagers. This highly-rated attraction offers training in a variety of circus skills, including juggling and wire dancing, or simply a place to have fun. ⊗ *5 locations around Berlin, see www.cabuwazi.de* • *(030) 611 92 75* • *Admission charge*

Puppentheater-museum

The small but excellent and inspirational Puppet Museum specializes in dolls and puppets. Children are allowed to perform their own puppet shows and have a go at being puppet theatre directors.

⊗ *Karl-Marx-Str. 135* • *Map J6* • *9am–4pm Mon–Fri, 11am–5pm Sun* • *(030) 687*

81 32 • *Admission charge*

Domäne Dahlem

This old manor house, built in 1680, offers a rare insight into rural life in the Berlin area 100 years ago. Next door is a farm with animals, fields and a vegetable garden. This historical farm is very popular, not just with city children. A small market creates a genuinely rural atmosphere, and children can try out country activities such as sowing and harvesting for themselves, watch cows being milked and horses being shooed, and get close to beehives. ⊗ *Königin-Luise-Str. 49* • *10am–6pm Wed–Mon* • *(030) 666 30 00*

At the Domäne Dahlem

Left **Neuer See** Centre **Landwehrkanal** Right **The 'Moby Dick" ferry on Wannsee**

Lakes, Rivers & Canals

Großer Wannsee

Wannsee has long been a popular destination for Berliners, and it is well worth visiting Strandbad Wannsee. Europe's largest inland beach, it attracts some 40,000 visitors a day who sunbathe on its beautifully white, artificial beach and swim in the lake. This is also a great place for people-watching, and in the summer you will see yachts, wind surfers and jet skis. In the middle of the large lake is Pfaueninsel (Peacock Island), which can be reached on the whale-shaped "Moby Dick" ferry.
꧁ *Am Großen Wannsee*

Teufelssee

The dark green waters of the Devils' Lake may conjure up evil, yet this is actually one of Berlin's cleanest lakes. It is also one of the most relaxed and easy-going places – nudists, gay Berliners and dog lovers enjoy peace and tranquillity on the reed-covered banks in the middle of the Grunewald woods.
꧁ *Teufelsberg, Grunewald*

Großer Müggelsee

Covering 766ha (1,900 acres), Berlin's largest lake is situated in the far southeast of the city. Berliners have nicknamed it the "large bathtub" – a good description, for thousands of Berliners congregate here in the heat of summer for a refreshing dip. You can also row, sail or surf on the lake *(see p146)*.

Schlachtensee

After Wannsee, Schlachtensee is the second most popular lake in Berlin. The small, elongated lake attracts mainly young people. To avoid the crowds on the sunbathing lawn right next to Schlachtensee S-Bahn station, just follow the embankment path around to the right. There you will find many small and slightly concealed green spaces perfect for sunseekers. The best time to go is during the week.
꧁ *Am Schlachtensee*

Spree River

One of Berlin's many epithets is that of "Athens on the Spree", so named because of its cultural heritage and the slowly meandering river. In total, the Spree measures 398 km (249 miles), of which 46 km (29 miles) run through Berlin. Its banks are attractive for rest and recreation, and guided boat tours, romantic evening cruises and walks along the riverside are pleasant ways to spend the day.
꧁ *Mitte, Tiergarten • Map J/K 1–6*

Boat trip to the Spree bend

Houseboats on Landwehrkanal

Lietzensee

The Bohemian population of Charlottenburg considers this their "local lake". It is not suitable for swimming, but idyllic meadows around the lake are ideally suited for sunbathing and snoozing. The shaded lakeside walks in the middle of the city are also popular with dog owners. In the evening, the few cafés on the east side offer a great view of the illuminated Funkturm.
Ⓢ *Am Kaiserdamm • Map A4*

Krumme Lanke

Although Krumme Lanke is commonly thought not to be clean enough for bathing, some people now think otherwise. In fact, it seems cleaner (though also colder) than the water in Schlachtensee.
Ⓢ *Am Fischerhüttenweg*

Landwehrkanal

Built in 1845–50, this is Berlin's oldest artificial waterway. The canal connects the Upper and the Lower Spree, running east to west through the western part of the centre. Take a boat trip along the canal and you will see some of Berlin's most attractive bridges. At some places, it is possible to lie on the green banks of the canal in the middle of the city, for example at the Paul-Lincke-Ufer in Kreuzberg.
Ⓢ *Lützowplatz • Map M/N5*

Ship's bell

Tegeler See

The northernmost lake in Berlin is situated in an elegant residential area. A particularly attractive walk is Greenwich Promenade, from Tegeler Hafen (harbour) to Schwarzer Weg. A small, slightly hidden lakeside path leads from here to the other side of the lake and to a peninsula. Here stands the Villa Borsig, built in 1905 for a family of industrialists. Today it is owned by a foundation and is closed to the public. If you continue southward along Schwarzer Weg, you will get to the Tegeler See lido. Ⓢ *Alt-Tegel*

Neuer See

Visitors will be surprised to discover the tranquil New Lake in the middle of the city, well hidden at the western end of the vast Großer Tiergarten park. On its banks is the Café am Neuen See *(see p101)*. A boat trip or a walk around the lake is a pleasant way to while away the day. Ⓢ *Großer Tiergarten • Map M3*

Berlin's Top 10

For parks and gardens in Berlin **see pp70–71**

Left **Inline-Skating in the Tiergarten** Centre **Trabrennbahn Mariendorf** Right **At Sport Oase**

Sport & Fitness Venues

1 Olympiastadion

The Olympic Stadium is worth a visit even if no particular sports events are scheduled. The giant edifice, constructed by Werner Mach for the Olympic Games in 1936, reflects the architectural style typical of the Nazi period. Two statues by Arno Breker flank the main entrance. Opposite the 80,000-seater stadium are the Maifeld, inspired by the architecture of ancient Rome, and a belltower from where you have fantastic views of Berlin. The stadium itself was renovated and partially covered in 2000–4. Berlin's premier-league football club, Hertha BSC, plays its home games here. An exhibition documents the history of the stadium *(see p84)*.

Hertha BSC playing in the Olympiastadion

2 Galopprennbahn Hoppegarten

Horse races take place against the historical backdrop of the Union Club 1867's traditional race track, considered to be the most attractive track between Moscow and Paris. In the audience, horse- and betting-mad Berliners mingle with the city's upper classes. ❧ *Goetheallee 1, Dahlwitz-Hoppegarten • races 2pm Sun • (03342) 389 30*

3 Trabrennbahn Mariendorf

Exciting trotting races such as the annual derby for the "Blue Ribbon" take place on the Trabrennbahn in Mariendorf. ❧ *Mariendorfer Damm 222 • races 6pm Wed, 1:30pm Sun • (030) 740 12 12*

4 Velodrom

This futuristic, silvery sports arena is the focal point for Berlin's cyclists. Every year in January, this is where the legendary Sechstagerennen (Six Day Race) takes place. ❧ *Paul-Heyse-Str. 26 • times vary depending on event • (030) 44 30 44 30*

5 Cycling

The large green spaces in Berlin and Potsdam are ideal for cycling excursions. Districts such as the Scheunenviertel or Dahlem are also well suited for exploration by bike. There are several places where you can hire a bicycle – for example, in the centre at Friedrichstraße station *(see p162)*.

Hertha BSC: **www.herthabsc.de**

Interior of the Neukölln swimming baths

Stadtbad Neukölln
The most attractive swimming baths in Berlin date back to the late 19th century. These luxuriously fitted Art-Nouveau baths make swimming a rather special experience. ◉ *Ganghoferstr. 3 • 2–9:30pm Mon; 6:45am–9:30pm Tue–Fri; 8am–9:30pm Sat–Sun • (030) 68 24 98 12*

Sport Oase
This charming badminton and squash centre is based in a former Schultheiss brewery. It has four halls with 23 courts on several levels; and there is also a bar. ◉ *Stromstr. 11–17 • Map D3 • 8am–11:30pm Mon–Thu; 9am–10pm Fri–Sun • (030) 390 66 20*

Jopp Frauenfitness
In the western centre of the city is this Fitness Centre for Women, which guarantees a relaxed and cheerful atmosphere for exercise on standard equipment as well as many specialist classes, away from prying eyes. The staff are very helpful. ◉ *Tauentzienstr. 13 • Map P5 • 7am–11pm Mon–Fri, 10am–8pm Sat, Sun • (030) 21 01 11*

Inline-Skating Tiergarten
The paths and tracks in the northern half of the Großer Tiergarten park, as well as around the perimeters of Straße des 17 Juni, are excellent for inline-skating away from the traffic. Skating in the busy city streets – though practised – is officially forbidden. ◉ *Tergarten • Map M5/6*

Aspria
Berlin's premier health and wellness club offers everything from a full-sized swimming pool and sauna to a beauty salon, a health-orientated restaurant, massages, and a rooftop relaxation area. ◉ *Karlsruher Str. 20 • 6am–11pm Mon–Fri, 8am–10pm Sat & Sun • (030) 890 688 80 • Admission charge*

Yoga at Aspria

Left **Britzer Schloss and Park** Centre **Neuer See** Right **Schlosspark Charlottenburg**

Parks & Gardens

Großer Tiergarten

Tiergarten – the green lungs of Berlin – is the most famous park in the city. It covers an area of 203 ha (500 acres) and is situated right in the centre of town. Originally designed, in 1833–40, by Peter Joseph Lenné as a hunting estate for the Elector, in the latter half of the 19th century the park became a recreation ground for all Berliners. Today it attracts a happy crowd of cyclists, joggers, sunbathers and Turkish families having barbecues, especially at weekends.
◈ *Tiergarten • Map M5/6*

Schlosspark Charlottenburg

The Palace Park is one of the most attractive and charming green spaces in Germany. Immediately behind Schloss Charlottenburg is a small but magnificent Baroque garden, and beyond this extends a vast park, dating back to the early 19th century. It was landscaped in the English style and boasts artificial lake and river landscapes, small hidden buildings and idyllic shaded groves on the banks of ponds and streams. The park is ideally suited for strolling, and it is also a favourite place for sunseekers *(see also pp28–31)*.
◈ *Schloss Charlottenburg, Spandauer Damm • Map A/B3 • from sunrise to sunset daily*

Grunewald and Teufelsberg

The Grunewald, or "green forest" as the public woods in the southwest of Berlin were known originally, is the least built-up area of woodland in the city. Parts of Grunewald are very quiet and isolated indeed, and there are even wild boar in the woods – which can be a nuisance to people who have gardens in the nearby district of Zehlendorf. Grunewald is excellent for hiking and horse-riding. ◈ *Grunewald*

Statue of Luise on Pfaueninsel

Pfaueninsel

Peacock Island, an island in the middle of Wannsee that can be reached only by ferry, is probably the most romantic spot in Berlin. In the 19th century, the island served as a love nest for King Friedrich Wilhelm II. His charming folly of a palace ruin was in keeping with the tastes of the time. Today dozens of proud peacocks live in the area around the building *(see p89)*.

Botanischer Garten

The 19th-century Botanical Garden is a paradise of flowers and plants in the centre of town. The vast area with 15 greenhouses was built in the late 19th century around gentle hills and picturesque ponds. In the Great Palm House by Alfred Koerner (closed until 2008) you can see

Botanischer Garten: www.bgbm.fu-berlin.de

and giant Victoria water lilies, reaching a diameter of over 2 m (6 ft). The museum introduces visitors to the world of micro-biology. ◈ *Unter den Eichen 5–10 (garden), Königin-Luise-Str. 6 (museum)* • *9am to sunset daily (garden); 10am–6pm daily (museum)* • *(030) 83 85 01 00* • *Admission charge*

Flowering hibiscus in Botanischer Garten

Viktoriapark and Kreuzberg

The old municipal park, originally designed in 1888–94 as a recreation area for local workers, is today one of Berlin's most popular green spaces. The meadows around Kreuzberg, which rises to 30 m (98 ft), are great for sunbathing. On top of the mountain, a monument recalls the Prussian Wars of Liberation *(see p105)*.

Volkspark Friedrichshain

The oldest park in Berlin (1840) is an artificial landscape of lakes and meadows and two heaps of rubble, one of which is jokingly called "Mount Klamott", meaning Mount Rubble. There is also a fairy-tale fountain with statues of the most popular fairy tale characters *(see pp146–7)*.

Tierpark Friedrichsfelde

This second, smaller zoo is situated in the idyllic palace park of Friedrichsfelde. Some 950 animal species live in the park; the lions are particularly worth seeing *(see p147)*.

Treptower Park

The 19th-century landscape garden on the banks of the Spree has become famous for the Soviet Memorial, which stands next to the graves of 5,000 Red Army soldiers *(see p146)*.

Britzer Schloss and Park

The Palace in Britz, dating from 1706, has been furnished with historical furniture from the Gründerzeit (after 1871). It is situated in a lovely park. ◈ *Alt-Britz 73* • *2–5:30pm Wed (guided tours of the palace), 9am to sunset daily (garden)* • *(030) 609 792 30* • *Admission charge*

For waterside recreation grounds **see pp66–7**

Berlin's Top 10

Left **Brandenburger Hof** Centre **Inside the Bristol Kempinski** Right **Lobby of the Regent Berlin**

🔟 Famous Hotels

Inside the famous Hotel Adlon

spacious rooms overlook the Marlene-Dietrich-Platz, but if this is too mundane for you, you can always enjoy the fantastic views of the entire city from the hotel's Olympus Wellness-Club.
🔍 *Marlene-Dietrich-Platz 2*
• *Map F4* • *(030) 25 53 12 34*
• *www.hyatt.com* • *€€€€*

1 Hotel Adlon Berlin
Berlin's top hotel ranks as one of the finest in Europe. A reconstruction of the historic Adlon hotel, it opened in 1997 and has become popular with celebrities and politicians from around the globe. Even if you are not going to stay here, you could have a cup of tea or coffee in the magnificent lobby.
🔍 *Unter den Linden 77* • *Map K3* • *(030) 226 10* • *www.hotel-adlon.de* • *€€€€*

2 Regent Berlin
Concealed behind the ultra-modern façade of this hotel is a late 19th-century building with thick carpets, sparkling chandeliers and tasteful wallpaper. Comfort of an international standard and discreet service are guaranteed.
🔍 *Charlottenstr. 49* • *Map K4* • *(030) 203 38* • *www. theregentberlin.com* • *€€€€*

3 Grand Hyatt
Japanese minimalism is the style that was chosen for this new building on Potsdamer Platz. The

4 Schlosshotel im Grunewald
This small and very expensive palace hotel is situated in a quiet part of Grunewald, some distance from the centre. The hotel is popular with filmstars and celebrities wishing to get away from the crowds. Karl Lagerfeld designed the interior – and for a mere €1,500 you can even rent his permanent bedroom suite.
🔍 *Brahmsstr. 10* • *(030) 89 58 40*
• *www.schlosshotelberlin.com* • *€€€€*

5 Kempinski Hotel Bristol Berlin
The grand old lady of West Berlin hotels, the splendid Kempinski is beginning to show her age a little, but the cosmopolitan glamour is still there and no hotel in town is better. All the rooms are furnished with a timeless elegance, while the lobby and bar are panelled in dark wood. In the Kempinski-Grill you can enjoy a glass of Sekt right on the Ku'damm while watching less fortunate mortals. A place where you can be pampered and spoilt *(see p179)*.

Regent Berlin porter

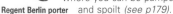

72

Online reservation service: **www.berlin.nethotels.com**

Hackescher Markt

One of Berlin's best hotels, the charming Hackescher Markt, is situated right in the popular Mitte district. Service and furnishings are of a four-star standard, yet the prices are moderate. Best of all is the hotel's central location in one of Berlin's liveliest areas: it is only a few steps away from the Hackesche Höfe and the Scheunenviertel.

🔵 *Große Präsidentenstr. 8*
• *Map J5 • (030) 28 00 30*
• *www.loock-hotels.com • €€*

Ritz-Carlton Berlin

The new Ritz-Carlton Berlin near Potsdamer Platz is an ultra-luxurious gem hidden behind a modern façade reminiscent of New York's Rockefeller Center. The lobby with its marble columns and tons of gold leaf is a stunning setting for the Curtain Club and the Desbrosses brasserie. Its rooms are sumptuously decorated, all decorated to Prussian Neo-Classical designs – there are even telescopes to enjoy the cityscape. 🔵 *Potsdamer Platz 3 • Map F4 • (030) 33 77 77 • www.ritzcarlton.com • €€€€*

Ritz-Carlton Berlin

Dorint Hotel am Gendarmenmarkt

A quiet and elegant hotel with great views over the historic square, the relatively small Dorint has real style and offers excellent service. All the rooms are first-class and feature elegant furnishings *(see p179)*.

Savoy Hotel

Greta Garbo used to stay at the Savoy, and the style of days gone by is celebrated throughout. Many filmstars are regulars in this hotel, which is justly proud of its service. The Savoy is famous for its Times Bar.

🔵 *Fasanenstr. 9–10 • Map N4 • (030) 31 10 30 • www.hotel-savoy.com • €€€*

Brandenburger Hof

An elegant town hotel, based in a 19th-century manor house. The lobby is traditionally furnished and the rooms are in a sobre Bauhaus-style. The Michelin-starred Quadriga restaurant specializes in French cuisine.

🔵 *Eislebener Str. 14 • Map P4 • (030) 21 40 50 • www. brandenburger-hof.com • €€€*

Left **Inside First Floor** Centre **Outdoor tables at Lutter & Wegner** Right **The super-trendy Vau**

Best Places to Eat

Vau
The best of international and Austrian cooking is served by Kolja Kleeberg at the stylishly designed Vau. The restaurant has been awarded a well-deserved Michelin star *(see p121)*. ◈ *Jägerstr. 54–55 • Map L4 • noon–2:30pm, 7–10:30pm Mon–Sat • (030) 202 97 30*

Vox
The exquisite food in this minimalist, elegant hotel restaurant is a sleek and modern fusion of Asian and international dishes, with an emphasis on Japanese (sushi) dishes and French-Italian creations. The show kitchen was one of the first in Berlin. Open for breakfast. ◈ *Marlene-Dietrich-Platz 2 • Map F4 • 6–11pm Tue–Sat • (030) 323 10 46*

Hugo's
The new shooting star in Berlin's gourmet firmament, Hugo's is a Michelin-starred restaurant with a stunning 270° view of the city skyline. Wood panelling and plush leather set the tone, while the international cuisine reveals the light touch of German master chef Michael Kammeier. The service is impeccable yet relaxed (no stiff upper lip here) and the wine list something to die for. ◈ *Budapester Str. 2 • Map N5 • 6pm–1am Mon–Sat • (030) 260 212 63*

Bocca di Bacco
Berlin's hippest Italian restaurant offers fresh fish and exceptional meat creations such as *Bresaola di Cavallo* (horse meat with salad and nuts). ◈ *Friedrichstr. 167–8 • Map K4 • noon–midnight daily • (030) 20 67 28 28*

Borchardt
Everyone of importance, including past Chancellors, dine at Borchardt. The historic room is furnished in Wilhelminian style (featuring tall columns, wall mosaics and tile flooring) – an appropriate setting for the classic French cooking that is served here. Without a reservation, however, even top politicians can't get a table *(see p121)*. ◈ *Französische Str. 47 • Map K4 • 11:30am–1am daily • (030) 81 88 62 62*

First Floor
This top gourmet restaurant, specializing in the creation of new German dishes, is a well-guarded secret. The menu features traditional Berlin fare such as *Eisbein mit Sauerkraut* (pork knuckle with sauerkraut) as well as new creations using fish, langoustines and truffles. The specials of the day are more moderately priced. ◈ *Hotel Palace, Budapester Str. 42 • Map N5 • noon–2:30pm, 6:30pm–10:30pm Tue–Sat • (030) 25 02 10 20*

Inside Hugo's

The popular Borchardt restaurant

Fischers Fritz

7 This high-profile establishment specializes in local and exotic fish dishes. Chef Christian Lohse, who has previously held two Michelin stars, prepares some of the best maritime dishes in the country. ◈ *Regent Berlin, Charlottenstr. 49 • Map K4 • noon–2pm, 6:30pm–10pm daily • (030) 203 363 63*

Facil

8 This Michelin-starred restaurant, in a green oasis on top of the Madison hotel, is a study in understated elegance. Chef Michael Kempf creates stylish Mediterranean dishes with a French accent *(see p101)*. ◈ *Potsdamer Str. 3 • Map L2 • 11–3pm, 7–11pm Mon–Fri • (030) 59 005 12 34*

Lutter & Wegner Gendarmenmarkt

9 In this old building, formerly the Berliner Sektkellerei (supposedly the place where sparkling wine, or *sekt*, was invented), Austrian cuisine is the star. Try the best *wiener schnitzel* in town, accompanied by a classic warm potato salad, at consistently low prices. In the summer, there are tables outdoors. ◈ *Charlottenstr. 56 • Map L4 • noon–2am daily • (030) 202 95 417*

Ana e Bruno

10 Ana e Bruno's is one of the best restaurants in Berlin, and certainly serves the best Italian food in the city. Don't be shocked when you see the menu: the numbers refer to the calories in a dish rather than to the price – although these are also at the top end *(see p87)*. ◈ *Sophie-Charlotten-Str. 101 • Map A3 • 6:30pm–10:30pm Tue–Sat • (030) 325 71 10*

At Ana e Bruno's

AROUND TOWN

BERLIN'S TOP 10

Left **On Savignyplatz** Centre **Front door in Charlottenburg** Right **On Breitscheidplatz**

Charlottenburg & Spandau

CHARLOTTENBURG IS THE ESSENCE OF BERLIN. *Here, the capital is more urbane and more cosmopolitan, more bohemian and more elegant than anywhere else. The historical streets off Ku'damm feature small cafés, restaurants, art galleries and boutiques, based in stout residential houses from the beginning of the 20th century. These streets and Charlottenburg's proud town hall remind us that this district was once the richest town in Prussia, which was only incorporated into the city of Berlin in 1920. Spandau, on the other hand, is rural in comparison, a part of Berlin with a special feel. Spandau's Late Medieval old town and the citadel make this district on the other side of the Spree and Havel seem like a small independent town.*

Prussian Eagle in Spandau

🔟 Sights

1. Kurfürstendamm
2. Schloss Charlottenburg
3. Zoologischer Garten
4. Zitadelle Spandau
5. Spandau Old Town
6. Savignyplatz
7. Fasanenstraße
8. Funkturm and Messegelände
9. Newton-Sammlung
10. Käthe-Kollwitz-Museum

1 Kurfürstendamm

The famous Berlin boulevard, the pride of Charlottenburg, is today more elegant than ever *(see pp24–5)*.

2 Schloss Charlottenburg

The Baroque and English-style gardens of this Hohenzollern summer residence are ideal for a stroll *(see pp28–31)*.
🌐 *Spandauer Damm • Map A /B3 • opening hours see p28 • (030) 32 09 11 • Admission charge*

3 Zoologischer Garten

Germany's largest and oldest zoological garden is a must for all families on a visit to Berlin *(see pp36–37)*.

4 Zitadelle Spandau

The only surviving fortress in Berlin, the citadel, at the confluence of the Havel and Spree Rivers, is strategically well placed. The star-shaped moated fortress, built in 1560 by Francesco Chiaramella da Gandino, was modelled on similar buildings in Italy. Its four powerful corner bastions, named Brandenburg, König (king), Königin (queen) and Kronprinz (crown prince) are especially remarkable. A fortress stood on the same site as early as the 12th century, of which the Juliusturm survives – a keep that served as

Zitadelle Spandau

a prison in the 19th century. At the time, Berliners used to say, "off to the Julio", when they sent criminals to prison. Later the imperial war treasures were kept here – the reparations paid by France to the German Empire after its defeat in the Franco-Prussian War of 1870–1. The Bastion Königin houses a museum of municipal history. 🌐 *Am Juliusturm • 9am–5pm Tue–Fri, 10am–5pm Sat, Sun • (030) 354 944 200 • Admission charge*

Inside Nikolaikirche, Spandau Old Town

5 Spandau Old Town

When walking around Spandau Old Town, it is easy to forget that you are still in Berlin. Narrow alleyways and nooks and crannies around Nikolaikirche are lined by Late Medieval houses, a sign that Spandau was founded in 1197 and is thus older than Berlin itself. Berlin's oldest house, the Gothic House, dating back to the early 16th century, stands here, in Breite Straße 32. 🌐 *Breite Straße, Spandau*

Spandau and Berlin

West Berliners consider the Spandauers to be rather different sorts of people, provincial and rough, and not "real" Berliners at all. But the Spandauers can reassure themselves that Spandau is 60 years older than Berlin, and proudly point to their independent history. The mutual mistrust is not just a consequence of Spandau's geographical location, isolated from the remainder of the city by the Havel and Spree Rivers. It is also due to the recent incorporation of Spandau in 1920. Today, still, Spandauers say they are going "to Berlin", even though the centre of the city is only a few stops away on the U-Bahn.

Left **A plaque in Savignyplatz** Centre **Literaturhaus Fasanenstraße** Right **Villa Grisebach**

Savignyplatz

One of Berlin's most attractive squares is right in the heart of Charlottenburg. Savignyplatz, named after a 19th-century German legal scholar, is the focal point of Charlottenburg's reputation as a district for artists and intellectuals and as a trendy residential area for dining out and entertainment. The square has two green spaces, either side of Kantstraße. It was built in the 1920s as part of an effort to create parks in the centre of town.

Balconies in Savignyplatz

Small paths, benches and pergolas make it a pleasant place for a rest. Dotted all around Savignyplatz are restaurants, street cafés and shops, especially in Grolman-, Knesebeck-, and Carmerstraße, all three of which cross the square. Many a reveller has lost his way here after a night's celebrating, which is why the area is jokingly known as the "Savignydreieck" (the Savigny Triangle). North of Savignyplatz it is worth exploring some of the most attractive streets in Charlottenburg – Knesebeck-, Schlüter- and Goethestraße. This is still a thriving Charlottenburg community; the small shops, numerous bookstores, cafés and specialist retailers are always busy, especially on Saturdays. South of the square, the red-tiled S-Bahn arches also lure visitors with their shops, cafés and bars; most of all the Savignypassage near Bleibtreustraße and the small passageway between Grolman- and Uhlandstraße on the opposite side of the square.

🔵 *An der Kantstraße • Map N3*

Fasanenstraße

This elegant street is the most attractive and trendiest street off Ku'damm. Designer shops, galleries and restaurants are tucked away here, a shoppers' paradise for all those who regard Kurfürstendamm as a mere retail strip catering for the masses. The junction of Fasanenstraße and Ku'damm is one of the liveliest spots in Berlin. One of the best known places

Statue in Savignyplatz

The Jewish House, in Fasanenstraße

Kempinski Hotel Bristol Berlin, Fasanenstraße

is the "Bristol Berlin Kempinski" *(see p72)* at the northern end of Fasanenstraße. The Lübbecke & Co bank opposite cleverly combines a historic building with a new structure. Next to it are the Jüdisches Gemeindehaus (Jewish Community House, *see p84)* and a little farther along, at the junction with Kantstraße, is the Kant-Dreieck *(see p41)*. Berliner Börse (stock exchange), based in the ultra-modern Ludwig-Erhard-Haus *(see p40)*, is just above, at the corner of Hardenbergstraße. The southern end of the street is dominated by residential villas, some of which may seem a little pompous, as well as the Literaturhaus, Villa Grisebach, one of the oldest art auction houses in Berlin, and the Käthe-Kollwitz-Museum *(see p83)*. There are also some very expensive fashion stores here, as well as a few cosy restaurants. At its southern end, the street leads to picturesque Fasanenplatz, where many artists lived before 1933.
Ⓢ *Charlottenburg • Map N/P4*

Shops in Fasanenstraße

A Day in Charlottenburg

Morning

🕐 Begin your tour of Charlottenburg at Breitscheidplatz and stroll down **Kurfürstendamm** *(see pp24–5)* in a westerly direction. Turn left into **Fasanenstraße** to visit the **Käthe-Kollwitz-Museum** *(see p83)* and to see the **Literaturhaus**. You could stop for a mid-morning breakfast at **Café Wintergarten** *(see p86)* in the Literaturhaus, before going back up Fasanenstraße in a northerly direction. On the left you will pass the **Kempinski Hotel Bristol Berlin**, and on the right you can see the Jewish House and the Ludwig-Erhard-Haus. Diagonally opposite, on the other side of Kantstraße, stands the **Theater des Westens** *(see p57)*. Continue along Kantstraße on the left side until you reach the shopping centre **Stilwerk** *(see pp60–61)*, a place no one has ever been known to leave without buying something!

Afternoon

🍴 A good place for lunch is the restaurant **Soultrane** in Stilwerk shopping centre. Afterwards, continue along Kantstraße to **Savignyplatz.** Now explore the small streets around the square, Grolman-, Carmer-, Knesebeck- and Mommsenstraße. Small shops invite you to browse and spend your money, and the **Café Savigny** *(see p86)* is a good place for a fruit flan with whipped cream and a cup of coffee. For the early evening, **Dressler** *(see p87)* is recommended, here you will find a range of dishes typical of a real French brasserie.

Around Town – Charlottenburg & Spandau

Ehrenhalle in the Messegelände

The Berliner Funkturm

8 Funkturm and Messegelände

The 150-m (492-ft) high Funkturm (TV tower), reminiscent of the Eiffel Tower in Paris, is one of the landmarks of Berlin that can be seen from afar. Built in 1924 to plans by Heinrich Straumer, it served as an aerial and as an air-traffic control tower. The viewing platform at 125 m (410 ft) provides magnificent views, while the restaurant, situated at 55 m (180 ft), overlooks the oldest part of the complex, the exhibition centre and the surrounding pavillions. The giant building in the

The History of Charlottenburg

The magnificent Charlottenburger Rathaus (town hall) on Otto-Suhr-Allee is a reminder of the time when this district of 200,000 people was an independent town. Charlottenburg, named after the eponymous palace, arose in 1705 from the medieval settlement of Lietzow. Towards the end of the 19th century, Charlottenburg – then Prussia's wealthiest town – enjoyed a meteoric rise following the construction of the Westend colony of villas and of Kurfürstendamm. Thanks to its numerous theatres, the opera and the Technical University, the district developed into Berlin's west end during the 1920s.

east is the Hall of Honour built to designs by Richard Ermisch in 1936, in the colossal Fascist architectural style.

On the opposite side rises the shiny silver ICC, the International Congress Centrum, built in 1975–9 by Ralf Schüler and Ursulina Schüler-Witte. It is still considered one of the most advanced conference centres in the world, with 80 rooms for more than 5,000 visitors. Berlin's vast exhibition grounds are among the largest in the world, covering an area of 160,000 sq m (40 acres). These play host to, among others, Grüne Woche (green week, an agricultural fair), Internationale Tourismusbörse (international tourism fair) and Internationale Funkausstellung (international TV fair). ◉ Messedamm 22 • Map A4/5 • 11am–9pm Mon, 10am–11pm Tue–Sun • (030) 30 38 29 96 • Admission charge

9 Newton Sammlung

Helmut Newton (1931–2004), the world famous photographer,

has finally returned to his home city. This new museum presents his complete works and centres on two shows called "Sex and Landscapes" and "Us and Them", which show his early fashion and nude photography as well as photos of the famous, rich and beautiful since 1947. ⓢ *Jebensstr. 2 • Map C4 • 10am–6pm Tue–Wed; 10am–6pm Fri–Sun; 10am–10pm Thu • (030) 318 648 56 • Admission charge*

⑩ Käthe-Kollwitz-Museum

The museum is dedicated to the work of the Berlin artist Käthe Kollwitz (1897–1945), who documented the misery of workers' lives in 1920s Berlin in numerous prints, graphics and sketches. After losing a son and a grandson in World War I, she concentrated on the themes of war and motherhood. The museum holds some 200 of her works, including several self-portraits.
ⓢ *Fasanenstr. 24 • Map P4*
• 11am–6pm Wed–Mon • (030) 882 52 10
• Admission charge

Mother and Child by Käthe Kollwitz

A Day in Spandau

Morning

Start with a journey on the U-Bahn. From the centre of town, take a U2 train in the direction of Ruhleben, and at Bismarckstraße station change to the U7 train in the direction of Rathaus Spandau. Ten minutes later you will have reached the centre of **Spandau Old Town** (see p79), where you can visit Breite Straße and Nikolaikirche.

Before returning to Charlottenburg, make sure you visit the **Zitadelle Spandau**. There, in the museum café, you can also enjoy a late breakfast. Return by U-Bahn. This time, get off the train at the Wilmersdorfer Straße station, one of the few pedestrianized areas in Berlin. This is a particularly good area for shopaholics and bargain hunters.

Afternoon

From Wilmersdorfer Straße a 20-minute walk along Kaiserdamm in a westerly direction will take you to the **Funkturm** and the **Messegelände** with the "Ehrenhalle". You could have lunch at the **Funkturm-Restaurant**, and enjoy the magnificent views. Nearby, the Haus des Rundfunks (broadcasting house) and the **Georg-Kolbe-Museum** (see p84) are worth visiting.
After your museum visit, if you still have some time and energy, you could take bus No. 218 from here to the **Olympiastadion** (see p68). In the evening, return to Charlottenburg and Savignyplatz by bus No. 149. Here you can enjoy the justly famed, delicious Franconian cooking at **Florian's** (see p87).

Left **In the Deutsche Oper** Centre **Denkmal Benno Ohnesorg** Right **In the Theater des Westens**

Best of the Rest

1 Olympiastadion
Built for the 1936 Olympic Games, the stadium is an example of Fascist architecture *(see p68)*. ◈ *Olympischer Platz • Apr–Oct: 10am–7pm daily • (030) 250 023 22*

2 Georg-Kolbe-Museum
Sculptures by Georg Kolbe (1877–1947) are exhibited in his home and workshop. ◈ *Sensburger Allee 25 • 10am–5pm Tue–Sun • (030) 304 21 44 • Admission charge*

3 Le-Corbusier-Haus
The apartment block where the French architect Corbusier lived was built for the 1957 Interbau trade fair. Designed to alleviate the acute housing shortage after World War II, it was highly innovative in its day. ◈ *Flatowallee 16*

4 Jüdisches Gemeindehaus
Berlin's Jewish community house stands on the site of the Charlottenburg synagogue. Damaged during "Reichskristallnacht" on 9 November 1938, it was mostly destroyed during World War II. Only the portal remains. ◈ *Fasanenstr. 79–80 • Map P4 • 11am–8pm daily • (030) 88 02 82 01*

5 Theater des Westens
This theatre is based in an attractive building from 1895–6. Renowned for its fare of light entertainment, it is regarded as one of Germany's best musical theatres *(see p57)*. ◈ *Kantstr. 12 • Map N4 • 8pm Tue–Sat, 6pm Sun • 0180 544 44*

6 Deutsche Oper
The German Opera, opened in 1961, specializes in Italian and German classics. ◈ *Bismarckstr. 34–37 • Map B4 • (030) 341 02 49 • Admission charge*

7 Denkmal Benno Ohnesorg
Alfred Hrdlicka's sculpture from 1971 commemorates the student Benno Ohnesorg, who was shot dead here during a demonstration on 2 April 1967. ◈ *Bismarckstr. • Map B4*

8 Technische Universität
Berlin's Technical University was founded in 1879. ◈ *Straße des 17. Juni • Map C4 • 8am–8pm Mon–Fri • (030) 31 40*

9 Universität der Künste
The School of Art is one of the best German universities for the fine arts, architecture and design. ◈ *Hardenbergstr. 32–33 • Map N4 • 8am–8pm Mon–Fri • (030) 318 50*

10 Erotik-Museum
Historic and new erotica. ◈ *Kantstr. 5 • Map N4 • 9am–midnight daily (from 1pm Sun) • (030) 886 06 66 • Admission charge (over 18 years only)*

 Deutsche Oper: www.deutscheoperberlin.de

Left **Zille-Hof** Centre **Butter Lindner** Right **Tee Gschwendner**

⒑ Shops & Markets

Stilwerk
A shopping centre specializing in stylish designer goods *(see p60)*. ◉ *Kantstr. 17 • Map C4 • (030) 31 51 50*

Antik- und Flohmarkt Straße des 17. Juni
Berlin's largest antiques, art and flea market, selling excellent items *(see p60)*. ◉ *Straße des 17. Juni • Map M4 • 10am–5pm Sat, Sun*

Peek & Cloppenburg
Offering five floors of men's, women's and children's clothing, this is one of Berlin's most popular department stores. ◉ *Tauentzienstr. 19 • Map P5 • 10am–8pm Mon–Sat • (030) 212 900*

Hallhuber
This huge upscale clothing store offers the latest designer labels for both men and women (DKNY, Paul Smith and the like) as well as its own less expensive house label. ◉ *Kurfürstendamm 13 • Map P4 • (030) 881 20 78*

Bücherbogen
Berlin's leading arts and photography bookseller is tucked away within three arches under the S-Bahn viaduct. ◉ *Savignyplatz • Map N3 • (030) 31 86 95 11*

Jil Sander
Simple, elegant designer fashions for men and women are for sale at this cool boutique. ◉ *Kurfürstendamm 185 • Map P4 • (030) 88 67 020*

Butter Lindner
This traditional Berlin store specializes in fresh, home-made foods and delicatessen. Of its numerous branches the most attractive one is in Charlottenburg. ◉ *Knesebeckstr. 92 • Map P3 • 8am–6pm Mon–Fri, 8am–1:30pm Sat • (030) 710 910*

Hellmann
Ladies' and gentlemen's fashions made from the best materials, including Hellmann's own collection and clothes from well-known designers. ◉ *Kurfürstendamm 53 & Bleibtreustr. 20 • Map P3 • 10am–7pm Mon–Fri, 10am–6pm Sat • (030) 882 25 65*

Tee Gschwendner
This tiny store is a haven for tea lovers, and upstairs you can try out a new flavour in their own tea room. ◉ *Kurfürstendamm 217 • Map P4 • 10am–8pm Mon–Fri, 10am–6pm Sat • (030) 881 91 81*

Zille-Markt
Old Berlin bric-à-brac market, with a vast, if expensive, selection. ◉ *Fasanenstr. 14 • Map P4 • 8am–5:30pm Mon–Fri, 8am–1pm Sat • (030) 313 43 33*

For more on shopping see p170

Left **Café Wintergarten** Centre **Reinhards at Kempinski** Right **Café Filmbühne am Steinplatz**

Cafés

1 Café Wintergarten im Literaturhaus

One of Berlin's most beautiful cafés is based in the conservatory of an old town house. In summer guests can sit outside, in the Literaturhaus garden. ✎ *Fasanenstr. 23 • Map P4 • 9:30am–1am daily • (030) 882 54 14 • no credit cards*

2 Café Savigny

This gay and lesbian café, with traditional interior, has a relaxed atmosphere; the fruit flans are particularly worth trying. ✎ *Grolmanstr. 53–54 • Map N3 • 9am–1am daily • (030) 32 89 06 61*

3 Reinhards at Kempinski

This new restaurant and café has great views of the Kurfürstendamm from its sunny terrace. ✎ *Kurfürstendamm 27 • Map P4 • 6:30am–midnight daily • (030) 20 45 45 45*

4 Café Kranzler

The new Café Kranzler is very different from the historic café of pre-World War II fame, yet the views over Ku'damm are just as amazing. ✎ *Kurfürstendamm 18 • Map P4 • 8:30am–8pm daily • (030) 887 18 39 25*

5 Café Filmbühne am Steinplatz

Other cafés may sell better cakes, but this coffee shop excels thanks to its student atmosphere. ✎ *Hardenbergstr. 12 • Map N3 • 9am–midnight daily • (030) 312 65 89*

6 Café Hardenberg

The Technical University's student café has a great atmosphere and reasonable prices. ✎ *Hardenbergstr. 10 • Map N3 • 9am–1am daily • (030) 312 26 44 • no credit cards*

7 Café Balzac

One of several modelled on the US Starbucks chain, this café is opposite the Technical University. ✎ *Hardenbergstr. 4 • Map M3 • 7:30am–8pm Mon–Fri, 7:30am–6pm Sat • (030) 31 80 01 82 • no credit cards*

8 Café Aedes

This modern café, based in an S-Bahn arch, forms part of an architectural gallery. ✎ *Else-Ury-Bogen • Map N3 • 8am–midnight Mon–Fri, Sat & Sun 9am–midnight • (030) 31 50 95 35*

9 Café Kleine Orangerie

A small garden café at the Charlottenburg Palace. ✎ *Spandauer Damm 20 • Map A3 • 10am–10pm daily • (030) 322 20 21*

10 Schwarzes Café

Alternative rock café, offering all-day breakfasts. ✎ *Kantstr. 148 • Map N4 • Open around the clock • (030) 313 80 38 • no credit cards*

Note: *All restaurants accept credit cards and offer vegetarian dishes unless stated otherwise.*

Price Categories

For a three-course meal for one with half a bottle of wine (or equivalent meal), taxes and charges included

€	under €20
€€	€20–30
€€€	€30–45
€€€€	€45–60
€€€€€	over €60

Left **Entrance of Paris Bar** Centre **Kuchi, on Kantstrasse**

Restaurants

Paris Bar
Berlin's most famous French restaurant boasts sophisticated cuisine and a fantastic atmosphere with many celebrities.
Ⓢ *Kantstr. 152 • Map N3 • noon–2am daily • (030) 313 80 52 • €€€*

Alt-Luxemburg
Chef Karl Wannemacher (one Michelin star) dishes up good international and German food.
Ⓢ *Windscheidstr. 31 • 5pm–midnight Mon–Sat • (030) 323 87 30 • €€€€*

Eiffel
A large but still charming French restaurant offering some traditional Berlin dishes and with outside tables. Ⓢ *Kurfürstendamm 105 • Map P1 • 9am–1am daily • (030) 891 13 05 • €€€*

Lubitsch
A small, elegant restaurant, serving German and Italian "fusion" food. Ⓢ *Bleibtreustr. 47 • Map N/P3 • 10am–midnight Mon–Sat, 6pm–midnight Sun • (030) 882 37 56 • €€*

Florian
Trendy and popular with film lovers; southern German food.
Ⓢ *Grolmanstr. 52 • Map N3 • 6pm–3am daily • (030) 313 91 84 • €€€*

First Floor
A 1920s-style restaurant, serving traditional Berlin and French food. Ⓢ *Budapester Str. 45 • Map N5 • noon–2:30pm and 6pm–10pm Sun–Fri, 6pm–midnight Sat • (030) 25 02 10 20 • €€€€€*

Dressler
Everything at Dressler's looks, smells and tastes as it would in a real French brasserie. In winter, the game and poultry dishes are well worth trying. Ⓢ *Kurfürstendamm 207–208 • Map C5 • 8am–1am daily • (030) 883 35 30 • €€€*

Austeria
This is a new homely fish and seafood restaurant with high ambitions and an outstanding choice of oysters. Ⓢ *Kurfürstendamm 184 • Map C5 • 11am–1am daily • (030) 881 84 61 • €€€*

Kuchi
Thanks mainly to its exquisite sushi and mixed Asian hot dishes, this minimalist restaurant has a loyal clientele. Ⓢ *Kantstr. 30 • Map M3 • noon–midnight daily • (030) 315 078 15 • €€*

Ana e Bruno
Warm, friendly and extremely tasteful, Ana e Bruno is the best – and most expensive – Italian restaurant in Berlin.
Ⓢ *Sophie-Charlotten-Str. 101 • Map A3 • 6:30pm–11:30pm Tue–Sat • (030) 325 71 10 • €€€€*

For more on restaurants in Berlin **see p74**

Left **Landing stage Wannsee** Centre **Castle ruins on Pfaueninsel** Right **Jacobsbrunnen Pfaueninsel**

Grunewald & Dahlem

BERLIN'S GREEN SOUTH, *which includes the districts of Grunewald and Dahlem, is dotted with numerous lakes, rivers, small castles, private estates and residential villas, leafy roads and cafés for daytrippers. Grunewald and Dahlem have managed to preserve their rural character, although affluent and famous Berliners have always built their houses here. There are many attractions in Berlin's southwest: visitors can enjoy extensive walks in the Grunewald forest, or ferry across the picturesque lake to Pfaueninsel, an island with romantic castle ruins – and a favourite destination for locals. The swimming baths at Wannsee, Europe's largest inland beach, welcomes up to 40,000 visitors a day for fun, games and a dip in the water and on its beautiful white beaches. The museum complex in Dahlem, too, with its outstanding ethnographic and art collections, is worth visiting. Meanwhile, the Alliiertenmuseum and the Haus der Wannsee Konferenz recall a more painful period in Berlin's history.*

A peacock on Pfaueninsel

🔟 Sights

1 Dahlem Museums
2 Pfaueninsel
3 Schloss Klein-Glienicke
4 Gedenkstätte Haus der Wannsee-Konferenz
5 Strandbad Wannsee
6 Alliiertenmuseum
7 Mexikoplatz
8 Dahlem Villas
9 Jagdschloss Grunewald
🔟 Museumsdorf Düppel

Dahlem Museums

These four museums in south Berlin, dedicated to foreign cultures and peoples, feature one of Germany'y best ethno-cultural collections. The Ethno-logical Museum holds around one million items from around the world, especially artistic and cult objects from Africa, as well as exhibits from North-American Indians. Full-scale wooden huts and boats from the island populations of the South Pacific as well as a large collection of ceramic and stone sculptures from the Mayas, Aztecs and Incas are particularly impressive. The Museum für Ostasiati-sche Kunst, focusing on 1,000 years of Far-Eastern culture, dis-plays mainly objects in porcelain and lacquer from Korea, China and Japan. The shiny green jade exhibits from ancient China are just as amazing. ✎ Lansstr. 8 (Muse-um Europäischer Kulturen: Im Winkel 6–8) • 10am–6pm Tue–Fri, 11am–6pm Sat, Sun • (030) 830 11 • Admission charge

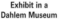

Exhibit in a Dahlem Museum

Pfaueninsel

Visitors are enchanted by the romantic palace ruins and the eponymous peacocks that run around here. The Wannsee island, which can only be reached by ferry, is one of the most charming spots for a walk in Berlin (see also p70). ✎ Pfaueninselchaussee • 10am–1pm & 1:30–5pm daily • (030) 80 58 68 30 • Admission charge

Gryffin at Schloss Klein-Glienicke

Schloss Klein-Glienicke

One of the most beautiful Hohenzollern palaces in Berlin, this romantic castle with its extensive park was built by Schinkel in 1824–60 as a summer residence for Prince Carl of Prussia. The land-scape garden, designed by Peter Joseph Lenné, hides many secrets – for example pavilions called "Große" and "Kleine Neugierde" (large and small curiosity), a garden house and a tea-house, a casino right on the water (a former apartment for guests) as well as the Orangerie (a greenhouse). ✎ Königstr. 36 • mid-Apr–mid-Oct: 10am–5pm Sat, Sun; mid-Oct–mid-Apr: 11am, 1pm, 3pm Sat–Sun (with tour only) • (030) 805 30 41 • Admission charge

Gedenkstätte Haus der Wannsee-Konferenz

It is hard to believe that some-thing as abhorrent as the Holo-

Neo-Baroque Gedenkstätte Haus

caust could have been planned at this elegant villa in a picturesque spot on Wann-see. Built in 1914–15 by Paul Baumgarten in the style of a small Neo-Baroque palace for the busi-nessman Ernst Marlier, it was here that the Nazi elite, among them the infamous Adolf Eich-mann, met on 20 January 1942 to discuss the details of the mass extermination of Jews. An exhibition at the memorial docu-ments both the conference and its consequences as well as the history of the villa. ✎ Am Großen Wannsee 56–58 • 10am–6pm daily • (030) 805 00 10 • Free admission

Prussia and Antiquity

From 1821, the landscape designer Peter Joseph Lenné and the architect Karl Friedrich Schinkel tried to turn the Potsdam countryside and its woods and lakes into an "island paradise". Their concept was based on Classical ideas of the harmonious ensemble of architecture and landscape, in accordance with the idealized views of antiquity prevalent in the Neo-Classical period. The architectural style of Prussian palaces thus harks back to Greek and Roman models and the Italian Renaissance.

Villa at No. 23 Toni-Lessler-Straße

flanked by elegant semi-circular Art-Nouveau apartment blocks, and in front of these stands Berlin's last remaining Art-Deco-style S-Bahn station. The yellow buildings are covered in green shingles and, in summer, the balconies are richly decked with greenery and flowers. Some of Berlin's most magnificent mansion houses line both sides of Argentinische and Lindenthaler Allee. Many celebrities live in the area around the square. ✪ *Mexikoplatz*

5 Strandbad Wannsee

Europe's largest inland beach is a surprisingly picturesque spot in the middle of the large city, attracting up to 40,000 visitors a day. The swimming baths were built in 1929–30 as a recreation area for workers in the neighbouring districts *(see p66)*.
✪ *Wannseebadeweg 25 • Apr–Sep: 10am–7pm Mon–Fri, 8am–8pm Sat, Sun • (030) 803 56 12 • Admission charge*

6 Alliiertenmuseum

Visitors stroll around this museum reminiscing and recalling the 50 or so years of partnership between Western Allies and West Berliners. The museum, based in a former US-barracks, employs uniforms, documents, weapons and military equipment to tell the story of Berlin's postwar history, though not only from the military point of view.
✪ *Clayallee 135 • 10am–6pm daily exc Wed • (030) 818 19 90 • Free admission*

7 Mexikoplatz

Idyllic Mexikoplatz in the southern district of Zehlendorf is one of the most atmospheric and architecturally fascinating squares in Berlin. The two round green spaces in the centre are

8 Dahlem Villas

Some of Berlin's most attractive villas, dating back to the 19th century, are found in the streets surrounding the Grunewald S-Bahn station. Especially worth seeing are Nos. 15 and 11 in Winklerstraße, the latter of which was built by Hermann Muthesius in the style of an English country mansion. Villa Maren, at No. 12 next door, is a beautiful example of the Neo-Renaissance style. The villas on Toni-Lessler-Straße and on Furtwänglerstraße are also worth a detour. ✪ *Am Großen Wannsee*

Villa at No. 11 Winklerstraße

Alliiertenmuseum: www.alliiertenmuseum.de

Jagdschloss Grunewald

Jagdschloss Grunewald

The small gleaming white palace in Grunewald, dating back to 1542, served as a hunting lodge for the Electors. The castle, built in the Renaissance and Baroque styles, houses a small collection of German and Dutch paintings. ⊗ *Hüttenweg 100, Grunewaldsee • Due to a major restoration project the palace will be closed to the public until 2009 • (030) 813 35 97 • Admission charge*

Museumsdorf Düppel

The open-air museum at Düppel is a reminder of the fact that Berlin once consisted of a series of villages, with one of the oldest settlements dating back to the 13th century. The lively museum is animated by actors, who are dressed and act out daily life as it would have been during the Middle Ages. There are fascinating live demonstrations of ancient crafts such as bread-baking, pottery and basket-weaving. Plants are grown as in medieval times for their various uses. ⊗ *Clauertstr. 11 • Apr–Oct: 10am–5pm Sun, 3–7pm Thu • (030) 802 66 71 • Admission charge*

At Museumsdorf Düppel

A Day in the South

Morning

Start your morning walk through Berlin's southern districts by taking the S-Bahn (lines S7 and S1) to **Mexikoplatz**. Here you can admire the beautiful villas and the lovely green square before dropping in to **Café Krone** in Argentinische Allee for a late breakfast. After refreshments, continue on foot or by bus (No. 211) southwards to the open-air museum **Museumsdorf Düppel**. From there, return by bus via Argentinische Allee to the **Alliiertenmuseum**. From the museum you can stroll across Königin-Luise-Straße and through the picturesque streets right up to the beer garden **Luise** *(see p93)* at the Free University, where you may like to have lunch.

Afternoon

Start your afternoon walk at the **Dahlem Museums** *(see p89)*. One you have enjoyed this cultural break, continue by U-Bahn (U2, Dahlem-Dorf) to Krumme Lanke, and from there, on foot, to the S-Bahn station Mexikoplatz. The S-Bahn will take you to Wannsee S-Bahn station, from where you can reach all the sights in southwestern Berlin. When the weather is right, visit **Strandbad Wannsee**, or visit the **Haus der Wannsee-Konferenz** *(see p89)* and then admire the park and **Schloss Klein-Glienicke** *(see p89)*. After your walk, allow yourself to be tempted by coffee and cake or supper at the **Remise in Schloss Klein-Glienicke** *(see p93)*. Your best option for the return journey is the S-Bahn from Wannsee.

Left **Onkel-Tom-Siedlung** Centre **St-Annen-Kirche** Right **Outside the Free University Berlin**

Best of the Rest

1 Stolpe

This small village has managed to retain its original character to the present day.

2 Grunewaldturm

Fantastic views can be had from the red Neo-Gothic brick tower, built in 1897 as a memorial to Kaiser Wilhelm I. It now houses a restaurant. ® *Havelchaussee*

3 Onkel-Tom-Siedlung

The "Uncle Tom's Hut" settlement, developed in 1926–32 according to designs by Bruno Taut and others, was intended to create a modern housing estate for workers, unlike their old narrow, dark tenement blocks. ® *Argentinische Allee*

4 Free University

The campus of Berlin's largest university, founded in 1948 as a rival to East-Berlin Humboldt University, covers large parts of Dahlem. It is worth looking at the 1950s Henry-Ford-Bau and the so-called *Rostlaube* (rusting hut), at present being redesigned by Sir Norman Foster. ® *Garystr.*

5 Teufelsberg

Both the hill and the lake, the dark green Teufelssee, are popular destinations for a day out at the weekend, for flying kites, biking and sunbathing.

6 St-Peter-und-Paul-Kirche

This charming stone church, built in 1834–7 by F A Stüler, resembles Russian-Orthodox churches. It is a popular venue for marriage ceremonies.
® *Nikolskoer Weg* • *11am–6pm daily*
• *(030) 805 21 00*

7 Blockhaus Nikolskoe

The log cabin, built in 1819, was a present from King Friedrich Wilhelm III to his daughter Charlotte and his son-in-law, future Tsar Nicholas I. The wooden Russian-style *dacha* was restored after a fire in 1985.
® *Nikolskoer Weg 15* • *10am–6pm Fri–Mon* • *(030) 805 29 14*

8 Heinrich von Kleist's Tomb

The German playwright Kleist and his companion Henriette Vogel committed suicide by shooting themselves in 1811; they are buried here together (near the S-Bahn overpass).
® *Bismarckstr. 3, Am Kleinen Wannsee*

9 St-Annen-Kirche

The 14th-century Gothic church is a typical Berlin country church. Attractive murals depict scenes from the life of Saint Anna. Also on display are 11 late-Gothic figures of saints and a Baroque pulpit. ® *Königin-Luise-Str./Pacelliallee*

10 Teltower Damm

The main shopping street of Zehlendorf has managed to preserve its village character and its 1768 Baroque church. ® *Zehlendorf, at S-Bahn station Zehlendorf*

Around Town – Grunewald & Dahlem

Left **Sign of the Wirtshaus Paulsborn** Right **Enjoying an outdoor meal at Blockhaus Nikolskoe**

TOP 10 Restaurants & Beer Gardens

1 Loretta am Wannsee
This restaurant, a favourite with day trippers to Wannsee, attracts visitors with its giant beer garden, shaded by chestnut trees. It always has a great atmosphere. ✆ *Kronprinzessinnenweg 260 • 11am–midnight daily • (030) 803 51 56 • €*

2 Forsthaus Paulsborn
This rustic restaurant next to Jagdschloss Grunewald is based in an old hunting lodge. ✆ *Hüttenweg 90 • summer: 11am–11pm Tue–Sun; winter: 11am–6pm Tue–Sun • (030) 818 19 10 • €€*

3 Wirtshaus Schildhorn
Nouvelle cuisine in Grunewald. In summer you can enjoy your *bratwurst* outside, in a picturesque spot right on the shoreline at Wannsee. ✆ *Havelchaussee/ Straße am Schildhorn 4a • summer: 11am–midnight daily; winter: 11am–10pm Sat, Sun • (030) 3088 35 00 • €€*

4 Blockhaus Nikolskoe
Traditional German fare is served in this historic log cabin, built as a Russian *dacha*. ✆ *Nikolskoer Weg 15 • from 10am Fri–Wed • (030) 805 29 14 • no credit cards • €€*

5 Wirtshaus zur Pfaueninsel
A small venue, serving rustic German food in the open air. This is an ideal place for refreshments before a visit to Pfaueninsel. ✆ *Pfaueninselchaussee 100 • summer: 9am–8pm daily; winter: 10am–6pm daily • (030) 805 22 25 • €€*

6 Alter Krug Dahlem
Large beer garden with a lengthy menu, offering excellent wines and desserts. ✆ *Königin-Luise-Str. 52 • 10am–midnight daily • (030) 84 31 95 40 • €€*

7 Luise
One of Berlin's nicest beer gardens, on the Free University campus, Luise's is crowded even at lunchtime and always boasts a good atmosphere. The delicious salads and sandwiches here are particularly worth trying.
✆ *Königin-Luise-Str. 40 • 10am–1am daily • (030) 841 88 80 • €*

8 Grunewaldturm-Restaurant
A great place for mushroom and game dishes, with views of Wannsee. ✆ *Havelchaussee 61 • summer: 11am–midnight daily; winter 10am–6pm daily • (030) 304 12 03 • €€*

9 Remise in Schloss Klein-Glienicke
This restaurant offers sophisticated cuisine and surroundings; light fish dishes and salads in summer, game and roasts in winter. ✆ *Königstr. 36 • Mar-Jan: noon-late Wed-Sun • (030) 805 40 00 • €€€*

10 Diekmann im Chalet Suisse
Swiss hospitality and a cosy atmosphere in Grunewald. Local and exquisite Swiss cooking.
✆ *Clayallee 99 • noon–10pm daily • (030) 832 63 62 • €€€*

Left **Haus der Kulturen der Welt** Centre **In Tiergarten** Right **Shell-Haus**

Tiergarten & Federal District

IN 1999, BERLIN'S GREEN *centre became the government district. Around Tiergarten, Berlin's largest and most popular park, stand the Reichstag, the Bundeskanzleramt and Schloss Bellevue, seat of the President of the Federal Republic of Germany. Tiergarten itself is a great place for strolling and cycling, and it also boasts the Neuer See, the Spree River and Berlin's Zoo. In summer, its lawns are used for soccer games and barbecue parties.*

The renovated Reichstag

🔟 Sights

1	Reichstag	6	Hamburger Bahnhof
2	Kulturforum	7	Sowjetisches Ehrenmal
3	Großer Tiergarten	8	Gedenkstätte Deutscher Widerstand
4	Siegessäule	9	Hansa-Viertel
5	Diplomatenviertel	10	Villa von der Heydt

Tiergarten: **www.tiergarten.de**

Reichstag
More than any other Berlin landmark, the Reichstag - seat of the German parliament – has come to symbolize German history (see pp10–11).

Kulturforum
This unique complex of buildings features the best museums and concert halls in Berlin (see pp32–5).

Großer Tiergarten
The Großer Tiergarten is Berlin's largest park, straddling an area of 200 hectares (494 acres) between the eastern and western halves of the town. Formerly the Elector's hunting grounds, it was redesigned in the 1830s as a park by Peter Joseph Lenné. At the end of the 19th century, the Siegesallee was established in the east of the park, more than 500 m (1640 ft) in length, lined by the statues of monarchs and politicians. After World War II, the starving and freezing population chopped down nearly all the trees for firewood and dug up the lawns to grow food. Thanks to reforestation work since the 1950s, Tiergarten today has become Berlin's favourite green space and the lungs of the city.
◈ Tiergarten • Map M5/6

Siegessäule
In the middle of Tiergarten stands the 62-m (203-ft) high Victory Column, erected to commemorate Prussian victory against Denmark in the war of 1864. After victory over Austria in 1866 and France 1871, the structure was crowned by a

Statue on Siegessäule

35-ton gilded statue of the goddess Victoria. There are excellent views from the viewing platform (see p39). ◈ Großer Stern • Map M6 • Apr–Oct: 9:30am–6:30pm daily; Nov–Mar: 9:30am–5:30pm daily • Admission charge

Diplomatenviertel
In the late 19th century, an embassy district sprang up. Its extent is still marked today by two pompous Fascist buildings (Italian and Japanese embassies of 1938 and 1943 respectively). Most structures were destroyed during World War II, and until the reunification of Germany the diplomatic buildings were left to decay. Since 1999, new life has been breathed into the diplomats' quarter and, thanks to its adventurous architecture, it has been transformed into one of the most interesting parts of Berlin. Especially worth seeing are the Austrian and Indian embassies on Tiergartenstraße as well as, on Klingelhöferstraße, the embassies of the Nordic countries (see p41) and of Mexico. ◈ Between Stauffenbergstr. and Lichtensteinallee as well as along Tiergartenstr. • Map E4

eft **Roof of the Japanese Embassy** Right **The Austrian Embassy**

For more on modern architecture **see pp40–41**

Peter Joseph Lenné

Lenné (1789–1866), regarded as Germany's most important landscape architect, was born into a family of gardeners in Bonn. He studied in Paris and joined the Royal Gardens in Potsdam as an apprentice in 1816. There he met Schinkel and, together, these two men set out to design the parks of Berlin and Potsdam in the harmonious style of the time.

Main entrance Bendlerblock

Hamburger Bahnhof

The former Hamburg railway station, now the "Museum of the Present Day", holds a cross-section of contemporary paintings and the latest multi-media works of art and installations. One of the highlights is the private collection of Erich Marx, including works by Beuys and others. Apart from well-known artists such as Andy Warhol, Jeff Koons and Robert Rauschenberg, it also shows works by Anselm Kiefer and Sandro Chiao. ✪ *Invalidenstr. 50–51 • Map F2 • 10am–6pm Tue–Fri, 11am–8pm Sat, 11am–6pm Sun • Admission charge*

Sowjetisches Ehrenmal

The giant Soviet Memorial near Brandenburg Gate was officially opened on 7 November 1945, the anniversary of the Russian October Revolution. It is flanked by two tanks, supposedly the first ones to reach Berlin. The memorial commemorates 300,000 Red Army soldiers who died during World War II in the struggle to liberate Berlin. The large column was constructed from marble blocks from Hitler's Reich Chancellery, which had just been torn down. The column itself, designed by Nicolai

Sergijevski, is crowned by the huge bronze statue by Lev Kerbel. Behind the memorial, 2,500 Russian soldiers are buried. ✪ *Straße des 17. Juni • Map K2*

Gedenkstätte Deutscher Widerstand

The 1930s complex, which is today known as Bendlerblock, lies behind the former Prussian Ministry of War. During World War II it served as army headquarters. It was here that a group of officers planned the assassination of Adolf Hitler. When the attempt failed on 20 July 1944, Claus Schenk Count von Stauffenberg and the others involved were arrested in the Bendlerblock, and many of them were shot in the courtyard during the night. A memorial, created by Richard Scheibe in 1953, commemorates these events. On the upper floor is a small exhibition documenting the German resistance against the Nazi regime. Today, the Bendlerblock has been incorporated into the Berlin branch of the Federal Ministry of Defence. ✪ *Stauffenbergstr. 13–14 • Map E4 • 9am–6pm Mon–Wed, Fri, 9am–8pm Thu, 10am–6pm Sat, Sun • (030) 26 99 50 00 • Admission charge*

Sowjetisches Ehrenmal

Lortzing Memorial in Tiergarten

Hansa-Viertel

The Hansa estate west of Schloss Bellveue was built for the "Interbau" trade fair in 1957. World War II bombs had flattened Tiergarten, and 36 residential complexes were erected in the park, designed by distinguished architects from around the world, including Walter Gropius (Händelallee 3–9), Alvar Aalto (Klopstockstr. 30–32) and Oscar Niemeyer (Altonaer Str. 4–14). ⚅ *Tiergarten, Hanseatenweg • Map D3*

Villa von der Heydt

The late-Neo-Classical Villa von der Heydt is one of the few surviving examples of the architectural villa style typical of Tiergarten. It was built in 1860–61, according to plans by Hermann Ende and G.A. Linke, for one of the most elegant residential areas in Berlin at the time. Since 1980, the Prussian Heritage Foundation has had its headquarters here. ⚅ *Von-der-Heydt-Str. 18 • Map E4*

Villa von der Heydt

A Day Out

Morning

Start your tour of Tiergarten at the **Reichstag** *(see pp10–11)*. Explore the government district from here starting with the Bundeskanzleramt (the Federal Chancellor's Office, diagonally opposite). Stop at **Restaurant Käfer** *(see p101)* in the Reichstag for breakfast. Via John-Foster-Dulles-Allee you will pass the Carillon and the Haus der Kulturen der Welt on the way to **Großer Tiergarten** *(see p97)*. Continue along one of the paths into the park, directly opposite the old Kongresshalle, until you reach Straße des 17. Juni. If you turn right here, you will be heading directly towards **Siegessäule** *(see p39)*. From there continue along Fasanerieallee in a southwesterly direction until you get to the **Café am Neuen See** *(see p101)*, where you could have lunch.

Afternoon

A stroll through the **Diplomats' Quarter** *(see p97)*: from Neuer See, it is only a few steps along Lichtensteinallee and Thomas-Dehler-Straße in an easterly direction until you get to Klingelhöferstraße with its Scandinavian embassies. On Tiergartenstraße you will pass, among others, the embassies of Japan, Italy, India and Austria. From here you could continue south along Klingelhöferstraße, making a small detour for refreshments at **Café Einstein** *(see p101)*. Continue along Lützowufer until you reach the **Kulturforum** *(see pp32–3)* via Potsdamer Brücke. A good place for an evening meal would be the **Vox** *(see p101)*.

Left **On Neuer See** Centre **The Löwenbrücke** Right **Estonian Embassy; Greek Embassy ruins**

Hidden Treasures

Neuer See
Shimmering in a mysterious emerald green, the largest lake in Tiergarten is perfect for rowing. Afterwards you can recover in the Café am Neuen See.
⊗ *S-Bahn station Tiergarten • Map M5*

Löwenbrücke
The Lion Bridge, which leads across a small stream near Neuer See, is "suspended" from the sculptures of four lions. This idyllic spot is a favourite meeting point for gays in Berlin.
⊗ *Großer Weg • Map M5*

Lortzing-Denkmal
There are 70 statues of philosophers, poets and statesmen in Tiergarten. The statue of the composer Lortzing, at one end of Neuer See, is one of the most beautiful.
⊗ *Östlicher Großer Weg • Map M5*

Houseboats
Docked on the banks of the Spree are some of the remaining few houseboats in Berlin – an idyllic haven in the middle of the city. ⊗ *Straße des 17. Juni, Tiergartenufer • Map M3*

Carillon
The *carillon*, officially dedicated in 1987, is the largest of its kind in Europe. The 68 bells are rung every day at noon and 6pm in the 42-m (138-ft) high black tower.
⊗ *John-Foster-Dulles-Allee (Haus der Kulturen der Welt) • Map E3*

Englischer Garten
The landscaped English-style garden near Schloss Bellevue is ideal for strolling.
⊗ *An der Klopstockstr. • Map M5*

Estonian Embassy
The old Estonian Embassy, in a quiet side street next to the ruined Greek Embassy, is characteristic of the diplomats' quarter.
⊗ *Hiroshimastr. • Map E4*

Locks
The two canal locks behind the zoo, taking visitors across the dammed Landwehrkanal, are popular resting places. ⊗ *At the Zoo, S-Bahn station Tiergarten • Map M5*

Gaslights in Tiergarten
With 80 historic gaslights along the paths, an evening stroll in Tiergarten is very romantic. ⊗ *At S-Bahn station Tiergarten • Map M5*

Landwehrkanal
The sloping, grass-covered banks of Landwehrkanal are ideal spots to chill out.
⊗ *Corneliusstr. • Map M/N5/6*

Price Categories

For a three-course meal for one with half a bottle of wine (or equivalent meal), taxes and charges included

€	under €20
€€	€20–30
€€€	€30–45
€€€€	€45–60
€€€€€	over €60

Left **In the Café am Neuen See** Right **Facil restaurant at the Madison Hotel**

Restaurants & Cafés

Café am Neuen See
Not a place of pilgrimage for gourmets but Berlin's most popular beer garden, serving salads, pasta and pizza *(see p53)*. ✆ *Lichtensteinallee 1 • Map M5 • (030) (03) 254 49 30 • no credit cards • €€*

Schleusenkrug
This small café, right next to a lock, has a rustic beer garden and is very popular with students. ✆ *Tiergarten-Schleuse • Map M5 • 10am–1am daily • (030) 313 99 09 • no credit cards • €*

Café Einstein
Based in the villa belonging to the film star Henny Porten, Café Einstein is the ultimate in Viennese elegance, serving Austrian food and boasting the best strawberry torte in town. ✆ *Kurfürstenstr. 58 • Map E5 • 9am–1am daily • (030) 261 50 96 • €€€*

Käfer im Reichstag
Ambitious restaurant, better known for its view than its food. ✆ *Platz der Republik • Map K2 • (030) 22 62 99 33 • €€€€*

Facil
Mediterranean gourmet food, stylishly presented, dominates the menu at this elegant eaterie. ✆ *Potsdamer Str. 3 • Map L2 • (030) 590 05 12 34 • €€€€€*

Vivo
A gourmet restaurant, influenced by Californian cooking and firmly on the way to receiving its first Michelin star. ✆ *Lützowufer 15 (Grand Hotel Esplanade) • Map N6 • (030) 254 78 86 30 • €€€€€*

Hugo's
This restaurant offers great views and Michelin-starred Mediterranean food. ✆ *Budapester Str. 2 • Map N4/5 • (030) 26 02 12 63 • €€€€€*

Brasserie Desbrosses
An appealing, historic French restaurant. Its seafood is particularly good. ✆ *Potsdamer Platz 3 (Ritz-Carlton) • Map F4 • 6:30am–11pm daily • (030) 33 77 76 340 • €€€€*

Paris-Moskau
A classic Berlin restaurant, in a timber-frame house, serving French food – especially game dishes. ✆ *Alt-Moabit 141 • Map J1 • (030) 394 20 81 • no credit cards • €€€*

Alte Pumpe
There is always an excellent atmosphere in this old Berlin restaurant, based in a pumping station and serving rustic German fare. ✆ *Lützowstr. 42 • Map E5 • noon–10pm Mon–Fri • (030) 26 48 42 65 • €€*

Note: All restaurants accept credit cards and offer vegetarian dishes unless stated otherwise.

Left **Martin-Gropius-Bau** Centre **Above a door in Schöneberg** Right **Shield, Jüdisches Museum**

Kreuzberg & Schöneberg

KREUZBERG IS POSSIBLY *Berlin's most famous district, and it definitely qualifies as its most colourful area.* Here, in historic tenement blocks that are slowly but surely being renovated, Turkish families live next door to drop-outs and alternatives, artists and students. Social tensions, still characteristic of Kreuzberg today, make this a varied and interesting district – but at the same time a problematic one. The neighbouring district of Schöneberg is markedly quieter; this part of town is not as experimental as Kreuzberg, neither is it as elegant as Charlottenburg – here Berlin is simply enjoyed by its inhabitants. Winterfeldtplatz is surrounded by many inviting pubs, and in the area around Nollendorfplatz entire roads have been taken over and transformed by Berlin's gay scene, with their shops, bars and night clubs.

Statue on Mehringplatz

🔟 Sights

1. Deutsches Technikmuseum
2. Jüdisches Museum
3. Checkpoint Charlie
4. Topographie des Terrors
5. Anhalter Bahnhof
6. Oranienstraße
7. Nollendorfplatz
8. Viktoriapark
9. Martin-Gropius-Bau
10. Riehmers Hofgarten

1 Deutsches Technikmuseum

The history of technology and crafts is the theme of this fascinating museum, located in the grounds of a former station. In a new building, visitors can learn about developments in aviation and admire 40 planes, including a Junkers Ju 52 and a "raisin bomber", the type of plane used for the Berlin airlift. Old ships and steam locomotives bring back the days of the Industrial Revolution. ◎ *Trebbiner Str. 9 • Map F5 • 9am–5:30pm Tue–Fri, 10am–6pm Sat, Sun • (030) 90 25 40 • Admission charge*

2 Jüdisches Museum

The Jewish Museum is not only unique architecturally, but it is also one of Berlin's most fascinating museums. Its collections present an overview of almost 1,000 years of German-Jewish cultural history; a special exhibition is devoted to everyday Jewish life in Berlin from the end of the 19th century *(see p46)*. ◎ *Lindenstr. 9–14 • Map G5 • 10am–10pm Mon, 10am–8pm Tue–Sun • (030) 25 99 33 00 • Admission charge*

3 Checkpoint Charlie

The Haus am Checkpoint Charlie, next to the former crossing point for the Alllied forces, has an exhibition on the history of the Berlin Wall and the various means people used in trying to

The old sign at Checkpoint Charlie

escape from East to West Berlin, ranging from a hot-air balloon to a car with a false floor. Only a replica of the control hut remains of the former border. ◎ *Friedrichstr. 43–45 • Map G4 • 9am–10pm daily • (030) 253 72 50 • Admission charge*

4 Topographie des Terrors

After 1934, three terrifying Nazi institutions had their headquarters in this area: the security service (Sicherheitsdienst, SD) was based at Wilhelmstraße 102 in the Prinz-Albrecht-Palais; the school of arts and crafts at Prinz-Albrecht-Straße 8 was occupied by the Gestapo; while Heinrich Himmler, head of the SS, resided next door at No. 9, at the Hotel Prinz Albrecht. After World War II, all the buildings were bulldozed except for the cellars where, in 1933–45, prisoners had been interrogated and tortured. An exhibition chronicles the troubled history of the area. ◎ *Stresemannstr. 110, entrance Niederkirchner Str. • Map F4 • May–Sep: 10am–10pm daily; Oct–Apr: 10am–6pm daily • (030) 25 48 67 03 • Free admission*

Left **Inside Deutsches Technikmuseum** Right **Exhibition of Nazi crimes at Topographie des Terrors**

Left **Plaque on Nollendorfplatz** Centre **Façade of the Metropol** Right **Ruins of Anhalter Bahnhof**

Anhalter Bahnhof

Only pitiful fragments remain of the railway station that was once the largest in Europe. The giant structure was erected in 1880 by Franz Schwechten as a showcase station: official visitors to the Empire were meant to be impressed by the splendour and glory of the German capital as soon as they reached the railway station. In 1943 the station was badly damaged by bombs and in 1960 it was pulled down. The waste ground behind the façade was meant to become a park; today the Tempodrom is based here, hosting concerts and cabaret shows.
§ *Askanischer Platz 6–7 • Map F5*

Oranienstraße

Oranienstraße is the heart of Kreuzberg. It is the wildest, most colourful and most unusual street of the district, where alternative shops and pubs jostle for space with doner kebab take-aways and Turkish greengrocers. All aspects of life and politics in Kreuzberg are centred around this road.
§ *Between Lindenstr. and Skalitzer Str. • Map H5*

Nollendorfplatz

Nollendorfplatz and neighbouring Winterfeldtplatz are right in the centre of Schöneberg. The former square has always been a focal point for the gay scene in Berlin, and a plaque at U-Bahn station Nollendorfplatz commemorates approximately 5,000 homosexuals killed in concentration camps by the Nazis. Today, gay life is concentrated more in the surrounding streets. Before World War II, Nollendorfplatz was also a centre of entertainment. The Metropol-Theater, today a discotheque, then boasted Erwin Piscator as its innovative director. And next door lived the writer Christopher Isherwood, whose novel formed the basis of the famous musical "Cabaret". § *Map E5*

Turkish Berlin

In the 1960s, thousands of Turkish *gastarbeiter* ("guest workers") came to Berlin in response to a shortage of labour. Today the Turkish community numbers around 190,000 and it is mainly their children who leave their mark on life in the city. There are few "guest workers" left; most Turkish Berliners own their own shops and consider themselves to be true Berliners. The rate of naturalization is still fairly low, and many German Berliners have no contact with everyday life in the Turkish community. At 40 per cent, the rate of unemployment among Turkish Berliners is depressingly high.

Flower stall on Winterfeldtmarkt

Memorial by Schinkel in Viktoriapark

Viktoriapark
8 This rambling park was set up as a recreational space for workers in Kreuzberg in 1888–94 to plans by Hermann Mächtig. It has an artificial waterfall, and the Neo-Gothic Schinkel memorial at the top of Kreuzberg, 66 m (216 ft) high, commemorates Prussian victory in the Wars of Liberation against Napoleon. ◊ *Kreuzbergstr.*
• *Map F6*

Martin-Gropius-Bau
9 The richly ornamented former museum of arts and crafts is one of Berlin's most attractive exhibition centres *(see pp46–7)*.
◊ *Niederkirchnerstr. 7* • *Map F4*
• *changing exhibitions and opening times, but usually 10am–8pm Wed–Mon* • *(030) 25 48 60* • *Admission charge*

Riehmers Hofgarten
10 Over 20 buildings make up this elegant estate, built as officers' quarters in the Gründerzeit (after the founding of the German Empire in 1871). Attractively restored in recent years, there is also a pleasant hotel with restaurant. ◊ *Yorckstr. 83–86*

Riehmers Hofgarten • *Map F6*

A Day in Kreuzberg

Morning
🕙 Start from the famous ruins of **Anhalter Bahnhof**, which you can reach by S-Bahn. From here continue along Stresemannstraße in a north-westerly direction to the **Martin-Gropius-Bau**. It is easy to while away a few hours in this impressive building if there is a special exhibition. You could take a break for refreshments in the museum café. A visit to the neighbouring exhibition, the **Topographie des Terrors** *(see p103)* afterwards will bring you face to face with the dark Nazi past of this area. Continue along Niederkirchnerstraße, past an original section of the Berlin Wall, to Wilhelmstraße. Then turn into Kochstraße to visit **Checkpoint Charlie** and the museum at the former border *(see p103)*.

Afternoon
You can buy a tasty lunch at **Sale e Tabacchi** *(see p109)* in Kochstraße. Continue along Kochstraße in an easterly direction and you will get to the heart of Kreuzberg. Make a detour south on Lindenstraße to the **Jüdisches Museum** *(see p103)* or carry on into **Oranienstraße**. Take the U-Bahn U6 from U-Bahn station Kottbusser Tor to Platz der Luftbrücke. The **Viktoriapark** nearby is a good place for a rest, while shopaholics prefer a stroll up and down Bergmannstraße. At the end, turn north into Baerwaldstraße and continue to Carl-Herz-Ufer, where you will be able to round off the day with a delicious evening meal at the **Altes Zollhaus** *(see p109)*.

Left **Rathaus Schöneberg** Centre **Oberbaumbrücke** Right **On Mariannenplatz**

Best of the Rest

1 Rathaus Schöneberg
It was from this Town Hall, on 26 June 1963, that the US President John F Kennedy made his famous speech, declaring "I am a Berliner" and expressing his commitment to the freedom of West Berlin.
◈ *John-F-Kennedy-Platz*

2 Mehringplatz
Once Kreuzberg's prettiest square, Mehringplatz was destroyed in World War II and is today surrounded by modern residential buildings. ◈ *Map G5*

3 Flughafen Tempelhof
Tempelhof, built in 1939 by Ernst Sagebiel and then Germany's biggest airport, survives as the largest Fascist structure in Europe. After years of debate the airport will close in late 2007. Future uses for it include as a medical research centre. ◈ *Platz der Luftbrücke • Map G6*

4 Mariannenplatz
This square is dominated by the Gothic-style artists' house Bethanien. A former hospital, it is today used as studio space by experimental artists. ◈ *Map H5*

5 Oberbaumbrücke
Pedestrians and cyclists can cross to the other side of the Spree River from Kreuzberg to Friedrichshain on this red-brick bridge, one of Berlin's loveliest, which was erected in 1894–6.
◈ *Warschauer/Skalitzer Str.*

6 Altes Mosse-Palais
One of Berlin's most important publishing houses was based in this Art Nouveau corner house in the former newspaper district. ◈ *Kochstr. • Map G4*

7 Friedhöfe Hallesches Tor
Numerous celebrities lie buried in the four cemeteries, including the composer Felix Mendelssohn Bartholdy. Also the writer E T A Hoffmann, whose work inspired Offenbach to write *The Tales of Hoffmann*.
◈ *Mehringdamm • Map G5*

8 Lapidarium
The former pumping station is open for visits; the sculptures in the garden once decorated the Siegesallee (alley of triumph).
◈ *Hallesches Ufer 78 • Map F5*

9 Kottbusser Tor
Kreuzberg in the raw: social misery tucked away in between new buildings in the Turkish heart of the district. ◈ *Map H5*

10 Kammergericht
In 1947–90, the magnificent supreme court, built in 1909–13, was used as Allied Control Council. ◈ *Potsdamer Str. 186 • Map E6*

Around Town – Kreuzberg & Schöneberg

Map labels: Mendelssohn-Bartholdy-Park, Kochstr., Anhalter Bahnhof, Hallesches Tor, Kottbusser Tor, Kleistpark, Eisenacher Str., Platz der Luftbrücke, Südstern

106

Rathaus Schöneberg: http://www.engr.psu.edu/ deutschlandsarchitektur/berlin/rathaeuser/schoeneberg.html

Left **A stall in Winterfeldtmarkt** Centre **Marheineke-Markthalle** Right **At Grober Unfug Comics**

🔟 Shops & Markets

Winterfeldtmarkt
At Berlin's largest and most wonderful weekday market you can buy fresh fruit and vegetables as well as other goods from around the world, such as clothes and New-Age items. ◈ *Winterfeldtplatz • Map E5 • 8am–2pm Sat*

Türkenmarkt Maybachufer
No other market in Berlin is quite as exotic. This is where Berliners and Turks alike buy their unleavened bread and fresh sheeps' cheese. ◈ *Maybachufer • Map H5 • noon–6:30pm Tue, Fri*

Molotow
Funky and trendy fashion from Berlin designers – perhaps not to everyone's taste, but guaranteed to cause a stir. ◈ *Gneisenaustr. 112 • Map G6 • (030) 693 08 18*

Oranienplatz and Oranienstraße
Kreuzberg's main square and unofficial high street specialize in all things alternative. ◈ *Oranienstr./ corner Oranienplatz • Map G5*

MaaßenZehn
Designer jeans or trendy belts – all with minor faults – at heavily reduced prices. ◈ *Maaßenstr. 10 • Map E5 • (030) 215 54 56*

Depot 2
This small boutique sells the latest streetwear and hip hop fashion of a local label. ◈ *Oranienstr. 9 • Map H5 • (030) 611 46 55*

High-Lite
If you're worried about standing out in the alternative crowd in Kreuzberg, this is the place to get your shades, body piercings and other essentials. ◈ *Bergmannstr. 99 • Map F/G6 • (030) 691 27 44*

Ararat
One of the best-stocked and trendiest stationery shops in Berlin, Ararat has many designer items for sale. ◈ *Bergmannstr. 99a • Map F/G6 • (030) 693 50 80*

Marheineke-Markthalle
One of the last remaining market-halls in Berlin. Visit the colourful fruit and vegetable stores to experience a genuine taste of Old Berlin. ◈ *Marheinekeplatz • Map G6 • 8am–6pm Mon–Sat*

Grober Unfug Comics
This store sells comic books of all periods and in various languages – its name means "complete rubbish". ◈ *Zossener Str. 32 • Map G6 • (030) 69 40 14 90*

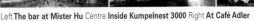

Left **The bar at Mister Hu** Centre **Inside Kumpelnest 3000** Right **At Café Adler**

🔟 Pubs, Bars & Discos

Kumpelnest 3000
A super-popular venue, based in a former brothel, complete with chintz wallpaper. Apart from the delicious Caipirinhas, the cocktails are not that special. ⍟ *Lützowstr. 23* • *Map E5* • *(030) 261 69 18*

Yorkschlösschen
A pub-restaurant with a great Old Berlin feel. Live jazz concerts at the weekend. ⍟ *Yorkstr. 15* • *Map F6* • *(030) 215 80 70*

Mister Hu
The locals would like to keep this secret to themselves: Mister Hu serves some of the greatest cocktails in town *(see p55)*. ⍟ *Goltzstr. 39* • *Map E5* • *(030) 217 21 11*

Van Loon
Enjoy a snack surrounded by nautical artifacts on this old barge moored in Urbanhafen. In summer you can sit on the green banks to drink your beer. ⍟ *Carl-Herz-Ufer 5–7* • *Map G5* • *(030) 692 62 93*

Green Door
A Berlin classic, this 1970s retro bar is very popular and always packed. It serves some of the best cocktails in the city. ⍟ *Winterfeldstr. 50* • *Map E5* • *(030) 215 25 15*

90 Grad
Rising with the ebb and flow of popularity in the Berlin club scene, this discotheque is always popular thanks to its changing club nights and great house music. ⍟ *Dennewitzstr. 37* • *Map E5* • *(030) 23 00 59 54*

Golgatha
A popular pick-up venue for students, this classic beer garden on the Kreuzberg also attracts an older clientele, bopping to funk on the small dance floor. ⍟ *Dudenstr. 48-64 (Viktoriapark)* • *Map F6* • *(030) 785 24 53*

Café M
A diehard, rough West Berlin classic with loud rock and indie music for a student, alternative and artsy crowd spilling out onto the pavement. ⍟ *Goltzstr. 34* • *Map E5* • *8am–late daily* • *(030) 216 70 92*

Würgeengel
The drinks at the "Angel of Death" are not in fact, lethal, but bar and clientele are straight out of a Buñuel film. ⍟ *Dresdner Str. 122* • *Map H5* • *(030) 615 55 60*

Café Adler
Time seems to have stood still at this pleasant pub–café with an affordable menu, it's next to the former border crossing at Checkpoint Charlie. ⍟ *Friedrichstr. 206* • *Map G4* • *(030) 251 89 65*

Price Categories

For a three-course meal for one with half a bottle of wine (or equivalent meal), taxes and charges included

€ under €20
€€ €20–30
€€€ €30–45
€€€€ €45–60
€€€€€ over €60

Left **In Storch** Right **The sign outside Sale e Tabacchi**

🔟 Restaurants & Cafés

1 Altes Zollhaus
International and German cuisine, served in a former border control point on the banks of the Landwehrkanal. Try the house speciality: *Brandenburger Landente aus dem Rohr* – a roast duck dish, or dishes with wild mushrooms, when in season. ⊗ *Carl-Herz-Ufer 30 • Map G5 • closed Sun & Mon • (030) 692 33 00 • €€€*

2 Joe Pena's Cantina y Bar
One of the best Mexican restaurants in town, serving a range of tortillas, borritos and enchiladas. ⊗ *Marheinekeplatz 3 • (030) 693 60 44 • €€*

3 Osteria No. 1
The Italian local par excellence: noisy and expensive, but serving unique pizzas and excellent pasta dishes. Later you can just decamp to the wine bar next door. ⊗ *Kreuzbergstr. 71 • Map F6 • (030) 786 91 62 • €€*

4 Hasir
One branch of the Turkish-Arabic fast food chain, serving falafels and other delicacies till late into the night. ⊗ *Maaßenstr. 10 • Map E5 • (030) 215 60 60 • no credit cards • €*

5 Sale e Tabacchi
Italian restaurant with elegant interior, popular with the media crowd. In summer, be sure to reserve a table in the central courtyard. ⊗ *Kochstr. 18 • Map G4 • (030) 25 29 50 03 • €€€*

6 Defne
An intimate restaurant serving modern Turkish food. ⊗ *Planufer. 92c • Map H5 • (030) 81 79 71 11 • no credit cards • €€*

7 Le Cochon Bourgeois
Top-quality French cooking at moderate prices, attracting a Bohemian local crowd and others. ⊗ *Fichtestr. 24 • Map H6 • (030) 693 01 01 • no credit cards • €€*

8 Merhaba
One of the best Turkish restaurants in Berlin, dishing up great lamb kebabs and other Turkish specialities. ⊗ *Wissmannstr. 32 • Map H6 • (030) 692 17 13 • €€*

9 Storch
The best dishes from the Alsace are served at this reliable, classic wood-panelled restaurant. Try one of the Flammkuchen. ⊗ *Wartburgstr. 54 • Map D5 • (030) 784 20 59 • €€€*

10 Pranzo e Cena
Unbeatable pizzas from the clay oven are the speciality in this Italian venue, popular with students and always busy. ⊗ *Goltzstr. 32 • Map E5 • (030) 216 35 14 • no credit cards • €€€*

Following pages: Gendarmenmarkt at night

Left **Portal of Kronprinzenpalais** Centre **Opernpalais** Right **Inside the Komische Oper**

Central Berlin: Unter den Linden

MOST VISITORS TO BERLIN *regard the magnificent boulevard of Unter den Linden as the heart of the small historic Mitte district. Many of Berlin's sights are concentrated along the grand avenue and around Bebelplatz, creating an impressive picture of Prussian and German history from the early 18th century until the present day. South of Unter den Linden is Gendarmenmarkt, one of Europe's most attractive squares. In recent years, many varied and elegant restaurants and cafés have appeared around the Neo-Classical square. Not far away, chic Friedrichstraße is lined with luxury shops and department stores as well as modern offices and apartments.*

Sculpture on Schlossbrücke

🔟 Sights

1. Brandenburger Tor
2. Deutsche Guggenheim
3. Forum Fridericianum
4. Gendarmenmarkt
5. Museumsinsel
6. Friedrichstraße
7. Holocaust-Denkmal
8. Wilhelmstraße
9. Schlossplatz
10. Museum für Kommunikation

1 Brandenburger Tor

Berlin's best-known landmark on Pariser Platz leads through to Unter den Linden *(see pp8–9).*
Ⓢ *Pariser Platz • Map K3*

2 Deutsche Guggenheim

This branch of the American Guggenheim museum, together with the Deutsche Bank branch Unter den Linden, show changing exhibitions of modern art of the highest standard from the US. During recent years, Deutsche Guggenheim has thus managed to become one of the most successful and popular art venues in the city, with an emphasis placed on installations. In 1999, the retrospective of works by Dan Flavin was a particular highlight. Treasures from the Deutsche Bank archives are also shown here. Pop into the small museum shop and refresh yourself with a coffee from the museum café. Ⓢ *Unter den Linden 13–15 • Map K4 • 11am–8pm Mon–Wed Fri–Sun, 11am–10pm Thu • (030) 202 09 30 • Admission charge, free on Mon*

3 Forum Fridericianum

The historic structures of this architectural complex in Unter den Linden are among the finest attractions in Berlin. From 1740, Frederick the Great commissioned the prestigious Early-Neo-Classical buildings for the

Altes Palais at Forum Fridericianum

area around today's Bebelplatz, and personally influenced their design: Deutsche Staatsoper, the first free-standing opera house in Europe; Catholic St Hedwigskathedrale, Alte Bibliothek and Prinz-Heinrich-Palais, later the Humboldt University. Bebelplatz itself is particularly interesting. A memorial set into the ground reminds of its dark past – in 1933, it was the venue for the Nazi book burning. Frederick's successors commissioned Altes Palais and a memorial statue of "the old Fritz", surrounded by "his" buildings. Christian Daniel Rauch created the 13.5-m (44-ft) high equestrian bronze figure in 1840. It portrays Frederick the Great wearing his trademark tricorn hat and coronation mantle and carrying a walking stick. The statue has always turned its back to the east – but wags claim that the East German government mistakenly set up the figure the wrong way around.
Ⓢ *Unter den Linden and Bebelplatz • Map K4*

Frederick as Architect

Forum Fridericianum was not only Frederick the Great's memorial to himself, it also ensured that Unter den Linden became one of the greatest boulevards in Europe. The king, who favoured a strict Neo-Classical style, drew up the plans for the Staatsoper and other buildings himself, and Knobelsdorff executed his ideas.

Deutsche Guggenheim, Unter den Linden

For more on Unter den Linden **see pp12–15**

Left **Inside the Konzerthaus** Centre **Deutscher Dom** Right **Front view of Altes Museum**

Gendarmenmarkt

This square, whose strict layout is reminiscent of an Italian Renaissance *piazza*, is probably the most beautiful in Berlin. To the left and right of Schauspielhaus – today's Konzerthaus – stand the twin towers of Deutscher and Französischer Dom (German and French cathedrals), dating back to the late 18th century. Gendarmenmarkt, named after a regiment of *gens d'armes* stationed nearby, was built at the end of the 17th century, as a market square. The Schauspielhaus (theatre) on the north side of the square, built by Schinkel in 1818–21, was used as a theatre until 1945. Damaged in World War II, it was reopened as Konzerthaus (concert hall) in 1984. A statue of the playwright Friedrich Schiller stands in front of the building. Französischer Dom, to its right, is a prestigious Late-Baroque

Figure of Athena in Pergamonmuseum

building; concealed behind it is the French Friedrichstadtkirche, a church serving Berlin's Huguenot community. The Deutscher Dom opposite, built in 1708 on the south side of the square for the Reformed Protestant Church, did not receive its first tower until 1785. Today it has an exhibition on democracy in Germany. ✪ *Mitte • Map L4*

Museumsinsel

Museum Island, a UNESCO World Heritage Sight, is one of the most important complexes of museums in the world, holding major arts collections and imposing full-scale ancient structures. Based here are the Pergamonmuseum, the Alte Nationalgalerie (the old national gallery), Bode-museum and Altes and Neues Museum. The Neues Museum will reopen in 2008 *(see pp20–23 and 46–9).* ✪ *Pergamonmuseum, Bodestr. 1–3 • Map J5 • 10am–6pm Tue–Sun, till 10pm Thu • (030) 20 90 55 55* ✪ *Alte Nationalgalerie • Bodestr.1–3 • Map J5 • 10–6pm Tue–Sun, until 10pm Thu • (030) 20 90 55 66 • Admission charge*

The Huguenots in Berlin

In 1685, the Great Elector issued the famous Edict of Potsdam, granting asylum in Berlin to around 20,000 Huguenots, who were persecuted in their native France because of their Protestant faith. Skilled academics and craftsmen, they moulded the social and cultural life of the city and enriched Berlin with the French art of living. Today, still, the French community worships in the Friedrichstadtkirche on Gendarmenmarkt.

Antique vase in the Pergamonmuseum

Konzerthaus in Gendarmenmarkt: www.konzerthaus.de

Quartier 206 in Friedrichstraße

Friedrichstraße

Friedrichstraße has risen to some of the glamour and vibrancy it possessed before World War II. Today, Berlin's Fifth Avenue once again boasts elegant shops, and some upmarket restaurants and cafés, which have opened here in recent years. Especially worth visiting are the three Quartiers 205, 206 and 207 within the Friedrichstadtpassagen, containing the Galeries Lafayette store and Department Store 206 respectively. At the northern end of the street is the famous Dussmann store (books, music, events), S-Bahn station Friedrichstraße, as well as the former entertainment district with the Friedrichstadtpalast, today housing the Metropoltheater.
⌕ Mitte • Map J–L4

Holocaust-Denkmal

This new memorial, officially called "Memorial to the Killed Jews of Europe", serves as Germany's national Holocaust memorial. After years of debate, US star architect Peter Eisenman completed the memorial in 2005. It is comprised of a large field with dark grey steles of varying heights up to 2 m (6 ft) high, which symbolize the six million Jews and others murdered by the Nazis in their concentration camps between 1933 and 1945. Underneath the memorial there is an information centre which explains the causes and history of the genocide.
⌕ Ebertstr. • Map L3

A Day of Culture

<u>Morning</u>

Unter den Linden begins at **Pariser Platz** in front of **Brandenburger Tor** *(see pp8–9)*. Stroll eastwards along the wide avenue, past Hotel Adlon Berlin. Then turn right into **Wilhelmstraße** *(see p116)*, the former political nerve centre. On the right-hand side you will pass the new building of the British Embassy. In Behrenstraße you can assess progress in the construction of the **Holocaust-Denkmal**. Turn left into Französische Straße, which will take you to **Friedrichstraße**. Here you can shop at the **Galeries Lafayette** *(see p119)* or in the **Department Store 206** *(see p119)*. After your shopping expedition, you may wish to recover over a snack lunch in the gourmet food department, which is situated in the basement of Galeries Lafayette.

<u>Afternoon</u>

Before you continue your exploration of Friedrichstraße, make a detour to **Gendarmenmarkt** with its Konzerthaus as well as Deutscher and Französischer Dom. From here return to **Friedrichstraße** and its modern buildings. Walk down the street to Leipziger Straße. Turn left into Leipziger Straße, and on the left you will see the giant structure of the former Ministry of Aviation. Today the Federal Ministry of Finance is based here. From here you can retrace your steps to Unter den Linden or return to Gendarmenmarkt. An evening meal at the Asian restaurant **Langhans** *(see p121)* is highly recommended.

Around Town – Central Berlin: Unter den Linden

Left **The former Ministry of Aviation, Wilhelmstraße** Centre **Hotel Adlon** Right **Stadtschloss**

Nazi Architecture

One of few surviving examples of the monumental architectural style favoured by Fascists is the former Reichsluftfahrtministerium (Ministry of Aviation), commissioned by Hermann Göring in 1935–6 from Ernst Sagebiel. At the time, the monotonous sandstone building was the world's largest and most modern office block, strengthened by steel girders against aerial attack. After reunification, the Treuhandanstalt was based here; today it houses the Federal Ministry of Finance.

Wilhelmstraße

8 In imperial Berlin, the centre of the German Empire's governmental power was based in Wilhelmstraße. Around 100 years later, nothing remains of the prestigious historic buildings which represented the equivalent of No. 10 Downing Street in London or Quai d'Orsay in Paris. All political decisions were made at Wilhelmstraße: both Chancellor (No. 77) and President (No. 73) of the German Reich lived here in old town houses. Their gardens became known

British Embassy, Wilhelmstraße

as "ministerial gardens". Adolf Hitler had the street systematically developed into the nerve centre of Nazi power. The Neue Reichskanzlei (the Chancellor's office) was built in 1937–9 to plans by Albert Speer, at the

corner of Vossstraße and Wilhelmstraße. It was blown up in 1945. Behind the Reichskanzlei was the so-called "Führerbunker" where Adolf Hitler committed suicide on 30 April 1945 (today it is a playground). Of the historic buildings, only the former Reichsluftfahrtministerium (Ministry of Aviation) remains. Today, Wilhelmstraße is lined by modern office buildings; and the British Embassy, built in 2000 by Michael Wilford, creates a link with the international importance of this street. ⊗ *Between Unter den Linden and Leipziger Str.* • *Map K/L3*

Schlossplatz

9 Today Schlossplatz seems deserted, but once the Stadtschloss (town residence) of the Hohenzollerns stood here. It was blown up by the East German government in 1950–51, and today just a few historic fragments of the original remain.

The debate about the reconstruction of the palace began in the early 1990s and, in 1993, a spectacular model was built; however the costs are prohibitive and make it unlikely that this venture will ever succeed. Remains include the façade of the doorway where Karl Liebknecht supposedly proclaimed the Socialist Republic in 1918. The portal has been incorporated into the former Staats ratsgebäude on the south side of the square. On its eastern side, Schlossplatz used to be bordered by the Palast der Republik (palace of the republic), the former seat of the East German parliament.

Portal of the Staatsratsgebäude

The building, dating from 1976, was demolished in 2006.
◑ *Mitte • Map G3, K5*

🔟 Museum für Kommunikation

The world's largest Post Office Museum was opened as early as 1872. Its excellent displays document the history of communication from the Middle Ages via the first postage stamps to today's satellite technology. Particularly worth seeing are a blue and a red Mauritius stamp, one of the first telephone installations (dating back to the year 1863) and three talking robots who interact with the visitors. Children – young and old – always enjoy the Computergalerie, where they can learn and gain new insights while playing.
◑ *Leipziger Str. 16 • Map L4 • 9am–5pm Tue–Fri, 11am–7pm Sat, Sun*
● *(030) 20 29 40 • Admission charge*

Museum für Kommunikation at night

A Day of Culture

Morning

🕘 Start your stroll on Unter den Linden, at the corner of Friedrichstraße. Once this spot was one of Berlin's liveliest street junctions, and there is still plenty to see today. For breakfast or refreshments, pop into **Café Einstein** *(see p121)*. Afterwards continue eastwards along the boulevard; you will pass numerous fascinating buildings, for example, on the right, the Deutsche Bank with the Kunstmuseum in **Deutsche Guggenheim** *(see p49)*. From here you can already see the equestrian statue of Frederick the Great, which marks the centre of **Forum Fridericianum** *(see p113)*. This area as well as Bebelplatz are right in the centre of Old Berlin, with Staatsoper, St Hedwigskathedrale, Altes Palais and Humboldt-Universität. You could have lunch in one of the restaurants based in the **Opernpalais**.

Afternoon

In the afternoon continue your stroll along Unter den Linden and, if you like, make a detour to the north to **Museumsinsel** *(see p114)*. Afterwards, if you still feel energetic enough, you could visit **Berliner Dom**. Opposite the cathedral you will see **Schlossplatz** *(see p115)*; its architectural future is still being hotly debated. You could round off your day of sightseeing in Mitte with a delicious evening meal at **Dressler Unter den Linden** *(see p121)*. To get there, just retrace your steps and return along Unter den Linden in a westerly direction.

Left **The "Tränenpalast"** Centre **At the Mohrenkolonnaden** Right **Admiralspalast**

10 Best of the Rest

Tränenpalast
1 The Palace of Tears witnessed much heartbreak, when Western visitors parted from family or friends in the East after a visit. The former checkpoint at S-Bahn station Friedrichstraße served as a concert hall, which is now closed. ◈ *Friedrichstr./Reichstagsufer 17 • Map J4*

Russian Embassy
2 This giant building, typical of Stalinist "wedding cake" style, was erected in 1948–53 on the site of the old Tsarist embassy. ◈ *Unter den Linden 63–65 • Map K3*

WMF-Haus
3 The former headquarters of the porcelain and cutlery manufacturer WMF has remarkable façades, decorated with beautiful mosaics. ◈ *Leipziger Str., corner Mauerstr. • Map L3*

Alte Kommandantur
4 An impressive classicist building designed by Schinkel and rebuilt in 2004 to house the Berlin offices of Bertelsmann. ◈ *Unter den Linden 1 • Map K5*

Maxim-Gorki-Theater
5 The renowned theatre was once Berlin's Singakademie, or singing school. Paganini and Liszt, among others, performed here. ◈ *Am Festungsgraben 2 • (030) 20 22 11 29 • Map K5*

S-Bahnhof Friedrichstraße
6 Remodelled several times, this has always been one of Berlin's most famous stations. In 1961–89, it was the principal crossing point between East and West. ◈ *Friedrichstr. • Map J4*

Admiralspalast
7 Newly re-opened, Berlin's most legendary venue, dating from the 1920s, stages musicals and comedy shows. ◈ *Friedrichstr. 101 • Map J4 • www.admiralspalast.de*

Palais am Festungsgraben
8 The Baroque palace of 1753 has maintained its original elegant interior. ◈ *Am Festungsgraben 1 • Map K5 • (030) 208 40 00*

Komische Oper
9 One of Germany's most magnificent opera houses, dating from 1892, is concealed behind a modern façade. All performances are in German. ◈ *Behrenstr. 55–57 • Map K3 • (030) 47 99 74 00*

Mohrenkolonnaden
10 The Neo-Classical arcades, designed in 1787 by Carl G. Langhans, originally adorned a bridge across the city moat. ◈ *Mohrenstr. 37b u. 40–41 • Map L4*

Left **Outside Kunstsalon** Centre **Fashion at Galeries Lafayette** Right **In Quartier 206**

🔟 Shops

Galeries Lafayette
1 Berlin's most attractive shop is the only branch of the luxury French store in Germany. Here you will find elegant fashion and gourmet foods on the lower level. ◈ *Friedrichstr. 76–78 • Map L4 • 10am–8pm Mon–Sat • (030) 20 94 80*

Department Store 206
2 Stylish Berliners shop here for up-to-the-minute and top-of-the-range designer clothes. ◈ *Friedrichstr. 71 • Map L4 • (030) 20 94 68 00*

Quartier 206
3 Apart from the department stores, many top designer shops, such as Gucci and DKNY, are based in Friedrichstadtpassagen. ◈ *Friedrichstr. • Map L4*

Kunstsalon
4 This shop offers art to touch and take home, including all sorts of paraphernalia (old costumes, for example), make ideal souvenirs. ◈ *Behrenstr. 14–16 • Map K4 • (030) 20 45 02 03*

Fassbender & Rausch
5 Giant chocolate sculptures of Reichstag and Brandenburger Tor adorn the windows and tempt visitors into this shop, a chocaholic's paradise. ◈ *Charlottenstr. 60 • Map L4 • (030) 20 45 84 43*

Berlin Story Wieland Giebel
6 Almost anything you've ever wanted to read about Berlin as well as photographs and souvenirs are available from Herr Giebel, who knows the town like no one else. ◈ *Unter den Linden 40 • Map K4 • (030) 20 45 38 42*

Kulturkaufhaus Dussmann
7 This multi-media store is a mecca for culture-junkies, offering everything from good books to computer games, and also boasting a large section of classical music on CD. The store is also open in the evening. ◈ *Friedrichstr. 90 • Map K4 • (030) 202 50*

Budapester Schuhe
8 Small branch of a chain, selling quality men's shoes. ◈ *Friedrichstr. 81 • Map L4 • (030) 20 38 81 10*

Escada
9 Stylish (and expensive) bespoke tailors for ladies, boasting a fantastic selection of luxurious materials. ◈ *Friedrichstr. 176–179 • Map L4 • (030) 238 64 04*

Juwelier René Kern
10 Well-known jeweller, selling quality watches and jewellery in this luxury outlet. ◈ *Friedrichstr. 176–179 • Map L4 • (030) 204 10 49*

119

Left **Café LebensArt** Centre **Opera Court** Right **Brauerei Lemke in an S-Bahn arch**

Pubs & Bars

Newton Bar
One of the trendiest bars in town. Sink into the deep leather armchairs and sip your cocktails, surrounded by Helmut Newton's photographs of proud women. ◎ *Charlottenstr. 57 • Map L4*
• 10am–3am daily • (030) 20 61 29 99

Opera Court
Afternoon teas, coffee and cake are served daily at the historic Opera Court, with its original glazed ceiling, in the luxurious Hotel de Rome. ◎ *Hotel de Rome, Behrenstr. 37 • Map K4 • (030) 460 60 90*

Operntreff
Completely furnished in leather, this small but elegant bar in the historic Opernpalais is an ideal stopping-off point for night owls looking for a place to go after an evening at the opera. ◎ *Unter den Linden 5 • Map K3*
• 8am–midnight daily • (030) 20 26 83

Emil
Café, pub and restaurant, especially popular with actors. ◎ *Schumannstr. 15 • Map J3*
• 5pm–1am daily • (030) 559 74 54

LebensArt
A café rather than a pub or bar, offering breakfast and afternoon cakes, this is one of the few places open at night on Unter den Linden.
◎ *Unter den Linden 69a • Map K4*
• 9am–8pm Mon–Sat, 10am–8pm Sun
• (030) 229 00 18

Café Einstein
Small and cosy branch of the Café in the western city, serving excellent wines and Austrian specialities. ◎ *Unter den Linden 42*
• Map K4 • 7am–1am Mon–Sun
• (030) 204 36 32

Ständige Vertretung
The name harks back to the permanent West German representation in East Berlin, but the drinks are bang up to date.
◎ *Schiffbauerdamm 8 • Map J3*
• 10am–1am daily • (030) 282 39 65

Q 205
This elegant underground bar offers cool drinks and piano music. ◎ *Quartier 205, Friedrichstr. 68 • Map L4*
• 10am–10pm daily • (030) 20 94 45 45

Brauerei Lemke
Atmospheric pub under the S-Bahn arches; courtyard. ◎ *Dirksenstr. S-Bahn arch No. 143 • Map J5*
• noon–1am daily • (030) 24 72 87 27

Windhorst
Trendy cocktail bar – classy, elegant, good. ◎ *Dorotheenstr. 65*
• Map K3 • from 6pm Mon–Fri, from 9pm Sat • (030) 20 45 00 70

Price Categories

For a three-course	€ under €20
meal for one with half	€€ €20–30
a bottle of wine (or	€€€ €30–45
equivalent meal), taxes	€€€€ €45–60
and charges included	€€€€€ over €60

Left **Outside Dressler Unter den Linden** Right **Theodor Tucher**

🔟 Restaurants & Cafés

Margaux
A newcomer among Berlin's top restaurants, Margaux serves sophisticated French-German nouvelle cuisine. ✪ *Unter den Linden 78 • Map K3 • 7pm–10:30pm Mon–Sat • (030) 22 65 26 11 • €€€€€*

Borchardt
Best of Berlin's trendy new restaurants, offering good French food in an historic setting. ✪ *Französische Str. 47 • Map K4 • 11:30am–1am daily • (030) 81 88 62 62 • €€€*

Vau
The chef, Kolja Seeberg, deserves his Michelin star with his top-class German food. Attractive interior. ✪ *Jägerstr. 54–55 • Map L4 • noon–2:30pm, 7–10:30pm Mon–Sat • (030) 202 97 30 • €€€€*

Fischers Fritz
Located in the sumptuous Regent Hotel, this Michelin-starred restaurant specializes in seafood and offers imaginative and sophisticated dishes. The crackling open fire in the dining room makes each meal a special experience. ✪ *Charlottenstr. 49 • Map K4 • 6:30am–2:30pm, 6–11:30pm daily • (030) 20 33 63 63 • €€€*

Dressler Unter den Linden
In season, this French brasserie is an excellent place for oysters. At other times, the inexpensive three-course set menu is recommended. ✪ *Unter den Linden 39 • Map K3 • 8am–1am daily • (030) 204 44 22 • €€€€*

Lutter & Wegner
Try this Austrian restaurant for the tastiest Wiener Schnitzel and potato salad in Berlin. ✪ *Charlottenstr. 56 • Map L4 • 11am–2am daily • (030) 202 954 17 • €€€*

Theodor Tucher
A nice little restaurant with book store next to the Brandenburg Gate, serving hearty Berlin food. ✪ *Pariser Platz 6a • Map K3 • 9am–1am daily • (030) 22 48 94 63 • €€*

Malatesta
Gourmet Italian food served in stylish, minimalist surroundings. ✪ *Charlottenstr. 59 • Map L4 • noon–midnight daily • (030) 209 450 70 • €€€*

Refugium
A cosy cellar restaurant next to the French cathedral. International and German dishes. ✪ *Gendarmenmarkt 5 • Map L4 • noon–11pm daily • (030) 229 16 61 • €€*

Aigner
Original Viennese restaurant serving typically Austrian food. ✪ *Französische Str. 25 • Map K4 • noon–11:30pm daily • (030) 203 75 18 50 • €€*

Note: All restaurants accept credit cards and offer vegetarian dishes unless stated otherwise.

121

Left **Hackesche Höfe** Centre **Tacheles, Oranienburger Straße** Right **In the Hackesche Höfe**

Central Berlin: Scheunenviertel

THE SCHEUNENVIERTEL, *literally the "barn quarter", Berlin's former Jewish quarter, has experienced a unique revival in recent years. Originally, the thriving Jewish community lived in neighbouring Spandauer Vorstadt, beyond the city limits, while the Scheunenviertel was better known as a red-light district. The Nazis, however, applied the name of "Scheunenviertel" to both areas, in order to tarnish the Jews. After World War II the district was much neglected and gradually fell into decay. Today, many of the historic merchants' yards and narrow side streets have been restored, reviving the Scheunenviertel's unique and lively character. Many pubs and restaurants, galleries and shops are now based here and the area has become very fashionable with locals and visitors alike, especially at night. The tragic history of its former inhabitants, however, remains unforgotten.*

Neue Synagoge

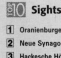 **Sights**

1. Oranienburger Straße
2. Neue Synagoge
3. Hackesche Höfe
4. Sophienstraße
5. Tacheles
6. Museum für Naturkunde
7. Dorotheenstädtischer Friedhof
8. Brecht-Weigel-Gedenkstätte
9. Gedenkstätte Große Hamburger Straße
10. Postfuhramt

Oranienburger Straße

Like no other street, Oranienburger Straße, in the centre of the old Scheunenviertel, symbolizes the rise and fall of Jewish culture in Berlin. Traces of its Jewish past are visible all along the street, such as the Neue Synagoge and several Jewish cafés and restaurants *(see p129)*. Some 18th- and 19th-century buildings bear witness to the street's former splendour – the Postfuhramt *(see p125)*, for example, or the house at No. 71–72, built in 1789 by Christian Friedrich Becherer for the Grand Lodge of the Freemasons of Germany. ✪ *Mitte, between Friedrich-str. and Rosenthaler Str.* • *Map J4/5*

Neue Synagoge

The New Synagogue, built in 1859–66, was once the largest in Europe. In 1938, it managed to survive "Reichskristallnacht" thanks to the vigilance of a brave guard, but it was damaged by bombs during World War II. Behind the Moorish façades are a prayer room and the Centrum Judaicum. ✪ *Oranienburger Str. 29–30* • *Map J4/5* • *10am–6pm Sun–Thu, 10am–2pm Fri* • *(030) 28 40 13 16* • *Free admission*

Hackesche Höfe

Berlin's largest and most attractive group of restored commercial buildings, Hackesche Höfe extends between Oranienburger and Rosenthaler Straße and up to Sophienstraße in the east. The complex of buildings, comprised of nine interconnecting courtyards, was designed around the turn of the 20th century by Kurt Berndt and August Endell, two leading exponents of Art Nouveau. The first courtyard especially features elements that are typical of this style: geometric patterns are laid out in vibrant colours on glazed tiles, covering the entire building from the foundations to the guttering. What had lain in ruin after 1945 has now been carefully restored, and forms today one of the most popular nightlife centres in the city. Restaurants and cafés *(see p128–9)*, the Varieté Chamäleon *(see p56)*, galleries and small shops have all settled in this area. ✪ *Rosenthaler Str. 40–41* • *Map I5*

Sophienstraße

Narrow Sophienstraße has been beautifully restored and now looks exactly as it did in the late 18th century. A number of shops and arts and crafts workshops are now based in the modest buildings and courtyards. Close by stands Sophienkirche, the first Protestant parish church, founded by Queen Sophie Luise in 1712. Next to the Baroque church is a small cemetery with some 18th-century tombs. ✪ *Große Hamburger Str. 29* • *Map I5*

The old Sophienkirche

Left **Bertolt Brecht's study** Right **Memorial on Große Hamburger Straße**

Tacheles

The ruins of the former Wilhelm-Einkaufspassagen, one of Berlin's most elegant shopping centres dating back to the turn of the 20th century, have been transformed by artists into an alternative arts centre. It now houses workshops and cafés and offers a regular programme of events.
⬡ Oranienburger Str. 54–56a
• Map F3 • (030) 282 61 85

Museum für Naturkunde

The Museum of Natural History – one of the largest of its kind – has the world's largest dinosaur skeleton: a brachiosaurus found in Tanzania. Also displayed are fossils, meteorites and minerals (see also p47). ⬡ Invalidenstr. 43 • Map F2 • 9:30am–5pm Tue–Fri; 10am–5:30pm Sat–Sun • (030) 20 93 85 91 • Admission charge

Dorotheenstädtischer Friedhof

Many celebrities have found their final resting place in this charming cemetery, dating back to 1762. To the left of the entrance are the graves of Heinrich Mann (1871–1950) and Bertolt Brecht (1898–1956); further along stand the pillar-like tombstones of the philosophers Johann Gottlieb Fichte (1762–1814) and Georg Wilhelm Friedrich Hegel (1770–1831). On Birkenallee (left off the main path) you can see the graves of master builder Karl Friedrich

Schinkel (1781–1841) and the architects Friedrich August Stüler (1800–65) and Johann Gottfried Schadow (1764–1850).
⬡ Chausseestr. 126 • Map F2 • summer: 8am–8pm daily; winter: 8am–4pm daily

Schinkel, Dorotheenstädtischer Friedhof

Brecht-Weigel-Gedenkstätte

Bertolt Brecht, one of the 20th century's greatest playwrights, lived here with his wife, Helene Weigel, from 1953–6. Original furnishings are on display alongside documents and photographs.
⬡ Chausseestr. 125 • Map F2 • 10–noon Tue–Sat exc Thu; 10–noon & 5–7pm Thu; 9:30am–2pm Sat; 11am–6pm Sun • (030) 283 05 70 44 • Admission charge

Jewish Berlin

In the 19th century, Berlin had a population of 200,000 Jews, the largest such community in Germany. Apart from wealthier Jews in the west of the city, it also attracted many impoverished Jews from Poland and Russia who settled in Spandauer Vorstadt. One part of the district, the criminal red-light district, was also known as Scheunenviertel. Nazi propaganda used the name to denote the entire Spandauer Vorstadt, in order to tarnish the Jews by association. Today, the Jewish quarter is still known under its "wrong" name as "Scheunenviertel", although very few Jews live here now. Only some 5,000 Jewish Berliners managed to survive between 1933–45 in hide-outs.

9 Gedenkstätte Große Hamburger Straße

Before 1939, this was one of the most important Jewish streets, with several Jewish schools, the oldest Jewish cemetery in Berlin and an old people's home. The latter achieved tragic fame during the Nazi period – the SS used it as a detention centre for Berlin Jews before transporting them to the concentration camps. A simple monument commemorates thousands of Jews who were sent to their death from here. To the left of the home is a Jewish school, on the site of an earlier school founded in 1778 by the Enlightenment philosopher Moses Mendelssohn (1729–86). To the right of the monument is the Jewish cemetery, where some 12,000 Jews were buried between 1672 and 1827. In 1943, the Nazis almost completely destroyed the cemetery. Only a few Baroque tombs, or *masebas*, survived; these are now embedded into the small original cemetery wall. The place presumed to be Moses Mendelssohn's tomb is marked by a new monument.
◈ *Große Hamburger Str.* • *Map J5*

10 Postfuhramt

The richly ornamented Postfuhramt (post office transport department) dates back to the 19th century. It is now an exhibition hall for alternative photography and art shows and a centre for performance art.
◈ *Oranienburger Str. 35* • *Map J4*

Frieze on the Postfuhramt façade

A Day in Scheunenviertel

Morning

🕐 Take the S-Bahn to Friedrichstraße and explore this road, Berlin's former entertainment district. Walk north along the street up to Reinhardstraße, and turn left here towards Bertolt-Brecht-Platz. Continue south to Albrechtstraße to the **Berliner Ensemble** *(see p126)*. Once you have admired the theatre where the great playwright used to work, you could make a detour to visit his home, **Brecht-Weigel-Gedenkstätte** in Chausseestraße. The best way to get there is on foot – walk along Chausseestraße. If you remain in Friedrichstraße and turn right behind Friedrichstadtpalast into **Oranienburger Straße** *(see p123)*, you will get to the heart of the fashionable Scheunenviertel. At the corner of the street rises the arts centre **Tacheles**, and a few steps to the east the shiny golden dome of the **Neue Synagoge** will come into view *(see pp45 and 123)*.

Afternoon

Before exploring the Scheunenviertel district, you should take some refreshments; not far from the Synagogue is **Café Oren** *(see p129)*. Walk along Tucholskystraße, then turn right into Auguststraße. Here you will find some of the most attractive courtyards, for example **Kunsthof** at the corner of Gartenstraße. Return along Auguststraße to **Gedenkstätte Große Hamburger Straße** and the **Hackesche Höfe** *(see p123)* to shop and for an evening meal.

Around Town – Central Berlin: Scheunenviertel

Left **The O & G club** Centre **Drinks at Yosoy** Right **Clärchen's Ballhaus**

Pubs, Bars & Discos

Riva
An elegant, cool and trendy bar free from hooligans, named after an Italian soccer player. ✆ *Dircksenstr., arch 142* • *Map J5* • *8pm–4am daily* • *(030) 24 72 26 88*

Bellini Lounge
Head this way for some of the most authentic tropical cocktails mixed north of the equator. ✆ *Oranienburger Str. 42* • *Map J4* • *4pm–5am Fri–Sat, 4pm–3am Sun–Wed* • *(030) 970 056 18*

Ambulance
Enjoy some of the best and most affordable drinks in town in a relaxed hip hop atmosphere. ✆ *Oranienburger Str. 27* • *Map J5* • *from 7pm daily* • *(030) 281 20 95*

Komfort
One of the newest and most fashionable dancing clubs in Berlin, playing R&B, house and electro music to an elegant, young urban crowd. ✆ *Dircksenstr. 40* • *Map J5* • *from 10pm Tue–Sat*

O & G
In a former socialist fruit store, O & G's DJs create a flirtatious atmosphere for young Mitte lovers. ✆ *Oraienburger Str. 48–49* • *Map J5* • *6pm–1am daily* • *(030) 25 76 26 67*

b-flat
Live jazz and occasionally dance are on offer at this small venue. ✆ *Rosenthaler Str. 13* • *Map J5* • *from 8pm daily* • *(030) 283 86 835* • *Admission charge*

Delicious Doughnuts
An old favourite among the hip new clubs of the district, promising to take you "back to the roots". Hot funk and soul rhythms are played. ✆ *Rosenthaler Str. 9* • *Map J5* • *10pm–5am Thu–Sun* • *(030) 28 09 92 74* • *Admission charge*

Clärchen's Ballhaus
One of Berlin's last remaining dancehalls, where dance-crazy Berliners of an uncertain age dance the waltz and sing along. ✆ *Auguststr. 24* • *Map G2* • *from 8pm Tue–Sat* • *(030) 282 92 95*

Yosoy
This attractively furnished Spanish restaurant serves tasty tapas, good wines and exciting cocktails – which is why it is crowded till late into the night. ✆ *Rosenthaler Str. 37* • *Map J5* • *from 11am daily* • *(030) 28 39 12 13* • *€€*

Wondratschek
This tiny champagne and cocktail bar in the basement of Schwarzraben restaurant *(see p129)* is a colourful hangout for the artsy Mitte crowd. ✆ *Neue Schönhauser Str. 13* • *Map G3* • *from 9pm Thu–Sat* • *(030) 283 916 98*

Price Categories

For a three-course meal for one with half a bottle of wine (or equivalent meal), taxes and charges included

€	under €20
€€	€20–30
€€€	€30–45
€€€€	€45–60
€€€€€	over €60

Left **Outside Oxymoron in the Hackesche Höfe** Right **La Fil in the trendy Mitte district**

Restaurants & Cafés

1 Pan Asia
Asian dishes, many with seared fish and vegetables – not too spicy – in minimalist 1960s surroundings. ◈ *Rosenthaler Str. 38 • Map J5 • noon–midnight daily • (030) 27 90 88 11 • €€*

2 Café Oren
This popular café serves authentic vegetarian Jewish food in the heart of the Scheunenviertel. ◈ *Oranienburger Str. 28 • Map J4/5 • 10am–1am Mon–Thu, 10am–midnight Fri–Sun • (030) 28 59 93 12 • €*

3 Schwarzenraben
Excellent pizzas and Italian specialities are on the menu at this long restaurant. ◈ *Neue Schönhauser Str. 13 • Map J5 • 11:30am–midnight Mon–Sat; 2pm–midnight Sun • (030) 28 39 16 98 • €€€*

4 Maxwell
Gourmet restaurant in a New-York-style loft; unfussy fusion food. ◈ *Bergstr. 22 • Map G2 • 6pm–11:30pm daily • (030) 280 71 21 • €€€*

5 Beth-Café
Small Jewish café of the Adass-Jisroel community, serving Jewish snacks. ◈ *Tucholskystr 40 • Map J4 • noon–8pm Sun–Thu • (030) 281 31 35 • no credit cards • €*

6 Hackescher Hof
Best restaurant in Hackesche Höfe serves traditional German fare. ◈ *Rosenthaler Str. 40 • Map J5 • 7am–2am Mon–Fri, 9am–2am Sat, Sun • (030) 283 52 93 • €€€*

7 Oxymoron
This small café and restaurant in Hackesche Höfe, featuring chintz decoration, serves light German meals. ◈ *Rosenthaler Str. 40 41 • Map J5 • 11am–1am daily • (030) 28 39 18 85/86 • €€€*

8 La Fil
This cosy Spanish restaurant offers simple and delicious Iberian fare, including the house speciality, *pinchos*, small pieces of bread with tapas-style toppings. ◈ *Gormannstr. 22 • Map G2 • 1pm–2am daily • (030) 285 990 26 • €€*

9 Modellhut
This new restaurant caters to Berlin's young fashion scene, so it specializes in lean cuisine. Stylish interior with gold walls and ceiling. ◈ *Alte Schönhauser Str. 28 • Map J5 • 6pm–2am Mon–Sun • (030) 97 00 50 58 • €€€*

10 Barist
A mixture of French, Italian and Austrian dishes are on offer here. There is always a good atmosphere under the S-Bahn arches; live jazz at weekends. ◈ *Am Zwirngraben 13–14 • Map G2 • 10am–3am daily • (030) 24 72 26 13 • €€*

Note: *All restaurants accept credit cards and offer vegetarian dishes unless stated otherwise.*

Left **Altar painting in Marienkirche** Centre **Frieze on the Münze** Right **Knoblauch-Haus**

Central Berlin: Around Alexanderplatz

THE AREA AROUND ALEXANDERPLATZ *is one of the oldest parts of the city; it was here that the twin towns of Cölln and Berlin merged to become one town in the 13th century. Berlin's oldest coherent quarter, the 18th-century Nikolaiviertel and its medieval Nikolaikirche, the city's oldest church, lie in the shadow of the TV tower, the pride of the "capital" of former East Germany. On the occasion of Berlin's 750th anniversary, in 1987, the East German government had the Nikolaiviertel restored. Very few of the original buildings are preserved, however; most houses were rebuilt from scratch. Only a few paces away from the alleyways of Nikolaiviertel extends Alexanderplatz, referred to by locals simply as "Alex". Before World War II, Alex defined the heartbeat of the city; after the ravages of war, it seemed vast and a little forlorn. Although the giant square is now livelier again, especially in summer, a chilly easterly wind still blows between the houses. The vibrancy of the square, as described by Alfred Döblin in his novel* Berlin Alexanderplatz, *is only slowly returning to the area. Much building and reconstruction work is planned for Alex in the coming years.*

Berliner Rathaus

🔟 Sights

1. Alexanderplatz
2. Berliner Rathaus
3. Berliner Fernsehturm
4. Nikolaiviertel
5. Marienkirche
6. Marx-Engels-Forum
7. Märkisches Museum
8. Ephraim-Palais
9. Neptune Fountain
10. Karl-Marx-Allee and Frankfurter Allee

Alexanderplatz on a 24-hour webcam:
www.berlinonline.de/spass/live_kamera/.html/alex.html

Alexanderplatz

1 The vast, largely desolate square in the centre of East Berlin, called "Alex" by Berliners, was one of the most vibrant places in Berlin before World War II – and no doubt it will be again some day. Alfred Döblin beautifully captured the rhythm of the city in his world-famous novel *Berlin Alexanderplatz*. Not much remains today of the once frenzied atmosphere, although there is plenty of hustle and bustle around the Kaufhof Galleria department store *(see p135)*.

Originally, Alex was a cattle and wool market. Not many of the prewar buildings survived – only Berolinahaus and Alexanderhaus, next to the historic S-Bahn station Alexanderplatz, remain, both dating back to 1929. The square was almost completely laid to waste in World War II, and most of the surrounding soulless tower blocks were built in the 1960s. There are now plans to build skyscrapers on Alexanderplatz. ◈ *Mitte • Map I6*

Berliner Rathaus

2 Berlin's proud town hall is the office of the Governing Mayor and is the political centre of power in Greater Berlin. The

Heraldic animal at the Rathaus

Rathaus was built in 1861–9, according to plans by Hermann Friedrich Waesemann on the site of an older town hall. It was designed to demonstrate the power and the glory of Berlin, and the architect took his inspiration for the new governmental building from Italian Renaissance *palazzi*.

The building is also known as the "Red Town Hall" – not a reminder of its Socialist past, but a reference to the red bricks from Brandenburg province from which it is built *(see also p38)*. ◈ *Rathausstr. 15 • Map K6 • 9am–6pm Mon–Fri • (030) 90 26 0*

Berliner Fernsehturm

3 The 365-m (1,197-ft) high TV tower is the tallest building in Berlin, affording views of up to 40 km (25 miles) in good weather. There is a viewing platform at 203 m (666 ft). The Tele-Café above rotates once around its own axis every 30 minutes. The tower, visible from afar, was erected in 1965–9 by the East German government to signify the triumph of East Berlin, their "capital". ◈ *Panoramastr. 1a • Map I6 • Mar–Oct: 9am–midnight, Nov–Feb: 10am–midnight • Tel. (030) 242 33 33 • Admission charge*

Left **Weltzeituhr (world time clock) on "Alex"** Right **Inside the Tele-Café of Fernsehturm**

Left **Nikolaikirche, Nikolaiviertel** Centre **Märkisches Museum** Right **A street in Nikolaiviertel**

Nikolaiviertel

Around the medieval Nikolaikirche *(see p44)*, the small Nikolaiviertel with its narrow nooks and crannies, Old Berlin restaurants and souvenir shops is one of the most charming parts of the city. The area extending between the banks of the Spree River and Mühlendamm was razed to the ground in World War II. The East German authorities restored it after the war – unfortunately not always successfully: some houses were covered in prefabricated façades.

Knoblauchhaus was one of few to escape destruction. Dating from 1835, it was the former home of the Knoblauch family (Neue Synagoge was designed by architect Eduard Knoblauch). Today it houses a museum depicting everyday life in Berlin, and includes a fully furnished apartment in the Biedermeier style. ◈ *Mitte, Knoblauchhaus: Poststr. 23 • Map K6 • 10am–6pm Tue–Sun • (030) 27 57 67 33 • Admission charge*

Marienkirche

Originally built in 1270, Marienkirche was extensively remodelled in the 15th century. Thanks to its Baroque church tower, designed by Carl Gotthard Langhans in 1790, it is one of Berlin's loveliest churches. Inside, the

Altar in Marienkirche

alabaster pulpit by Andreas Schlüter (1703) and the main altar (1762) are particularly worth seeing. The 15th-century Gothic font and a 22-m (72-ft) long fresco, *Der Totentanz* (The Dance of Death) from 1485 are its two oldest treasures. The church was a thorn in the side for the East German government because the cross on its tower is reflected in the TV tower. ◈ *Karl-Liebknecht-Str. 8 • Map K6 • May–Sep: 10am–9pm daily; Oct–Apr: 10am–6pm daily • (030) 242 44 67*

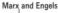

Marx and Engels

Marx-Engels-Forum

Shortly after German reunification in 1989, the motto "Next time it will all be different" was scrawled onto this monument to Karl Marx and Friedrich Engels, the fathers of Socialism. The bronze statues, created by Ludwig Engelhart in 1986, adorn the centre of a square. ◈ *Map K5/6*

Märkisches Museum

Berlin's municipal museum displays architectural treasures such as doorways and the head of one of the horses from the top of the Brandenburg Gate, plus various items relating to theatre and music in Berlin. ◈ *Am Köllnischen Park 5 • Map L6 • 10am–6pm Tue–Sun, noon–8pm Wed • (030) 30 86 60 • Admission charge*

Ephraim-Palais

Ephraim-Palais

The curved Baroque palace, built in 1766 for the wealthy merchant Nathan Veitel Heinrich Ephraim, was once regarded as the city's most beautiful spot. Rebuilt after the demolition of the old palace, it is now a museum, showing paintings by local artists. ⬡ *Poststr. 16* • *Map K6* • *10am–6pm Tue & Thu–Sun, noon–8pm Wed* • *(030) 24 00 20* • *Admission charge*

Neptune Fountain

The green Neo-Baroque fountain, dating from 1895, depicts the sea god Neptune. He is surrounded by four female figures, symbolizing Germany's Rhine, Weichsel, Oder and Elb Rivers. ⬡ *Am Rathaus* • *Map K6*

Karl-Marx-Allee and Frankfurter Allee

This road, lined by Soviet-style buildings, was built as a show-piece for Socialism in 1949–55. Known then as "Stalinallee", it provided ultra-modern apartments. ⬡ *Mitte/Friedrichshain*

Neptune Fountain

A Day around Alexanderplatz

Morning

Start your day by going to **Alexanderplatz** *(see p131)* where you can watch the crowds in the square and perhaps do a spot of shopping before strolling to **Marienkirche**. Not far from here you can chill out at **Neptune Fountain** and then admire the statues of Marx and Engels in the **Marx-Engels-Forum**. From there it is only a few steps to the **Berliner Rathaus** *(see p131)*. The basement restaurant, or Ratskeller, is an excellent place for an early lunch, or you could stroll to the nearby historic Nikolaiviertel, and enjoy a meal, for example at **Reinhard's** *(see p137)*, which serves rustic fare.

Afternoon

Experience the historic ambience of the **Nikolaiviertel** by exploring on foot, if possible, its narrow alleyways. Nikolaikirche and the Knoblauchhaus are especially worth a visit. From here walk back to Alexanderplatz and – if the weather is nice – take the lift up to the viewing café in the **Berliner Fernsehturm** *(see p131)*. After refreshments you can continue on foot or take the U-Bahn from Alex to Strausberger Platz to admire the products of Socialist architecture in **Frankfurter Allee** *(see p133)*. On Grunerstraße you will reach the opposite bank of the Spree River, where you can immerse yourself in Berlin's municipal history at the **Märkisches Museum** just around the corner. In the evening, go for a posh meal at **Ermelerhaus** *(see p137)*.

Around Town – Central Berlin: Around Alexanderplatz

Left **Stairs of the Stadtgericht** Centre **Palais Podewil** Right **Ruins of Franziskanerkirche**

Best of the Rest

Stadtgericht

The imposing municipal courts building boasts extravagant stairs in the lobby area, with curved balustrades and elegant columns. ✿ *Littenstr. 13–15 • Map K6 • 8am–6pm Mon–Fri*

Franziskanerkirche

The ruins, remnants of a 13th-century Franciscan abbey, are surrounded by lawns, making this a picturesque spot for a rest in the city centre.
✿ *Klosterstr. 74 • Map K6*

Stadtmauer

A fragment of the 13th–14th-century town wall that once surrounded the twin towns of Berlin and Cölln. ✿ *Waisenstr. • Map K6*

Palais Podewil

The light yellow Baroque palace, built in 1701–4, has been transformed into Podewil, a cultural centre and one of the best places for contemporary music.
✿ *Klosterstr. 68 • Map K6 • 11am– 10pm Mon–Sat • (030) 24 74 96*

Parochialkirche

This church, by Johann Arnold Nering and Martin Grünberg, was one of Berlin's most charming Baroque churches, but the magnificent interior was destroyed in World War II, and the bell tower collapsed. Recently, it has become a venue for contemporary music concerts.
✿ *Klosterstr. 67 • Map K6*

Märkisches Ufer

This picturesque riverside promenade gives a good impression of the city in the late 18th century. ✿ *Map L6*

Heiliggeistkapelle

The 13th-century hospital church is a beautiful example of Gothic brick architecture.
✿ *Spandauer Str. 1 • Map K6*

Ribbeckhaus

The only Renaissance house in central Berlin, with a remarkable, lavishly ornamented façade.
✿ *Breite Str. 36 • Map K5*

Palais Schwerin and Münze

Two adjoining buildings with elegant 18th-century façades: Palais Schwerin has beautiful window cornices; Münze (the mint) is decorated with a Neo-Classical frieze. ✿ *Molkenmarkt 1–3 • Map K6*

Historic Port

Historic barges and tugboats that once operated on the Spree River are moored here. Boat tours of the harbour can be booked.
✿ *Märkisches Ufer • Map L6 • Apr–Oct: 2–6pm Tue–Fri; 11am–6pm Sat, Sun • (030) 21 47 32 56*

Left **Kaufhof Galeria façade** Centre **Inside Die Puppenstube** Right **Der Teeladen in Nikolaiviertel**

🔟 Shops & Markets

Kaufhof Galeria
The largest department store in East Berlin stocks everything your heart could desire. Its food department entices customers with a range of international gourmet foods. ⊗ *Alexanderplatz 9* • *Map I6* • *9am–8pm Mon–Sat* • *(030) 24 74 30*

Die Puppenstube
Adorable dolls made from porcelain and other materials await window shopper and buyer alike, as do mountains of cute fluffy teddy bears. ⊗ *Propststr. 4* • *Map K6* • *10am–6:30pm Mon–Sat, 11am–6pm Sun* • *(030) 242 39 67*

Teddy's Spielwaren
An old-fashioned toy store, with probably the best selection of teddy bears in the city. ⊗ *Propststr. 4* • *Map K6* • *(030) 247 82 44*

Der Teeladen
A charming specialist tea shop opposite Nikolaikirche, always steeped in delicious scents. ⊗ *Propststr. 3* • *Map K6* • *10am–6:30pm Mon–Sat* • *(030) 242 32 55*

Hessisches Haus (Gallery of Antiques)
One of the city's best antique shops, specializing in furniture. Expert advice is guaranteed.
⊗ *Poststr. 12* • *Map K5 /6* • *11am–6:30pm Tue–Sun* • *(030) 208 25 54*

U- and S-Bahnhof Alexanderplatz
This bustling area has a selection of shops for daily needs, plus late-opening fast food outlets and German *imbisse* (food stands). ⊗ *Alexanderplatz* • *Map J6*

Berlin Carré
The snack bars based in this small shopping arcade offer delicious foods that you can buy or sample on the spot. ⊗ *Karl-Liebknecht-Str. 13* • *Map I6*

Thüringischer Weihnachtsmarkt
A vast array of stalls laden with Christmas gifts and traditional wooden decorations at the Thuringian Christmas Market. ⊗ *Propststr. 8* • *Map K6* • *(030) 241 12 29*

Wohltat'sche Buchhandlung
This large bookstore sells remainders and second-hand books, postcards and calendars of Berlin, as well as videos, CDs and DVDs. ⊗ *Alexanderplatz 2* • *Map I6* • *9am–8pm Mon–Sat* • *(030) 242 68 54*

Saturn
Branch of a large multi-media chain, selling CDs, PC games and all sorts of electronic games and entertainment. ⊗ *Alexanderplatz 8* • *Map I6* • *9:30am–8pm Mon–Fri, 9am–8pm Sat* • *(030) 24 75 16*

Left **Brauhaus Georgbräu** Centre **Zur letzten Instanz** Right **Zum Nußbaum**

Pubs, Cafés & Beer Gardens

1 Zur letzten Instanz
Berlin's oldest pub dates back to 1621, and former guests include Napoleon, the German artist Heinrich Zille and former Soviet leader Mikhael Gorbachev. The interior is charmingly aged. ◎ *Waisenstr. 14–16 • Map K6 • noon–1am Mon–Sat, noon–11pm Sun • (030) 24 25 528 • €€*

2 Brauhaus Georgbräu
This beer garden attracts not only Bavarians "in exile" but also many tourist groups. On offer are rustic fare and beer from both Berlin and Munich. ◎ *Spreeufer 4 • Map K5/6 • summer: 10am–midnight daily; winter: from noon Mon–Fri • (030) 242 42 44 • €€*

3 Zum Nußbaum
A charming historic pub in Nikolaiviertel, serving draft beers and Berliner Weiße in summer. ◎ *Am Nußbaum 3 • Map K6 • noon–11pm daily • (030) 242 30 95 • €€*

4 Sky Club
It's the gambling that draws punters to Sky Club but, at night, the views of Berlin from the 42nd floor are truly spectacular. ◎ *Dircksenstr. 98–100 • Map I/K5/6 • from 11pm daily • no credit cards • no phone*

5 Alex Café
The Alex Café, below the TV tower, has a huge breakfast buffet – start your tour of East Berlin here. ◎ *Panoramastr. 1a • Map K6 • 9am–1am Sun–Thu, 9am–3am Fri, Sat • (030) 24 04 76 30 • €€*

6 Heinrich
Home-made cakes make the little café diagonally opposite Nikolaikirche an irresistible stopping point. ◎ *Poststr. 13 • Map K6 • 10am–1am daily • (030) 24 72 60 41 • €*

7 Café Ephraim's
Coffee and cakes plus good views of the Spree River attract locals and tourists. ◎ *Spreeufer 1 • Map K5/6 • noon–10pm daily • (030) 24 72 59 47 • no credit cards • €€*

8 Telecafé Fernsehturm
Enjoy a snack in the skies above Berlin; the café does a full rotation every 45 minutes. ◎ *Panoramastr. 1a • Map J6 • 10am–midnight daily • (030) 242 33 33 • €€*

9 Zum Fischerkietz
Atmospheric pub-restaurant, serving beer and the speciality, Berliner Weiße. ◎ *Fischerinsel 5 • Map L6 • 11am–midnight daily • (030) 201 15 16 • €€*

10 Historische Weinstuben
A tiny wine bar/pub where you can enjoy beer and simple German food in historic surroundings. ◎ *Poststr. 23 • Map K6 • noon–midnight daily • (030) 242 41 07 • €*

Hackescher Markt

Alexanderplatz

Klosterstr.

Jannowitzbrücke

Märkisches Museum

Price Categories

For a three-course meal for one with half a bottle of wine (or equivalent meal), taxes and charges included	**€** under €20
	€€ €20–30
	€€€ €30–45
	€€€€ €45–60
	€€€€€ over €60

Left **Restaurant Zur Gerichtslaube** Right **Reinhard's in Nikolaiviertel**

Restaurants

Reinhard's
One of the most charming restaurants in the Mitte district. Savour the international food, surrounded by photos and paintings of famous contemporaries. *Poststr. 28 • Map K6 • 9am–midnight daily • (030) 24 25 295 • €€€*

HEat
The ultra-chic fusion restaurant at the SAS Radisson *(see p179)* serving an imaginative blend of Oriental and European tastes. *Karl-Liebknecht-Str. 3 • Map K5 • 6am–11pm daily • (030) 238 28 0 • €€€*

Zur Gerichtslaube
The former court building is a stylish setting for traditional Berlin specialities. *Poststr. 28 • Map K6 • 11:30am–1am daily • (030) 241 56 98 • €€€*

Le Provencal
Baked oysters, scallop soup and other seafood delicacies are served in this cosy family-run French restaurant. *Spreeufer 3 • Map K6 • noon–midnight • (030) 302 75 67 • €€*

Zum Paddenwirt
A mecca for fans of traditional Berlin food, including fried herrings and brawn, and a strong beer. *Nikolaikirchplatz 6 • Map K6 • noon–midnight daily • (030) 242 63 82 • no credit cards • €€*

Zillestube
Named after the folksy Berlin painter Heinrich Zille, this tiny pub serves hearty Berlin food and traditional beers, in a rustic setting. *Propststr. 9 • Map K6 • daily from 11am • (030) 242 52 4/ • €€*

Marcellino
The best Italian restaurant in the area, with terrace and a large inviting garden, offering shade on a hot summer's day. Excellent pasta dishes and specials. *Poststr. 28 • Map K6 • noon–midnight daily • (030) 242 73 71 • €€*

La Riva
A more upmarket Italian venue in Nikolaiviertel, offering delicious pasta dishes, which can be enjoyed outside in summer, with a view of the Spree River. *Spreeufer 2 • Map K6 • 11am–11pm daily • (030) 242 51 83 • €€*

Kartoffelhaus No. 1
The menu is dominated by fish and hearty meat dishes. *Poststr. 4 • Map K6 • noon–midnight daily • (030) 24 72 09 45 • €€*

Mutter Hoppe
Delicious traditional German food, served in gigantic portions, makes up for the service, which is not always the friendliest. *Rathausstr. 21 • Map K6 • 11:30am–midnight daily • (030) 24 72 06 03 • €*

Note: *All restaurants accept credit cards and offer vegetarian dishes unless stated otherwise.*

Left **The façades of restored houses in Hagenauer Straße** Right **The Jewish Cemetery**

Prenzlauer Berg

BERLIN'S PRENZLAUER BERG DISTRICT *attracts locals and tourists like virtually no other part of town because it has undergone the most dramatic changes in recent years. Today, the old tenement blocks in the former workers' district of East Berlin have been taken over by cafés, pubs and restaurants, and the nightlife is exciting and vibrant. Even when Berlin was still a divided city, Prenzlauer Berg was an area favoured by artists and an alternative crowd – and it exerts a similar pull today. Many houses in the quiet side streets have not yet been renovated and give a genuine impression of what Berlin once used to be like. But Prenzlauer Berg is undergoing a transformation. Since the reunification of the city, this quarter has become one of the most popular residential areas. Many West Germans, decried as "yuppies" by the locals, settle here, restore the buildings and buy up the apartments. The standard of life in the district has risen noticeably. Trendy bars, restaurants and cafés are clustered mainly around Kollwitzplatz and Husemannstraße. And so a visit to Prenzlauer Berg today is at the same time a journey back in time to the days immediately following reunification.*

Wasserturm

🔟 Sights

1. Kollwitzplatz
2. Schönhauser Allee
3. Prater
4. Kulturbrauerei
5. Jewish Cemetery
6. Husemannstraße
7. Zionskirche
8. Wasserturm
9. Synagoge Rykestraße
10. Gethsemanekirche

Prater: www.praterteam.de

Kollwitz monument in Kollwitzplatz

Kollwitzplatz

Once a quiet square, Kollwitzplatz is today the noisy and turbulent heart of the district. All around the green square, locals congregate in numerous cafés, pubs, bars and restaurants; in summer especially, the fun carries on till late at night. From the appearance of the lavishly restored façades it is hard to tell that Kollwitzplatz was once one of Berlin's poorest areas. The impoverished past of the district and its 19th-century tenement blocks is today only recalled by the name of the square. The artist Käthe Kollwitz (1867–1945) *(see p51)* once lived and worked at Kollwitzplatz 25 (now destroyed) and spent much of her life in the district, where she highlighted the poverty of the local workers in her sculptures, drawings and sketches.
Ⓢ *Prenzlauer Berg • Map H2*

Schönhauser Allee

Schönhauser Allee, 3 km (2 miles) long, is the main artery of the district. In the centre of the dual carriageway is the high-level viaduct of U-Bahn line U 2, painted green. Schönhauser Allee, which runs north-east from Rosa-Luxemburg-Platz to the edge of town, is lined with shops and a few pubs. Many buildings have not yet been restored and give

a good impression of the "old" Prenzlauer Berg – especially the buildings between Senefeld-erplatz and Danziger Straße.
Ⓢ *Prenzlauer Berg • Map H1/2*

Prater

The Prater is one of the few remaining entertainment complexes that were once common in Germany's big cities. It was built in 1837 just outside the original city gates, and was first jokingly called "Prater" by Berliners after its world-famous counterpart in Vienna. A concert hall was added in 1857 and by the turn of the century it had become so popular that the nickname stuck. Today, you can enjoy beer and food at the restaurant of the same name *(see p143)*. Ⓢ *Kastanienallee 7–9 • Map G2 • 6pm–midnight Mon–Sat, noon–midnight Sun • (030) 448 56 88*

Kulturbrauerei

The giant building originally housed Berlin's Schultheiss brewery, one of the few remaining breweries that once made Prenzlauer Berg famous. The complex of buildings, parts of which are more than 150 years old, was designed by Franz Schwechten. It was completely restored in 1997–9, and has become a lively and popular meeting point for locals. Restaurants, cafés, pubs, a cinema, small shops and even a theatre have sprung up within the complex of red and yellow brick buildings and now line its numerous interior courtyards. Ⓢ *Schönhauser Allee 36–39 (entrance: Knaackstr. 97) • Map H1 • (030) 44 31 50*

Kulturbrauerei tower

Left **A house in Kollwitzplatz** Centre **At the Prater** Right **In Kollwitzstraße**

Jewish Cemetery

The small Jewish cemetery is one of the most charming cemeteries in the city. The tombstones lie or stand here amid dense scrub and high trees. The cemetery was set up in 1827, when the former Jewish cemetery in Große Hamburger Straße was closed. Two of the famous personalities who have found their final resting places here are the painter Max Liebermann (1847–1935) and the composer Giacomo Meyerbeer (1791–1864). ◈ *Schönhauser Allee 23–25 • Map H2*

Husemannstraße

The East German regime undertook a perfect restoration of this idyllic street for Berlin's 750th anniversary celebrations. A stroll through the leafy roads lined with houses from the

Gründerzeit (the years after the founding of the German Empire in 1871) is one of the nicest ways to experience Prenzlauer Berg. Ancient-looking street lamps and signs, cobbled streets, antiquated shop signs and a few atmospheric pubs take the visitor back to the late 19th century. ◈ *Between Wörther and Danziger Str. • Map H1/2*

Zionskirche

Zionskirche, dating from 1866–73, and the square of the same name form a tranquil oasis in the middle of the lively district. The Protestant church has always been a political centre, too. During the Third Reich, resistance groups against the Nazi regime congregated here and, during the East German period, the alternative "environment library" (an information and documentation centre) was established here. Church and other opposition groups who were active here played a decisive role in the political transformation of East Germany in 1989–90, which eventually led to reunification.
◈ *Zionskirchplatz • Map G2 • noon–4pm Sun, 10am–11am, 4–5pm Wed, 4–6pm Thu • (030) 449 21 91*

Zionskirche

Wasserturm

The unofficial symbol of the district is the giant, 30-m (98-ft) high Water Tower in Knaackstraße, built in 1877 as a water reservoir, but shut down in 1914. The engine house in the tower was used as an unofficial prison by the SA in 1933–45 – a period recalled by a commemorative plaque. The tower stands on Windmühlenberg (windmill hill), where some of the windmills that had made Prenzlauer Berg famous in the 19th century once stood. Today the round brick building has been converted into trendy apartments.

Synagoge Rykestraße

The synagogue, built in 1904, is one of the few Jewish places of worship to have survived "Reichskristallnacht" on 9 November 1938, the violent destruction of Jewish shop premises by the Nazis. The historic interior of the synagogue was built from red bricks in the shape of a basilica. Today it is part of an apartment block. ◈ *Rykestr. 53 • Map H2 • by prior arrangement • (030) 442 59 31*

Gethsemanekirche

Outside this red-brick church, dating back to 1891–3, East German secret police beat up peaceful protesters. It was the starting point for the collapse of the East German regime. ◈ *Stargarder Str. 77 • Map H1 • May–Oct: 5–7pm Wed, Thu (otherwise by prior arrangement) • (030) 445 77 45*

Entrance to Gethsemanekirche

A Day in Prenzlauer Berg

Morning

🕐 Set off from U-Bahn station Senefelderplatz – one of the lively spots in Prenzlauer Berg. From here, explore the old tenement blocks and backyards. Now continue in a westerly direction along Fehrbelliner Straße to **Zionskirchplatz** with its eponymous church. There are numerous cafés on the square, such as **Commode**, where you could stop for a capuccino. Continue along Zionskirchstraße, then turn left into Kastanienallee. This is one of the most colourful streets in the quarter. At the end of the street you could pop into **Prater** *(see p143)*; now turn right into Oderberger Straße, one of the best preserved streets of the district. Continue along Srzedzkistraße in an easterly direction until you reach **Husemannstraße**. Have a good look around the Old Berlin streets, you may find something interesting to buy.

Afternoon

You could have lunch at one of the many restaurants in **Kollwitzplatz** *(see p139)*: **Gugelhof** and **Zander** are both worth recommending *(for both see p143)*. Continue along Knaackstraße to the small **Synagoge Rykestraße**. From here it is only a few paces to the **Wasserturm** in Knaackstraße. Give your feet a rest on the small green space around the tower, before continuing along Belforter and Kollwitzstraße to Schönhauser Allee. You will find perfect tranquillity there in the **Jewish Cemetery**.

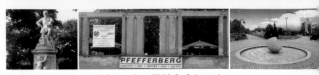

Left **Senefelderplatz** Centre **Pfefferberg** Right **ZEISS-Großplanetarium**

Best of the Rest

Greifenhagener Straße
Not the most beautiful street of Old Berlin, but one of the best preserved. Map H1

Pfefferberg
This alternative cultural centre hosts concerts, performance art events and festivals. Schönhauser Allee 176 • Map H2 • (030) 44 38 31 10

Senefelderplatz
The wedge-shaped square is dedicated to Alois Senefelder, a pioneer of modern printing techniques. At its centre is "Café Achteck". Map H2

ZEISS-Großplanetarium
A trip to outer space – see stars, planets and galaxies under the silvery dome of the Planetarium. Prenzlauer Allee 80 • 9:30am and 11am Tue–Fri; also pm Wed, Sat, Sun • (030) 42 18 45 12

Mauerpark
The vast sporting terrain near the former border, comprising Max Schmeling Hall and Jahn Sports Park, was built for the Berlin Olympics in 2000. Today it hosts sports and music events. Am Falkplatz • Map G1 • (030) 44 30 44 30

Helmholtzplatz
All around this square, time seems to have stopped in 1925. The residential buildings are reminiscent of a social housing programme. Map H1

Prenzlauer Berg Museum
The small lively museum documents the history of the district and its poor working-class inhabitants in the 19th century. Prenzlauer Allee 227–228 • Map H2 • 10am–6pm Tue–Wed & Sun, noon–8pm Thu • (030) 902 953 081

Konnopke
This legendary Currywurstimbiss was opened in 1930 under the U-Bahn steel viaduct. The spicy sausages are among the best in the city. At the southern exit of U-Bahn Schönhauser Allee • Map H1 • 7:30am–6pm Mon–Fri • (030) 9 25 25 76

Oderberger Straße
This tree-lined street has remained almost completely unchanged. The old municipal swimming baths of Prenzlauer Berg are also located in this road at No. 84. Map G/H1

Thälmannpark
One of few parks in the northeast of the city, dominated by Socialist prefabricated buildings. It has a giant monument to Ernst Thälmann, a communist who was murdered by the Nazis. Prenzlauer Allee • Map H1

Price Categories

For a three-course	€	under €20
meal for one with half	€€	€20–30
a bottle of wine (for	€€€	€30–45
equivalent meal), taxes	€€€€	€45–60
and charges included	€€€€€	over €60

Left **Italian restaurant BellUno** Right **Café November**

ᴛᴏᴘ Restaurants, Pubs & Bars

1 Drei
Yuppies and West Germans congregate at this trendy eaterie, serving international and Asian food. ✪ *Lychener Str. 30 • Map H1 • 5pm–1am Mon–Sat • (030) 417 157 18 • no credit cards • €€*

2 Gugelhof
Bill Clinton was once a guest at this restaurant, which draws clients from all over Berlin. The menu features an original combination of German and French dishes. ✪ *Knaackstr. 37 • Map H1/2 • 4pm–1am Mon–Fri, 10am–1am Sat–Sun • (030) 442 92 29 • €€*

3 Zander
A small restaurant, offering imaginative new interpretations of local fish specialities. The three-course set menu is one of the best and least expensive in the district. ✪ *Kollwitzstr. 50 • Map H2 • 6–11pm Tue–Sun • (030) 44 05 76 78 • €€€*

4 BellUno
Lively Italian restaurant with large terrace – ideal for people-watching in the open air. ✪ *Kollwitzstr. 66 • Map H2 • 10am–1am daily • no credit cards • (030) 441 05 48 • €€€*

5 Prater
Surprises at Prater include a beer garden, a rustic restaurant in the courtyard, and free live concerts. ✪ *Kastanienallee 7–9 • Map G2 • 6pm–midnight Mon–Sat, 10am–midnight Sun • (030) 448 56 88 • no credit cards • €€€*

6 Knaack-Club
Almost legendary club, playing rock and indie to an alternative crowd. ✪ *Greifswalder Str. 224 • Map H2 • from 10pm Fri, Sat • (030) 442 70 60 • no credit cards*

7 Restauration 1900
This venerable restaurant still pulls in the crowds with its deliciously light German cuisine. ✪ *Husemannstr. 1 • Map H1/2 • 10am–2am daily • (030) 442 24 94 • €€*

8 Pasternak
Go Russian at this Moscow-style venue, with borshch, Russian music and vodka. ✪ *Knaackstr. 22 • Map H1/2 • 10pm–midnight daily • (030) 441 33 99 • no credit cards • €€*

9 Café November
Popular restaurant and bar on the Prenzlauer Berg hill. ✪ *Husemannstr. 15 • Map H1/2 • 10am–1am Mon–Fri, 9am–2am Sat & Sun • (030) 442 84 25 • €€*

10 Anita Wronski
One of the district's oldest pubs, attracting students, would-be revolutionaries and locals. ✪ *Knaackstr. 26 • Map H1/2 • 9am–2am Mon–Fri, 10am–2am Sat, Sun • (030) 442 84 83 • no credit cards*

Note: All restaurants accept credit cards and offer vegetarian dishes unless stated otherwise.

Left **Normannenstraße** Centre **Schloss Friedrichsfelde** Right **Köpenick's coat of arms**

Berlin's Southeast

ERLIN'S EAST AND SOUTH *are remarkably different in character. Fried-richshain, Lichtenberg and Hohenschönhausen in the east are densely built-up, former working-class areas, while green Treptow and idyllic Köpenick in the far southeast seem like independent villages. The tenement blocks of East Berlin were steeped in history during World War II and later under the East German regime. Historic Köpenick and Großer Müggelsee, meanwhile, are popular daytrip destinations.*

 Sights

1 Köpenicker Altstadt	**6** Großer Müggelsee
2 Köpenicker Schloss	**7** Treptower Park
3 Gedenkstätte Normannenstraße	**8** Volkspark Friedrichshain
4 Deutsch-Russisches Museum	**9** Tierpark Friedrichsfelde
5 East Side Gallery	**10** Gedenkstätte Hohenschönhausen

Köpenick Town Hall

Pool in Köpenicker Altstadt

Köpenicker Altstadt

Köpenick is a small, quiet, self-absorbed world. This island community has a venerable history: as early as the 9th century, people had settled on Schlossinsel. The former fishing village stayed independent until 1920, and its coat of arms still features two fish, as do many of the house façades. The Old Town, on the banks of the Dahme River, is still characterized by cobbled streets and low fishermen's huts from the 18th and 19th centuries, taking the visitor back in time. Schüßlerplatz, Grünstraße and Alter Markt, too, still have some older buildings.

Hauptmann von Köpenick

Old Köpenick became famous on 16 October 1906. Wilhelm Voigt, a homeless man dressed up as a captain, commanded a troop of soldiers, marched into the town hall, arrested the mayor and confiscated the municipal coffers. Today the "Hauptmann von Köpenick" (Captain of Köpenick) is commemorated by a statue in front of the Rathaus (town hall). The vast red-brick structure, dating from 1901–4, is a typical example of Gothic brick architecture from Brandenburg province. ◈ Rathaus: Neue Krugallee 4 • 8am–6pm Mon–Fri, 10am–6pm Sat & Sun • (030) 617 20

Köpenicker Schloss

The Köpenick palace, which is situated on Schlossinsel (palace island) in the south of the district, was built in 1677–81 to plans by the Dutch architect Rutger van Langervelt for Frederick, heir to the throne and future King Frederick I. In the 17th century, the charming Baroque palace was extended by Johann Arnold Nering and others. Today it houses part of the collections of the Berliner Kunstgewerbemuseum (arts and crafts museum) *(see p47)*.
◈ Schlossinsel • 10am–6pm Tue–Sun • (030) 656 617 49

Gedenkstätte Normannenstraße

The former headquarters of the much-feared "Stasi", East Germany's secret police, is now a memorial, commemorating the thousands of victims of the East German regime and of Erich Mielke, the minister in charge of the secret police. Visitors can see his offices, the canteen and various pieces of spying equipment, revealing the methods used by the Socialist big-brother regime.
◈ Ruschestr. 103, Haus 1 • 11am–6pm Mon–Fri; 2–6pm Sat, Sun • (030) 553 68 54 • Admission charge

Deutsch-Russisches Museum

World War II ended here on 8 May 1945, when Germany signed its unconditional surrender. Documents, uniforms and photographs, displayed in the former officers' casino, relate the story of the war.
◈ Zwieseler Str. 4 • 10am–6pm Tue–Sun • (030) 50 15 08 10 • Admission charge

Left **East Side Gallery** Centre **Inside Köpenicker Schloss** Right **Volkspark Friedrichshain**

East Side Gallery

A fragment of the Berlin Wall, 1.3 km (1,422 yards) long, was left standing next to the Spree River. In 1990, 118 artists from around the world painted colourful images onto the grey concrete wall, making it a unique work of art. Particularly famous is a picture by the Russian artist Dmitri Vrubel, showing Leonid Brezhnev and the East German leader Erich Honecker, exchanging fraternal Socialist kisses. Much has faded due to exhaust fumes, but it is now being restored.
§ At Mühlenstr./ Ober-baumbrücke • Map H4

Großer Müggelsee

Großer Müggelsee, known as Berlin's "bathtub", is the largest of the city's lakes, covering an area of 766 hectares (1,892 acres). Müggelsee is not as popular as Großer Wannsee, its West Berlin counterpart, mainly because it is so far from the centre of town, in the southeast corner of the city. The lake is known for the beer gardens on its south side, which can be reached by boat from Friedrichs-hagen. Further south, Müggel-turm (tower) offers magnificent views over Berlin and the surrounding Brandenburg province. All around the lake there are excellent paths for walking and cycling. You can also swim in the lake, for example at the beach resort of Rahnsdorf.
§ Friedrichshagen: Müggelturm: Straße zum Müggelturm 1 § 10am–6:30pm daily • (030) 674 36 79

Treptower Park

Treptower Park, established in the 19th century as a recreation area for Berlin's working-class communities, is today best known for the giant Sow-jetisches Ehrenmal (Soviet Memorial). In April 1945, 5,000 Red Army soldiers, who died during the liberation of Berlin, were buried here. Beyond the mass graves rises a 12-m (39-ft) bronze statue of a Russian soldier, holding a child in one arm and a sword in the other, which he has used to destroy a swastika. § Alt-Treptow

Memorial in Treptower Park

Volkspark Friedrichshain

Berlin's oldest landscaped gardens, the people's park, was designed by Joseph Peter Lenné in 1840. Today it provides an oasis of tranquillity in the middle of the densely built-up district of Friedrichshain. World War II has left its traces here, too. Kleiner and Großer Bunkerberg – two heaps of rubble (the latter nick-named "Mount Rubble") reaching a height of 78 m (256 ft) – were piled up here after the war. Less traumatic is the Märchenbrunnen a charming Neo-Baroque fairy-tale fountain created by Ludwig

East Side Gallery: www.eastsidegallery.com/deutsche.htm

Aviary in Tierpark Friedrichsfelde

Hoffmann. It is decorated with 106 richly ornamented figures from popular fairy tales.
🔧 Am Friedrichshain • Map H2

9 Tierpark Friedrichsfelde

This small zoological garden is situated in the middle of a beautiful park next to Friedrichsfelde Palace. The animal park is particularly worth visiting for the lions and Siberian tigers, which are kept in rocky outdoor enclosures. The elephant house, too, attracts many visitors. Matibi, a baby elephant, is the star among the pachyderms.
🔧 Am Tierpark 125 • Apr–Oct: 9am–7pm daily; Nov–Mar: 9am till sunset daily • (030) 51 53 10 • Admission charge

10 Gedenkstätte Hohenschönhausen

This former secret police prison for "political" prisoners was in use until 1990. Before 1951, it served as a reception centre for the Red Army. On a guided tour, you can visit the watchtowers and the cells – particularly horrifying are the so-called "submarine cells", rooms without windows used for solitary confinement, where inmates were interrogated and tortured.
🔧 Genslerstr. 66 • Guided tours 11am and 1pm daily and by prior arrangement • (030) 98 60 82 30

A Day in Berlin's Green Southeast

Morning

Begin your tour of Berlin's Southeast at Alexanderplatz, from where you can take the S-Bahn to the various sights, which are not always near each other.

First, take S-Bahn line S3 to Karlshorst, where you can visit the **Deutsch-Russisches Museum** (see p145). From here it is not far to the **Stasi-Museum Normannenstraße** (see p145) – return to S-Bahn station Ostkreuz, then take S-Bahn line S4 and U-Bahn line U5 to Magdalenenstraße. After visiting all these museums you could recover outdoors. Take U-Bahn line U5 to **Tierpark Friedrichsfelde**, where you can visit both the zoological garden and Friedrichsfelde Palace.

Afternoon

For the afternoon make an excursion to Köpenick. Take S-Bahn line S3 to Köpenick, and enjoy a typically German meal in the **Ratskeller** (see p149), the town hall cellar. Afterwards explore **Köpenick Old Town**. The centre of the old fishing village is especially worth a visit. There are many cafés near **Köpenicker Schloss** (see p145), where you could stop for a coffee and a piece of cake, for example **Café Kietz** (see p148). Continue your journey by S-Bahn to Friedrichshagen, the access point for **Großer Müggelsee**. From here take one of the tourist boats to the restaurant **Müggelseeperle**, where you can round off the day with a tasty evening meal.

Left **Eierschale Haus Zenner** Centre **Altstadtcafé Cöpenick** Right **Kietz Café and Restaurant**

🔟 Cafés & Snack Bars

Around Town – Berlin's Southeast

1 Altstadtcafé Cöpenick
This tiny café in Köpenick's Old Town serves coffee and cakes, outdoors, in summer, on a small veranda. ✆ *Alt Köpenick 16* • *10am–6:30pm daily* • *(030) 65 47 40 69* • *no credit cards*

2 Eierschale Haus Zenner
One of the classic day-trip destinations: families once used to "bring and brew their own coffee". Today it is a popular outdoor café. ✆ *Alt-Treptow 14–17* • *10am–10pm Mon–Thu, 10am–4pm Fri & Sat, 10am–10pm Sun* • *(030) 533 73 70* • *no credit cards*

3 Café L & B
Not far from the swimming baths, this café serves local fish dishes, as well as afternoon coffee and cakes. ✆ *Am Kleinen Müggelsee 1* • *summer: 11am–10pm daily; winter: 11am–9pm Sat & Sun* • *(030) 659 82 24* • *no credit cards*

4 Neu-Helgoland
A favourite day-trippers' restaurant on the lake, where locals and visitors alike enjoy the game and fish dishes. ✆ *Odernheimer Str., Kleiner Müggelsee* • *11am–midnight daily* • *(030) 659 82 47* • *no credit cards*

5 Seerestaurant Rübezahl
This beer garden, on the piers of Müggelsee, is a great place to aim for on a day out. You can reach the outdoor restaurant by ferry. ✆ *Am Großen Müggelsee* • *Oct–Apr: 11:30am–6pm daily; May–Sep: 11:30am–10pm daily* • *(030) 65 88 24 70*

6 Schloss-Café
A tranquil oasis where you can enjoy coffee and cakes overlooking the Dahme River after a visit to Kunstgewerbemuseum (arts and crafts museum) on Schlossinsel. ✆ *Köpenicker Schloss, Schlossinsel* • *10am–11pm Tue–Sun* • *(030) 650 185 85* • *no credit cards*

7 Kietz Café and Restaurant
A pleasant café, serving superb home-made cakes and snacks. A great draw in summer is the waterside terrace. ✆ *Müggelheimer Str. 1* • *9am–1am daily* • *(030) 651 71 09* • *no credit cards*

8 Café Liebig
Charming, richly ornamented Art-Nouveau café in a historic building, dating back more than 130 years. The summer terrace overlooks Grünau regatta course. ✆ *Regattastr. 158* • *3pm–11pm Mon–Fri, noon–11pm Sat–Sun* • *(030) 67 82 09 36* • *no credit cards*

9 Restaurantschiff Hoppetosse
A picture-book ship restaurant, serving everything including fish dishes. ✆ *Eichenstr. 4* • *from noon Mon–Sat, from 11am Sun* • *(030) 53 32 03 40* • *no credit cards*

10 Hanff's Ruh
Sticking to an old tradition, guests can brew their own coffee here. The mushroom dishes are highly recommended. ✆ *Rabindranath-Tagore-Str. 25* • *11am–9pm Wed–Mon* • *(030) 674 33 68* • *no credit cards*

Price Categories

For a three-course meal for one with half a bottle of wine (or equivalent meal), taxes and charges included

€	under €20
€€	€20–30
€€€	€30–45
€€€€	€45–60
€€€€€	over €60

Left **Restaurant freiheit fünfzehn** Right **The Ratskeller in Köpenick's Old Town**

🔟 Restaurants

1 freiheit fünfzehn
German and French cuisine are served aboard a schooner moored at the pier. There is also occasional cabaret and live music. If you prefer dry land, you can enjoy your meals in the beer garden. ⊗ *Freiheit 15 • 6pm–midnight Tue–Sat, 11am–midnight Sun • (030) 65 88 78 26 • €€*

2 Ratskeller Köpenick
Traditional Berlin fare is served in the vast vaulted cellars where Wilhelm Voigt once famously took advantage of gullible local civil servants *(see p145)*. ⊗ *Alt-Köpenick 21 • 11am–11pm daily • (030) 655 56 52 • €€*

3 Klipper Schiffsrestaurant
This two-master, dating back to 1890, has been turned into a cosy restaurant; the menu features French-inspired international meals. ⊗ *banks of the Spree River, close to Insel der Jugend • 10am–1am daily • no credit cards • €€*

4 Schrörs Biergarten
Popular, informal beer garden near the lake, specializing in hearty food from the grill. ⊗ *Josef-Nawrocki-Str. 16 • summer: from 11am daily; winter: 11am–6pm Tue–Sun • (030) 64 09 58 80 • no credit cards • €*

5 Die Spindel
This rustic restaurant serves traditional German food as well as a large selection of fondues, which need to be ordered in advance. ⊗ *Bölschestr. 51 • 11:30am–10pm daily • (030) 645 29 37 • €*

6 Ellis
One of the few American-style restaurants in Berlin, with authentic decor and American regional dishes. ⊗ *Fürstenwalder Allee 17 • 5pm–midnight Mon–Sat, 1pm–midnight Sun (closed Mon Jan–Feb) • (030) 65 89 181 • €€*

7 Krokodil
Situated in the Old Town, near the river baths in Gartenstraße, this is one of the nicest garden venues, especially in summer. ⊗ *Gartenstr. 46–48 • 5pm–midnight Mon–Sat, 11am–11pm Sun • (030) 65 88 00 94 • no credit cards • €€*

8 Bräustubl
A typical Berlin beer garden and restaurant, belonging to the Berliner Bürger-Brau brewery, which serves game dishes. ⊗ *Müggelseedamm 164 • noon–midnight Tue–Sat, 11am–midnight Sun • (030) 645 57 16 • €€*

9 Lehmofen
Meat and vegetarian dishes, freshly cooked in an antiquated clay oven, are the top attractions in this restaurant with summer terrace. ⊗ *Freiheit 12 • noon–midnight daily • (030) 655 70 44 • €€*

10 Al Borgo
This is an intimate, family-run Italian restaurant in southwest Berlin. It's a great place in summer to enjoy alfresco dining. ⊗ *Borgmannstr. 5 • noon–midnight Tue–Sun • (030) 64 95 87 11 • no credit cards • €€*

Note: All restaurants accept credit cards and offer vegetarian dishes unless stated otherwise.

Left **Inside Schloss Charlottenhof** Centre**Chinese tea-house** Right **Vestibül in Neues Palais**

Potsdam & Sanssouci

OTSDAM IS AN IMPORTANT PART OF EUROPEAN *cultural history – a splendid centre of European Enlightenment, which reached its climax in the 18th century in the architectural and artistic design of Frederick the Great's palace. The palace complex of Sanssouci, with its beautiful, extensive park, is both magnificent and playful and has been designated a World Heritage Centre of Culture by UNESCO. Every year, it enchants millions of visitors from around the world. The town of Potsdam, numbering some 300,000 inhabitants, is the capital of the federal province of Brandenburg. This former garrison town has much to delight its visitors, including small palaces and old churches, idyllic parks and historic immigrant settlements.*

Frederick the Great playing the flute in Sanssouci

🔟 Sights

1	Schloss Sanssouci	6	Marmorpalais
2	Neues Palais	7	Holländisches Viertel
3	Schlosspark Sanssouci	8	Nikolaikirche
4	Schloss Cecilienhof	9	Marstall (Filmmuseum)
5	Schloss Charlottenhof	10	Filmpark Babelsberg

Preceding pages **The stairs leading up to Schloss Sanssouci**

Schloss Sanssouci

The Prussian King Frederick the Great wished to live "sans souci", in a palace outside the boundaries of the hated city – the French phrase means "without worries". In 1745, Frederick commissioned his favourite architect Georg Wenzeslaus von Knobelsdorff to plan and construct this magnificent Rococo palace according to his own designs.

The main building with its yellow façade rises proudly above the former terraced vineyards, leading up to the domed building and its elegant marble hall at the centre of the palace complex. In both its design and shape, the marble hall pays homage to the Pantheon in Rome. To its left and right are some very attractive rooms designed by von Knobelsdorff and Johann August Nahl; these include the famous concert room, adorned with paintings by Antoine Pesne, and Frederick's library. In this wing, the monarch liked to play the flute or to philosophize with Voltaire. Valuable paintings by Frederick the Great's favourite painter, the French artist Antoine Watteau, adorn the palace walls.
◈ *Zur historischen Mühle • Apr–Oct: 9am–5pm Tue–Sun; Nov–Mar: 9am–4pm Tue–Sun; guided tour obligatory •(0331) 969 41 90 • Admission charge*

Vase in Park Sanssouci

Neues Palais

To the north of Sanssouci palace park rises the Baroque Neues Palais. One of Germany's most beautiful palaces, it was built in 1763–9 for Frederick the Great according to designs by Johann Gottfried Büring, Jean Laurent Le Geay and Carl von Gontard. The vast two-storey structure comprises 200 rooms, including the Marmorsaal (marble hall), a lavishly furnished ballroom, and the Schlosstheater, where plays are once more performed today. Frederick's private chambers are equally splendid, especially his study furnished in Rococo style, the upper gallery with valuable parquet flooring and the Oberes Vestibül, a room clad entirely in marble. ◈ *Am Neuen Palais • Apr–Oct: 9am–5pm Sat–Mon; Nov–Mar: 9am–4pm Sat–Mon; guided tour obligatory • (0331) 969 43 61 • Admission charge*

Schlosspark Sanssouci

It is easy to while away an entire day in the extensive palace park, which covers 287 hectares (709 acres) of land. Of the many charming buildings hidden in the lavishly designed landscape garden, the Rococo-style Chinesisches Teehaus, built in 1754–6 by Johann Gottfried Büring, is especially worth seeking out.

Left **Neues Palais** Right **Concert Hall in Schloss Sanssouci**

S-Bahn S7 goes to Potsdam from Berlin. The journey takes about 45 minutes.

Left **A street in Holländisches Viertel** Centre **Marmorpalais** Right **Marstall (Filmmuseum)**

Originally it served as a tea-house and dining room, and it now houses an exhibition of porcelain pieces from East Asia.

The Römische Bäder (Roman Baths), a group of pavilions next to the lake, are also inspired by historic models. Modelled on an Italian Renaissance villa, they were built between 1829 and 1840 by Friedrich Karl Schinkel as guest and bathing houses.

The Orangerie, constructed in 1851–60 by Friedrich August Stüler, was also originally intended to accommodate the king's guests. Today it houses a small gallery of paintings.

⊗ *Chinesisches Teehaus: ökonomieweg*
• *mid-May–mid-Oct: 10am–5pm Tue–Sun*
• *(0331) 969 42 02*
⊗ *Römische Bäder: Lennéstr.*
• *mid-May–mid-Oct: 10am–5pm Tue–Sun*
• *(0331) 969 42 02*
⊗ *Orangerie: Maulbeerallee • mid-May–mid-Oct: 10am–5pm Tue–Sun*
• *(0331) 969 42 02*

The Potsdam Conference

In July and August 1945, the heads of government of the United States (Harry Truman), the USSR (Joseph Stalin) and Great Britain (Winston Churchill) met in Schloss Cecilienhof, in order to seal the future of Germany in a treaty. Vitally important points such as the demilitarization of Germany, the level of reparations to be paid, the punishment of war criminals, the resettlement of Germans from Poland and the new borders of Germany were decided here.

Schloss Cecilienhof

This little palace, built in the style of an English country manor house, entered the history books in 1945, when Germany's fate was sealed by the Potsdam Conference. Built in 1914–17, the palace is now used as a hotel. It also houses a small exhibition documenting the Conference and the palace's furnishings. ⊗ *Am Neuen Garten*
• *Apr–Oct: 9am–5pm Tue–Sun;*
Nov–Mar: 9am–4pm Tue–Sun • (0331)
969 42 44

Schloss Charlottenhof

A small Neo-Classical palace in Park Sanssouci, built in 1829 by Schinkel for the heir to the throne, Friedrich Wilhelm IV. Particularly worth seeing is the tent-like Humboldtsaal.
⊗ *Geschwister-Scholl-Str. • mid-May–mid-Oct: 10am–5pm Tue–Sun*
• *(0331) 969 42 28*

Marmorpalais

This small, early Neo-Classical palace at the side of the lake was built in 1791–7 by Carl Gotthard Langhans and others. It features an elegant concert hall as well as contemporary furniture and porcelain. ⊗ *Heiliger See (Neuer Garten) • Apr–Oct: 10am–5pm Tue–Sun; Nov–Mar: 10am–4pm Sat, Sun • (0331) 969 42 46*

Holländisches Viertel

A pleasant way to explore the district of Potsdam is a walk through the historic Old Town,

Nikolaikirche on Alter Markt

with its art galleries, cafés and restaurants. Built between 1733 and 1742, the area originally served as a settlement for Dutch workers after whom it is now named. The small red-brick buildings are decorated with attractive stucco ornaments. ⊗ *Friedrich-Ebert-, Kurfürsten-, Hebbel-, Gutenbergstr.*

Nikolaikirche

Potsdam's most attractive church was designed by Schinkel in 1830 in an early Neo-Classical style. Its giant dome is particularly striking. ⊗ *Am Alten Markt • summer: 10am–7pm daily; winter: 10am–5pm daily • (0331) 270 86 02*

Marstall (Filmmuseum)

The small museum, based in the Baroque former stable buildings of the king's town residence, uses old cameras, props and projectors to document the history of German film. ⊗ *Am Alten Markt • 10am–6pm Mon–Sun • (0331) 27 18 10*

Filmpark Babelsberg

The Filmpark offers visitors a tour of the legendary UFA Studios, which were among the world's most important when they operated here in Babelsberg from 1917 to 1945. Exciting U-boat trips, stunt performances and special effects are shown. ⊗ *Großbeerenstr. • Apr–Oct: 10am–6pm daily • (0331) 721 27 50*

A Day in Potsdam

Morning

Begin your exploration in the **Schlosspark Sanssouci** (see pp153–4) as early as possible in order to get ahead of the daily influx of visitors. Start with **Schloss Sanssouci** and **Neues Palais** (see p153) then visit Chinesisches Teehaus, Römische Bäder and Orangerie. From the orangery's viewing terrace you will have magnificent views over the entire palace complex. If you are up for it, you could also climb up to Schloss Belvedere on top of the hill. From Schlosspark walk along Voltaireweg to Neuer Garten in the northeast of Potsdam, where you can rest and recover over a tasty lunch at **Schloss Cecilienhof** (see p157).

Afternoon

Start the afternoon with a stroll through Neuer Garten. Visit **Schloss Cecilienhof** and, if you like, stop for a break at Heiliger See. Afterwards walk or drive into the centre of Potsdam, starting with the **Holländisches Viertel** (Dutch quarter) where you could pop into one of the numerous cafés. Then continue on a circular walk, strolling past Peter-und Paul-Kirche, the French church, **Nikolaikirche** and the town hall. Finish your day of sightseeing with a visit to the **Marstall** and the film museums in Potsdam and Babelsberg. Take a look at the palace and the telegraph hill. A delicious evening meal awaits you at **Villa Kellermann** (see p157) to round off your day in Potsdam.

Left **Schloss Babelsberg** Centre **Alexandrowka-Haus** Right **Wasserwerk Sanssouci**

Best of the Rest

1 Alexandrowka

A detour to the Russian colony in Potsdam feels like a journey to Russia itself. Decorated log cabins with picturesque gardens were built here in 1826 for a Russian military choir. ⓢ *Russische Kolonie/Puschkinallee*

2 Wasserwerk Sanssouci

This building, resembling a mosque with minarets, houses the water pumping station for Schlosspark Sanssouci. The ancient pump, dating from 1842, can be inspected in the building. ⓢ *Breite Str. • mid-May–mid-Oct: 10am–5pm Sat, Sun • (0331) 969 42 01*

3 Telegrafenberg

If you're prepared to climb telegraph hill, you could visit the elegant Einstein tower at the top. It was designed in 1920 by Erich Mendelssohn for the observation of the sun. ⓢ *Albert-Einstein-Str. • Guided tours Einsteinturm: (0331) 29 17 41 • Admission charge*

4 Schloss Babelsberg

Built by Schinkel in 1833–5, this Gothic palace is situated in an idyllic park on the banks of the Havel River. ⓢ *Park Babelsberg • Apr–Oct: 10am–12:30pm, 1–5pm Tue–Sun; Nov–Mar: 10am–4pm Sat, Sun • (0331) 969 42 50 • Admission charge*

5 Potsdam-Museum

A small museum presenting the history of the town of Potsdam, from prehistoric times to the present day. The museum is based in the historic Hiller-Brandtsche Häuser. ⓢ *Benkertstr. 3 • 10am–6pm Tue–Sun • (0331) 289 68 00 • Admission charge*

6 Altes Rathaus

The old town hall, built in 1753, is decorated with sculptures and Potsdam's coat of arms – two gilded Atlas figures, each carrying a globe. ⓢ *Am Alten Markt*

7 Luisenplatz

This small square with its plain, restored buildings gives a good impression of Potsdam in the early 19th century. ⓢ *Luisenplatz*

8 Französische Kirche

In 1752, Johann Boumann built this elliptical Huguenot church with its giant columned portico, while Schinkel designed the beautiful interior in the 1830s. ⓢ *Am Bassinplatz • 2:30–5pm Tue–Sun • (0331) 29 12 19*

9 St-Peter-und-Paul-Kirche

The Catholic church of saints Peter and Paul, modelled on Haghia Sophia in Istanbul, was built in 1867–70 by Stüler. ⓢ *Am Bassinplatz • May–Oct: 10am–6pm Tue–Sat; Oct–Apr: by prior arrangement • (0331) 230 79 90*

10 Brandenburger Tor

The most attractive of five former town gates was built by Gontard and Unger in 1770 in the Neo-Classical style to celebrate Prussian victory in the Seven Years' War. ⓢ *Luisenplatz*

Around Town – Potsdam & Sanssouci

Left **Schloss Cecilienhof serves delicious food**

Restaurants & Cafés

Speckers Zur Ratswaage
The combination of Prussian interior, friendly service and a light international cuisine make Ratswaage one of Potsdam's best restaurants. ® *Am Neuen Markt 10* • *noon–3pm, 6–10pm daily* • *(0331) 280 43 11* • *no credit cards* • *€€€*

Cecilienhof
The historic palace is now the home of a luxury hotel. Its restaurant serves solid German food. ® *Am Neuen Garten* • *11am–11pm daily* • *(0331) 370 50* • *€€€*

Villa Kellermann
You can enjoy an excellent meal in this town house directly on Heiliger See, with great views of the Marmorpalais and Schloss Cecilienhof. The menu is dominated by Italian dishes. ® *Mangerstr. 34–36* • *noon–midnight Tue–Sun, 6pm–midnight Mon* • *(0331) 29 15 72* • *€€€*

Restaurant Juliette
A former manor house has been taken over by this French restaurant, one of the most charming in the city, serving top-quality French classics. ® *Jägerstr. 39* • *noon–3:30pm, 6pm–midnight daily* • *(0331) 270 17 91* • *€€*

Brau- und Brennhaus
This rustic restaurant, set in the brewery of a historic country manor, Krongut Bornstedt, serves hearty meals with local fish, game, sausages, and local beers. ® *Krongut Bornstedt, Ribbeckstr. 6–7* • *11am–11pm daily* • *(0331) 550 650* • *€€*

Maison Charlotte
Olde-worlde wine bar in a simple redbrick Dutch house, specializing in German and French country fare and excellent wines. ® *Mittelstr. 20* • *noon–11pm daily* • *(0331) 280 54 50* • *€€*

Barokoko
Fashion designer Wolfang Joop is a regular at this venue, which is based in an historic building and serves fresh Italian food, with delicious pasta dishes. ® *Friedrich-Ebert-Str. 30* • *noon–1am daily* • *(0331) 280 14 38* • *€€*

Waage
Attractive historic restaurant in a central location. Regional game and fish dishes in unusual new variations are particularly worth trying. ® *Am Neuen Markt* • *noon–midnight Tue–Sun* • *(0331) 817 06 74* • *€€*

Café Heider
A lovely café in the middle of Potsdam's Old Town. Fantastic breakfast selection, which you can enjoy outside on the terrace in summer. ® *Friedrich-Ebert-Str. 29* • *8am–1am Mon–Fri, 9am–1am Sat, 10am–1am Sun* • *(0331) 270 55 96* • *€*

La Madeleine
A little bistro, serving all sorts of crêpes, such as sweet with jam or savoury with ham, ideal for a quick snack. ® *Lindenstr. 9* • *noon–midnight daily* • *(0331) 27 05 400* • *no credit cards* • *€*

Note: All restaurants accept credit cards and offer vegetarian dishes unless stated otherwise.

STREETSMART

BERLIN'S TOP 10

Left **In Kurfürstendamm** Right **The Christopher Street Day Parade in June**

🔟 Planning your Trip

1 When to Go and Climate

The weather in Berlin is better than its reputation. The continental climate, which characterizes the entire region, guarantees mild and dry weather for the main holiday period from May to September. In spring and autumn it can be cold and wet, and it may be advisable not to travel to Berlin between November and February, when it is often cloudy, and a bitingly cold, easterly wind whistles through the city.

2 What to Wear

In the summer months you'll need only lightweight clothing. In spring and autumn you should definitely pack a rain- and windproof jacket as well as an umbrella. Locals dress informally and more flamboyantly than other German urbanites – anything you like goes. The capital has, however, gone more upmarket and you may feel out of place in many restaurants or theatres without a jacket and tie or evening dress.

3 Money

If you're arriving from abroad, you'll be able to buy euros at all banks and bureaux de change (many are based around Bahnhof Zoo). Credit cards, traveller's cheques and EC-cards are accepted everywhere in the centre of town.

4 Insurance

All travellers are well advised to buy insurance cover for accidents, illness and theft. Cancellation insurance may also be worth taking out.

5 Driving Licence

UK, US, Canadian and Australian driving licences are recognized in Germany.

6 Visa and Customs

All visitors to Berlin need valid passports. If you're staying in Berlin for 90 days or less, you will not normally need a visa. Ask your German Embassy for details. Non-EU citizens may import 200 cigarettes and one litre of spirits per adult.

7 Electrical Appliances

The electric current is 220 volt; but remember to bring an adaptor with two round pins.

8 Time Difference

Berlin is in the Central European time zone, which means that it is one hour ahead of Greenwich Mean Time, six hours ahead of US Eastern Standard Time and 11 hours behind Australian Eastern Standard Time.

9 Children's Needs

If you are travelling with children, book into child-friendly accommodation. Always look out for family reductions. It can be a lot of fun to explore the city together with children, but you are advised to avoid the rush hours on U-Bahn and buses, especially if you are travelling with babies or very young children.

10 Pupils and Students

Many museums, theatres and other cultural establishments offer up to 50 per cent reductions for pupils and students on production of a valid student card.

Embassies

Australian Embassy
Wallstr. 76–79 • Map L4 • (030) 880 08 80

British Embassy
Wilhelmstr. 70–71
• Map K3
• 030) 20 45 70

Canadian Embassy
Leipziger Platz 17
• Map L4
• (030) 20 31 20

New Zealand Embassy
Friedrichstr. 60
• Map L4
• (030) 20 62 10

South African Embassy
• Tiergartenstr. 18
• Map L4
• (030) 22 07 30

US Embassy
Clayallee 170
• Map K3
• (030) 23 85 174

Left **Flughafen Tegel** Centre **The ICE to Berlin** Right **Three typical road signs**

Arriving in Berlin

Flughafen Tegel

Berlin's largest airport is situated a mere 8 km (5 miles) to the north-west of the city centre. Though it is a relatively small airport, Lufthansa, Deutsche BA, British Airways, KLM, Air France, Iberia and Alitalia and others all operate direct flights here. There are no intercontinental flights to Berlin. A taxi from the airport to Ku'damm costs around €13 and takes about 20–30 minutes (depending on traffic). Less expensive and nearly as fast is the journey by bus – Nos X09 or 109 (about €2.10) stop everywhere in the centre. ◈ *Airport information: (01805) 00 01 86*

Flughafen Schönefeld

Located approximately 20 km (12 miles) southeast of Berlin, in Brandenburg province, this airport is served by low cost, charter and East European airlines. The fastest way into the city is via the Airport Express train, which takes just over 20 minutes to Alexanderplatz and 31 minutes to Bahnhof Zoo. ◈ *Airport information: (01805) 00 01 86*

Flughafen Tempelhof

The small historic city airport south of Kreuz-berg (which is scheduled to close in late 2007) provides regional connections to medium-sized German towns and to Scandinavia. From Flughafen Tempelhof take U-Bahn line U6 from Platz der Luftbrücke station or bus No. 119 to Ku'damm. ◈ *Airport information: (01805) 00 01 86*

Airlines

Lufthansa has an office downtown on Ku'damm, while other airlines like Deutsche BA have ticket offices at Tegel airport. ◈ *Lufthansa: Kurfürstendamm 45 (Neues Kranzler-Eck)* • *Map P4* • *10am–7pm Mon–Fri* • *(030) 88 75 38 00* ◈ *Deutsche BA: Flughafen Tegel* • *(0900) 11 00 322* • *8am–8pm Mon–Fri, 9am–6pm Sat, Sun*

Hauptbahnhof

The city's grand, new central station is officially called Hauptbahnhof – Lehrter Bahnhof. Located in the government district, it is the arrival and departure destination for all long-distance trains. ◈ *Invalidenstraße* • *Map F2* • *(030) 118 61*

Zoologischer Garten

The Bahnhof Zoo is no longer a long-distance train station (some trains do make a quick stop). It remains an important local transportation hub due to its many S- and U-Bahn lines and bus routes which connect here. ◈ *Hardenbergplatz* • *Map N4* • *(030) 118 61*

Bahnhof Lichtenberg and Ostbahnhof

Trains from Southern and Eastern Europe stop at these stations. This is the best place to arrive if your final destination is in the eastern part of the city. ◈ *Weitlingstr. 22* • *(030) 118 61* ◈ *Straße der Pariser Kommune*

Zentraler Omni-busbahnhof (ZOB)

The coach station near Funkturm in Charlotten-burg offers fast and inex-pensive coach connec-tions to all German and European cities. ◈ *Masurenallee 4–6* • *Map A4* • *(030) 302 53 61*

Motorways

If you're travelling to Berlin by car, you will have to get there via Berliner Stadtring, an orbital motorway around the city. From the north you will reach the city motorway on the A111 motorway via Stolpe in the direction of Auto-bahndreieck Funkturm; from the south you will reach the centre on the A115 – the famous Avus motorway.

By Car

The speed limit on the orbital Berliner Ring is mostly 100 km/h (62.5 miles per hour); on the urban motorways in Berlin you are limited to 80–100 km/h (50–62.5 miles per hour). There are frequent radar checks.

Left **S-Bahn** Centre **At a bus stop** Right **Exploring Berlin by Velotaxi**

Getting Around Berlin

U-Bahn
The Berlin U-Bahn, or underground railway, has one of the largest networks in Europe, providing the fastest and most convenient means of getting around the city. There are ten U-Bahn lines each sporting their own colour. The U-Bahn runs from 5am to 1am; at weekends lines U1 and U9 run throughout the night. The station indicated on the platform is the final destination of the train. ✎ *BVG customer service (030) 194 49*

S-Bahn
The S-Bahn or Stadtbahn (city railway) has 15 lines, connecting the centre with the suburbs, They run at 5- to 10-minute intervals. Many lines share tracks so you will need to pay attention to indicator boards. ✎ *Information S-Bahn • Bhf. Alexanderplatz • 7am–7pm Mon–Fri, 9:15am–6:30pm Sat, Sun • (030) 29 74 33 33*

Buses
Berlin has a dense network of bus routes. The famous yellow double-decker buses operate mostly in the centre. Bus lines have three-digit numbers, except for express services, which have a preceding "X". Buses and tram lines starting with an "M" service areas without direct U- or S-Bahn links. On boarding, you have to use the front door (unless you have a buggy, in which case use the back entrance) and present your ticket, or the money for a new one, to the driver. ✎ *BVG customer service centre (030) 194 49*

Tickets
Tickets for U- and S-Bahn trains and for buses in Berlin are available at all stations and bus stops as well as from bus drivers. Berlin is divided into three zones: A, B and C. The best value for money is a day ticket at €6, which is valid until 3am the following day and covers all three zones. A single journey, costing €2.10, is valid for unlimited travel for two hours. A "Kurzstrecke" (short distance) counts as up to three U- or S-Bahn stations or six bus stops, and costs €1.20. Children under 14 years pay a reduced rate; those under six travel free. You have to stamp your ticket in a red machine in the station or on the bus before starting the journey. ✎ *BVG customer service (030) 194 49*

Trams
Trams – operating only in the eastern part of the city – are part of the same network (BVG).

Taxis
There are taxi stands all over Berlin. It is not always easy to hail a passing taxi. The basic starting price is €2.50, and a further €1.02–1.52 is charged per km (2/3 of a mile). A short-distance tariff also exists: if you hail a taxi in the street, you can travel for up to 2 km (1 mile) for €3. ✎ *Taxi: (030) 26 10 26, 443 322, (030) 21 01 01.*

Car Hire
You can hire a car from any of the large operators on production of a valid driving licence, passport and credit card; some only accept customers aged 21 years or over. There are car hire places at all airports and in central Berlin. ✎ *Avis: (01805) 557 755; Europcar: (0180) 580 00; Hertz: (01805) 333 535; Sixt: (01805) 252 525*

Velotaxis
An unusual way to explore Berlin is by velotaxi – a bicycle rickshaw. These can be found in the city centre (from April to October only).

Bicycle Hire
There are several bike hire places. ✎ *Bicycle station Bhf. Dorotheenstr. • Mar–Oct: 8am–8pm Mon–Sat; Nov–Feb: 10am–7pm Mon–Sat • (030) 204 545 00*

Berlin on Foot
It can be rewarding but exhausting to explore Berlin on foot. You should, however, make sure you stroll along Ku'damm and Unter den Linden. Take particular care when crossing the cycle paths, which are marked in red.

Left **Berlin city guides** Centre **A newspaper kiosk** Right **The logo of tourist information offices**

🔟 Information & Advice

1 Berlin Tourismus Marketing GmbH

The municipal tourist information service BTM has offices in the Europa-Center, near Brandenburg Gate and in Tegel airport. There you can obtain up-to-date information. ⊛ *Berlin Tourismus Marketing GmbH, Am Karlsbad 11 • Map E4 • (030) 25 00 25, Fax (030) 25 00 24 24 • www.berlin.de* ⊛ *Brandenburger Tor, southern bldg • Apr–Nov: 9:30am–6pm daily; Nov–Apr: 10am–6pm daily* ⊛ *Fernsehturm, Alexanderplatz • Apr–Nov: 9:30am–6pm daily; Nov–Apr: 10am–6pm daily* ⊛ *Hauptbahnhof, Europapl 1, Level 0, northern entrance • 8am–10pm daily* ⊛ *Neues Kranzler-Eck, Kurfürstendamm 21 • 10am–8pm Mon–Sat, 10am–6pm Sun*

2 Berlin's State Museums

Detailed up-to-date information on the state museums and all the establishments on Museumsinsel can be obtained from a bilingual phoneline. Here you will also find out about the current programme of events – for example about the "long night of the museums". ⊛ *(030) 266 36 66*

3 Sanssouci

The visitors' advice service for the palaces and gardens of Potsdam and Sanssouci supplies accurate information and tips as well as guided tours and more via their own telephone service. ⊛ *(0331) 969 42 02*

4 Potsdam Information

Potsdam has its own tourist information service, offering brochures, an accommodation service and guided tours. ⊛ *Brandenburger Str 3 • Apr–Oct: 9:30am–6pm Mon–Fri, 9:30am–1pm Sat & Sun; Nov–Mar: 10am–6pm Mon–Fri, 9:30am–2pm Sat & Sun • Tel (0331) 275 580, Fax (0331) 275 58 29*

5 Where to Stay

The Berlin Tourismus Marketing GmbH (BTM) has a telephone hotline which will help reserve a room (for a fee). Several offices also arrange private accommodation, where visitors book into shared apartments for a period of several days or weeks. ⊛ *Tel (030) 25 00 25, Fax (030) 2500 24 24. From abroad: 0049 302 500 25*

6 What's On

There are two fortnightly city magazines with detailed information on all kinds of events – *tip* and *zitty*. The monthly *Berlin-Programm* with detailed events listings is also worth consulting. For younger readers, the magazines *prinz* and *030* contain information on nightclubs and bars. Daily newspapers such as *Tagesspiegel*, *Berliner Zeitung* and *Berliner* *Morgenpost* usually publish listings of cultural events on Wednesdays and Thursdays respectively, while tips and reviews can be found in the papers every day.

7 Radio Stations

For radio news in English, you can tune into Inforadio (93.1 MHz), the BBC World Service (90.2 MHz) or the multilingual SFB 4 Multikulti (106.8 MHz).

8 Television

In addition to the national TV stations, the RBB offers a regional programme; tv berlin, a private TV station, also broadcasts information on what's on. Thanks to cable and satellite you can also easily tune into English programmes.

9 Advice for Foreign Nationals

This Senate Office, which deals with the concerns of foreign nationals who live in Berlin, is also a good point of advice for foreign visitors. ⊛ *Potsdamer Str. 65 • Map E5 • 9am–1pm Mon–Fri except Wed, plus 2–6pm Thu • (030) 90 17 23 72*

10 Advice for Gay Visitors

Advice and information for gay and lesbian visitors is always available at Mann-o-Meter *(see p58)*. ⊛ *Bülowstr. 106 • 5–10pm Mon–Fri, 4–10pm Sat, Sun • (030) 216 80 08*

Left **Parking for the Disabled** Centre **Adapted bus door** Right **Lift to the U-Bahn station**

🔟 Berlin for Disabled Visitors

1 Streets and Pavements
Nearly all pavements in Berlin are sloped at junctions to make them suitable for wheelchair users. However visitors in wheelchairs will need to watch out for cyclists using the red cycle tracks, often in both directions.

2 Stations
Most underground stations in the centre, including those that are actually above ground in high-level stations on viaducts, are equipped with lifts, giving wheelchair users easy access from the road to the platform.
🖎 BVG service for disabled access to stations
• (030) 25 62 20 96
🖎 S-Bahn service for disabled access to stations
• (030) 29 74 33 33

3 U- and S-Bahn
Underground trains are accessible to wheelchair users although they are a little narrow. If you wish to travel by U-Bahn, wait at the head of the platform. After the train has stopped, the driver will put up a ramp to bridge the difference in height between platform and train. If you wish to travel by S-Bahn, speak to the station manager before the arriva0l of the train; he or she will install the ramp you need to board the train.
🖎 Berliner Verkehrsbetriebe
• around the clock

• (030) 194 49.
🖎 Deutsche Bahn Berlin
• around the clock
• (030) 118 61

4 Buses
All buses displaying a wheelchair symbol are specially equipped for disabled access; most buses in the centre have one door with a ramp that can be lowered down to the pavement. At certain times, however, these buses run only at 20-minute intervals.

5 Cars Services and Guided Tours
Disabled visitors wishing to explore Berlin and Brandenburg province on their own by car, or to share a car with driver with other disabled visitors, can contact several specialist travel agents.
🖎 BBV Tours Behindertenfahrdienst, Bizetstr. 51–55
• (030) 92 70 36 30
🖎 Micky Tours, Sewanstr. 2
• (030) 515 33 36
🖎 Berlin Erkundungen Gangart Berlin, Potsdamer Chaussee 21A • (030) 32 70 37 83
🖎 Reisebegleitung E. Schielzeth, Parchimer Allee 55c • (030) 601 01 07

6 Kobinet.De
The internet website www.kobinet.de gives information on wheelchair access to restaurants, hotels and shops in Berlin. This association also offers interactive guided tours of the city, covering the areas that

are most popular with tourists, and it provides information on disabled access to sights.
🖎 www.kobinet.de

7 Berliner Behindertenverband e V
This charitable association gives advice and support on all issues concerning disabled people in Berlin.
🖎 Information hotline (030) 204 38 47 • Call times: noon–5pm Wed, Fri

8 Landesamt
Berlin's Regional Office for Health and Social Security runs a citizen's advice bureau with a telephone helpline. 🖎 Albrecht-Achilles-Str. 62 • Map B5
• (030) 90 12 61 14
• Information for young disabled people
• (030) 26 54 24 03
• Service for the disabled and senior citizens
• (030) 859 40 10

9 Wheelchair Hire
The Regional Office (see above) also rents out wheelchairs. Order one in advance by telephone.
🖎 (030) 204 38 47

10 Sight-impaired Visitors
Berlin's charitable association for the blind and sight-impaired advises on facilities that are available for blind visitors.
🖎 Allgemeiner Blinden- und Sehbehindertenverein, Auerbacherstr. 7
• (030) 89 58 80

Left **Historic letter box** Centre **Modern card telephone** Right **Bureau de change**

🔟 Banking & Communications

Streetsmart (vertical side tab)

1 Banks

All the large German banks have branches in the centre of town. Most banks open 9am–6pm Mon–Fri; many open for shorter periods on Fridays and Wednesdays.
◎ *Commerzbank, Europa-Center, Tauentzienstr. 9* • *Map N/P5* • *9am–6pm Mon & Wed, 9am–4pm Tue & Thu, 9am–2pm Fri*
◎ *Deutsche Bank, Otto-Suhr-Allee 6–16* • *Map M3* • *10am–6pm Mon, Tue & Thu, 10am–4pm Wed & Fri*
◎ *Berliner Sparkasse, Rankestr. 33–34* • *Map P4* • *9am–6pm Mon–Fri*

2 Changing Money

Money is changed at a *Wechselstube* (bureau de change); you can find these near Bahnhof Zoo, at the airports or at a bank. Make sure you ask about commission and charges, as these vary from place to place. Hotels will also change money, but may charge higher fees.
◎ *American Express, Bayreuther Str. 37* • *Map P5* • *9am–7pm Mon–Fri, 10am–1pm Sat* • *(030) 21 47 62 92.*
◎ *Reise Bank Bahnhof Zoo* • *Map N4* • *7:30am–10pm daily* • *(030) 881 71 17.*
◎ *Travel Ex, Friedrichstr. 56* • *Map I 4* • *Apr–Oct: 9:30am–6pm Mon–Fri, 11am–2pm Sat* • *(030) 20 16 59 16*

3 Credit Cards

Everywhere in the centre of Berlin you'll be able to use a standard credit card, such as Visa

or Euro/MasterCard, to pay at most restaurants, cafés and shops. American Express and Diner's Club are less commonly accepted. You can also use your credit or EC card (plus PIN number) to withdraw money from a machine. Should you lose your card, tell your bank or provider immediately.
◎ *American Express* • *(069) 97 97 10 00* ◎ *EC Cards* • *(069) 74 09 87*
◎ *Eurocard and MasterCard* • *(069) 79 33 19 10* ◎ *Diner's Club* • *(01805) 533 66 95*
◎ *Visa* • *(0180) 361 76 170*

4 Telephones

There are public phones (both enclosed cells and open phones) all over the centre of town. These are almost exclusively card phones. Telephone cards can be bought from post offices, in department stores and at kiosks.

5 Post Offices and Letter Boxes

Post offices are hard to miss – they are painted a bright yellow. As elsewhere in Germany, Berlin letter boxes are also yellow, but there are some blue "historic" boxes.
◎ *Center-Filiale, Joachimstaler Str. 7* • *Map P4* • *8am–midnight Mon–Sat, 10am–midnight Sun and holidays.*
◎ *Bahnhof Friedrichstr., Georgenstr. 12* • *Map K4* • *6am–10pm Mon–Fri, 8am–10pm Sat, Sun*

6 Postage

A standard letter (up to 20 g) to anywhere in the EU costs €0.55; a compact letter (up to 50 g) €1.44; a postcard €0.45. Stamps can be bought at the post office, from card shops and machines.

7 Internet Cafés

You can surf the internet and pick up your e-mails anywhere. Easy-everything is one of the largest internet cafés.
◎ *easy-everything, Kurfürstendamm 224* • *Map P4* • *around the clock* • *(030) 88 70 79 70*

8 Secretarial Services

If your hotel does not offer secretarial services, you could use an independent service. Details of such services are listed in the "Yellow Pages" of the telephone directory.

9 Travellers' Cheques

Travellers' cheques made out in euros or any other currency can be exchanged at all larger banks or at branches of the issuers. Most banks charge a fee.

🔟 Important Numbers

Important Deutsche Telekom helpline numbers are as follows:
• *national directory enquiries 118 33*
• *international directory enquiries 118 34*
• *operator (0180) 200 10 33*

Left **Ambulance** Centre **A pharmacy in the centre of Berlin** Right **A police van**

🔟 Security & Health Tips

1 Emergencies
As elsewhere in Germany, the emergency phone numbers are 112 for ambulance and fire brigade, and 110 for the police. These can be dialled free of charge from public phone boxes.

2 Safety
Berlin is a fairly safe city. As in any other metropolis, however, you are advised to follow a few golden rules. Keep an eye on your valuables, such as your wallet or handbag, at all times, especially on U- and S-Bahn trains and on buses. At night, the following areas are best avoided: the area behind the Gedächtnis-Kirche, U-Bahn line U9 north of the Zoo, the districts Lichtenberg (especially the station) and Fried-richshain. Eastern areas can be less safe; black or openly homosexual visitors are also advised not to take the S-Bahn at night east of Alexander-platz or to Brandenburg.

3 Theft
Ask the hotel to place your documents and valuables in a safe if possible, or carry them close to your body. Even if you are making a short visit, it is worth taking out insurance unless you are already covered by your household insurance. Be sure to inform the police immediately of any theft; you'll usually easily find

police officers patrolling the streets in the centre.
Ⓢ *Polizeipräsidium, Platz der Luftbrücke 6*
• *(030) 69 93 64 44*

4 Lost Property
The Zentrales Fundbüro (central lost-property office) keeps anything that has been lost and found anywhere in Berlin. If you have lost an item on public transport, enquire with the Fundbüro der BVG. The Fundbüro der Deutschen Bahn AG is responsible for all items lost on the S-Bahn or the railways.
Ⓢ *Zentrales Fundbüro, Platz der Luftbrücke 6*
• *(030) 756 031 01*
Ⓢ *Fundbüro der BVG, Potsdamer Str. 182*
• *(030) 194 49*
Ⓢ *Fundbüro der DB*
• *(01805) 990 599*

5 Hospitals
Visitors from EU countries are covered for emergency treatment, but British visitors should obtain form E111 from a post office before leaving home. Non-EU visitors should buy special travel insurance to cover medical emergencies.

6 Chemists
There are numerous *Apotheken* (chemists or pharmacies) all over town. After 8pm, an emergency phone line will give you information on where to find the nearest open chemist.
Ⓢ *(030) 31 00 31*

7 Dentists
The dental emergency phone line will refer you to the nearest dentist for treatment.
Ⓢ *(030) 89 00 43 33*

8 Emergency Services
There are several other important numbers for emergencies, which usually operate throughout the night. These will provide telephone advice or inform you of other emergency services if necessary.
Ⓢ *Doctors on call*
• *(030) 310 031*
Ⓢ *German Red Cross Rescue Service*
• *(030) 85 00 52 08*
Ⓢ *Emergency Poison Helpline*
• *(030) 192 40*
Ⓢ *Narcotics Emergencies*
• *(030) 192 37*
Ⓢ *Telephone helpline for emotional problems*
• *0800 111 0 111* • *0800 111 0 222 (spiritual help)*

9 Embassies
Foreign visitors who have lost their passport or need legal advice or help with their visa should contact their embassy *(see p160)*.

10 Women travelling on their own
Berlin is quite safe for women on their own, but avoid parks and dark, quiet streets at night, as well as the outer districts of East Berlin. Ⓢ *Confidential helpline for women* • *(030) 615 42 43*

Left **By S-Bahn to the outer districts** Centre **Travelling on Havel and Spree** Right **In Spreewald**

🔟 Excursions & Days Out

1 Spreewald
The river landscape around the little towns of Lübben and Lübbenau, southwest of Berlin, is a unique and unspoilt area of natural beauty. From here you can explore by boat the old settlements of the Sorbs, a Slavic people. Make sure you also enjoy the specialities of the region – fresh fish and vegetables, but most of all the famous pickled Spreewald gherkins. ✪ *Tourismusverband Spreewald e V, Lindenstr. 1, Raddusch • (035433) 722 99*

2 Sachsenhausen concentration camp
A visit to Sachsenhausen, Germany's first Nazi concentration camp, is a haunting experience. It was opened in 1933 as a "wild camp" for political prisoners. From 1936 to 1945, some 100,000 people were murdered here. Next to the camp is an exhibition. ✪ *Gedenkstätte und Museum Sachsenhausen, Straße der Nationen 22 • Apr–Sep: 8:30am–6pm Tue–Sun; Oct–Mar: 8:30am–4:30pm Tue–Sun • (03301) 20 00*

3 Schloss Rheinsberg
This small palace is an excellent destination for a day-trip. The palace was made famous by the love story of Kurt Tucholsky. Today the palace is a home for senior citizens and can be seen only from the outside. ✪ *Fremdenverkehrsamt Rheinsberg, Markt-Kavaliershaus • (033931) 20 59*

4 Werder
Surrounded by the Havelland fruit orchards, this small village celebrates Baumblütenfest, the blossoming of the fruit trees in April and May. ✪ *Potsdam-Information, Am Neuen Markt 1 • (0331) 27 55 80*

5 Caputh
This picturesque small village near Potsdam, surrounded by numerous lakes, boasts a charming Baroque palace as well as Albert Einstein's summer residence at No 7 Waldstraße. ✪ *Potsdam-Information, Am Neuen Markt 1 • (0331) 27 55 80*

6 Frankfurt/Oder
The other Frankfurt, on the Oder River, about 70 km (43 miles) east of Berlin, is well worth visiting, if only for its superb museum, devoted to the playwright Heinrich von Kleist. ✪ *Faberstr. 7 • 10am–5pm Tue–Sun • (0335) 53 11 55*

7 Bad Saarow
An old spa town and once a celebrity haunt, Bad Saarow's thermal springs and hotel invite you for a relaxing weekend. ✪ *Kur- und Fremdenverkehrs-GmbH, Am Kurpark 1 • (033631) 868 100 (tourist information)*

8 Buckow
The small village of Buckow is the centre of the so-called Märkische Schweiz (the Swiss Mark). A landscape of lakes and hills, which seems almost untouched, it is a good place for walking, swimming and boating. The best area is around Schermützelsee. Also at Buckow, the summer residence of Bertolt Brecht can be visited. ✪ *Umwelt- und Fremdenverkehrsamt Märkische Schweiz, Wriezener Str. 1a • (033433) 57 500*

9 Sacrow
North of Potsdam is the tiny village of Sacrow. It has become a favourite tourist spot because of its dreamy Saviour's Church, on the lake of the same name. ✪ *Potsdam-Information, Brandenburger Str. 3 • (0331) 27 55 80*

10 Königs Wusterhausen
A beautiful landscape of lakes stretches all around Königs Wusterhausen, 27 km (17 miles) southeast of Berlin. There are numerous romantic villages such as Grünau and Zeuthen, and one of its most attractive spots is the village of Teupitz, on Teupitz lake. The Schlosshotel is an ideal place to relax. ✪ *Kultur- und Tourismusverband Dahmeland, Am Bahnhof, Königs Wusterhausen • (03375) 25 200*

Left **A historic double-decker bus** Centre **Sightseeing by bus** Right **Visiting the city by velotaxi**

Guided Tours

Sightseeing by double-decker bus

Nothing is more fun than a sightseeing tour of the city on the double-decker nostalgia bus, which is open-top in summer. Buses depart from the corner of Ku'damm and Rankestraße. English and German commentary is available. ◎ *Stadtrundfahrtbüro Berlin, Kurfürstendamm 236 • (030) 261 20 01*

Buses 100 and 200

The cheapest and fastest way to see the city is a journey on buses Nos 100 or 200. These double-deckers go from Bahnhof Zoo and Alexanderplatz right into Prenzlauer Berg, passing all the important sights between West and East *en route*. A Berlin tour for only €2.10.

StattReisen

StattReisen was one of the first agencies in Germany to offer informative themed walks through the city. Among the most popular themes for guided tours are "Jewish Berlin" and a guided overview tour of the centre (lasting up to three hours). ◎ *Malplaquetstr. 5 • (030) 455 30 28*

Sightseeing Bus Tours

Traditional sightseeing tours by bus, with commentary in up to eight different languages, are good for getting a quick overview. The tours

depart from Kurfürstendamm (corner of Meinekestr. or Rankestr.), and in summer they leave every hour. These bus tours usually last between two and four hours, and take in all the most important sights of Berlin. There are special tours to Potsdam. Departure points:
◎ *Berolina Berlin-Service, Kurfürstendamm 220 • (030) 88 56 80 20*
◎ *Severin & Kühn, Kurfürstendamm 216 u. Alexanderplatz • (030) 880 41 90*
◎ *Bus Verkehr Berlin (BVB), Grenzallee 13–15 • (030) 683 89 10*

art:berlin

This agency cuts a swathe through Berlin's artistic jungle. Small, well-conducted tours lead visitors through the museums, galleries, cultural events and – of course – to the city's most exciting architectural treasures. ◎ *Oranienburger Str. 32 • (030) 28 09 63 90*

Boat Tours

Berlin's waterways – Havel and Spree Rivers, Landwehrkanal and the lakes Wannsee and Müggelsee – can all be explored by boat. Many tours allow you to take in Berlin's historic sights between Charlottenburg and the centre from the water. Tours last two or three hours, and there are piers at Schloss Charlottenburg, next to the Haus der Kulturen der Welt in

Tiergarten, next to the bridge Schlossbrücke as well as in Treptow. ◎ *Stern- und Kreis-Schiffahrt, Puschkinallee 15 • (030) 536 36 00.* ◎ *Weiße Flotte Potsdam, Lange Brücke • (0331) 275 92 10*

Berlin from the Air

Several enterprises offer sightseeing trips over Berlin and Brandenburg province by helicopter and in historic planes. ◎ *Kanzler International Executive Services, Kommandantenstr. 14 • (030) 694 94 90* ◎ *Air Service Berlin, Flughafen Tempelhof • (030) 695 35 90*

Berlin Walks

This small agency conducts themed English-language walks, departing daily from the taxi rank outside Zoologischer Garten. ◎ *Bahnhof Zoo • 10am daily (summer also 2:30pm) and by prior arrangement • (030) 301 91 94 • www.berlinwalks.com*

Velotaxis

An inexpensive, and personalized way to see the town is by velotaxi *(see p162).*

Berlin Underground

A very special sort of tour are these guided walks through the spooky under belly of Berlin, making your way through bunkers and ancient tunnels. ◎ *(030) 49 91 05 17*

Official guided tours: **www.stattreisen.berlin.de** *or:* **www.severin-kuehn-berlin.de**

Left **Relaxation can be found in one of the city's many parks** Right **Exploring Berlin on foot**

Top 10 Ways to Escape the Crowds

1 Rush Hours
If you're driving around Berlin, try to avoid the main rush hours – between 7am and 9am in the morning, and between 4:30pm and 7pm in the evening. Buses, U- and S-Bahn, too, are very crowded at these times.

2 Lunchtime
At restaurants, cafés and snack bars in the centre, you will often have to stand in line or wait to be seated if you arrive between 12:30pm and 2pm. Most venues in Berlin, though, will continue to serve the same dishes. So, if you wish to enjoy your meal in peace and quiet, set off after 1:30pm.

3 Evenings Out
Popular restaurants, particularly those around Savignyplatz, Gendarmenmarkt and Kollwitzplatz are often booked up between 7pm and 8pm, especially in summer, even during the week. You are therefore best advised to reserve a table in advance, or to arrive a little later, after about 9pm.

4 Early Risers
Many of the popular sights get very crowded, especially from Thursdays to Sundays. It's a good idea to arrive early, and to start your visit as soon as a place opens – especially the Reichstag.

5 Weekends
Most tourists come to Berlin for weekends, and so Ku'damm and Friedrichstraße are completely overrun by visitors on a Saturday morning. In the evening, many events, especially concerts by the Berlin Philharmonic Orchestra and performances in the best theatres, will be sold out. If possible arrange for your visit to start on a Sunday and take in the first few days of the week.

6 Holidays
High season for Berlin visitors is the period from May to July. From the end of July or the beginning of the school holidays, however, the town gets noticeably quieter, as many locals go on holiday then. You'll easily find parking spaces and many restaurants are much emptier than usual – especially in August. The only disadvantage is that theatres and concert halls close then for a summer break.

7 Berlin Parks
If, after a couple of days, you're tired of the hustle and bustle of the big city, go to one of the parks to chill out – Viktoriapark in Kreuzberg, Jungfernheide in Charlottenburg and the area around Tegeler See are picturesque places where you can relax in peace and quiet.

8 Sunday Morning
Even the central areas in Berlin are often completely deserted early on Sunday mornings – the ideal time for a quiet stroll down Kurfürstendamm or Unter den Linden. Most cafés and museums open at 10am, so you won't miss out on either cultural discoveries or refreshment.

9 Reservations
Whether you wish to visit the theatre, the opera, the Philharmonie concert hall, a multiplex cinema or a special event, it is almost always worth trying to book tickets as early as possible by phone or at one of the agencies – you'll rarely be lucky enough to buy tickets for the most popular events on the day.

10 Nights
Berlin is a city that never sleeps – it is "open" 24 hours a day. If you don't have to stick to particular times, for your evening meal, for example, make the most of your freedom – in most restaurants you can still enjoy a good meal after 11pm. The same is true of pubs and bars – many close at 3am or 4am, or not at all. Nightclubs and discos don't get going until midnight or later, even during the week. And some museums stay open late, until 10pm, on Thursdays.

Left **In the Europa-Center** Centre **Inside Galeries Lafayette** Right **A stand selling souvenirs**

🔟 Shopping

Shopping Streets

Kurfürstendamm, Tauentzienstraße and Friedrichstraße are the main three shopping streets in Berlin. You'll find inexpensive shops around Tauentzienstraße and Alexanderplatz. The Galeries Lafayette department store as well as the west side of Ku'damm are upmarket. A good mix of shops can be found in the arcades at Potsdamer Platz, Schlossstraße in the south of Berlin and the Gesundbrunnen-center in the north.

Opening Hours

Normally, shops are open between 10am and 8pm on Mondays to Saturdays. Smaller shops, however, close at 2 or 4pm on Saturdays, except in the four weeks before Christmas when they stay open until 6pm. Following a liberalizing of the law affecting opening hours, larger shops often stay open until 10pm at weekends. During special events (for example during the IFA International Broadcasting Exhibition or the Berlinale Film Festival) special opening hours may be in force.

How to Pay

Most shops in the city centre accept credit cards such as Visa, Mastercard and American Express, less commonly Diner's Club. Almost all shops take EC-cards.

Consumer Protection

If you feel that you are not being treated fairly or if a product you have bought proves to be faulty (and an exchange is refused), you can contact the consumer protection association. Ⓢ *Verbraucherzentrale Berlin, Bayreuther Str. 40 • 9am–1pm Mon, 9am–4:30 Tue & Fri, 9am–8pm Wed & Sun • (030) 21 48 50*

Sales

End-of-season sales take place at the end of January and the end of July. But you'll be able to find bargains throughout the year in the department stores and shops, often laid out on special stands right next to the main entrance.

Fashion

The best fashion and designer stores, selling coveted labels such as Gucci, Versace, Jil Sander, DKNY or Prada, can be found on the west side of Ku'damm and in Friedrichstraße. Kaufhaus des Westens sells a good large range of ladies' and gentlemen's fashions *(see p60)*.

Music

Apart from large multi-media and CD-store chains such as Saturn, MediaMarkt, Promarkt and Kaufhof, you will find a vast selection of CDs at Kulturkaufhaus Dussmann *(see p119)*, at

Wertheim, as well as in the department store Kaufhaus des Westens or KaDeWe *(see p60)*.

Gifts and Souvenirs

If you're looking for gifts and souvenirs to take home, try the Europa-Center *(see p24)* and the KaDeWe *(see p60)*. There are also souvenir shops in Unter den Linden (near Pariser Platz), on Potsdamer Platz as well as at Checkpoint Charlie.

Art and Antiques

Most antiques shops are clustered south of Nollendorfplatz *(see p104)* and in the smaller streets off Kurfürstendamm. However, the flea and art fair on the Straße des 17 Juni *(see p60)* and the antiques shops in the S-Bahn arches between Friedrichstraße and Museumsinsel are often much better value and offer a wider range of goods and antiques.

Around Berlin

In Potsdam as in other small towns, there are many excellent places to shop for arts and crafts items or clothes. A good place for bargain hunters is the "B96" shopping centre, situated on the national road with the same number. Here many fashionable items are sold at heavily discounted prices. Ⓢ *B96, exit Elstal • 10am–8pm Mon–Fri, 9am–4pm Sat*

 For more on shops & markets see pp60–1

Left **Theatre ticket office** Right **Enjoy Berlin's parks for free**

🔟 Berlin on a Budget

Accommodation
For low-cost accommodation you can check into inexpensive youth hostels, hostels run by the YMCA, or a backpacker hostel. Or try a Mitwohnzentrale, an agency arranging shared accommodation in private homes at a low cost *(see also p163)*.

Restaurants
As in Britain, Indian and Turkish restaurants are often particularly good value. Another cheap alternative are Turkish doner kebab snack bars and German curry sausage stands – these often also sell other snacks at low prices.

Museums
Berlin's municipal museums, especially those on Museumsinsel, can all be visited on a three-day ticket costing only €6. Admission is also free on the first Sunday of every month.

WelcomeCard
The BVG Welcome-Card offers the best and cheapest way of visiting exhibitions and museums in Berlin and using public transport throughout the city. The WelcomeCard costs €16 for one adult and up to three children under the age of 14 (children under 6 travel free). It provides two or three days of free travel on all buses and trains of the Berlin-Brandenburg

public transport network operating anywhere within the A, B and C fare zones, as well as up to 50 per cent reductions for many tourist attractions.

Reduced Tickets
Theatres and the opera house sell reduced tickets at the door on the day of the performance, mainly for pupils and students who can show a valid student card. Alternatively, tickets can be bought cheaply in advance by anyone from ticketing agencies such as Hekticket. ✆ *Hekticket (030) 230 99 30*

Street Artists
Berlin has always been a good place for street artists, especially on Breitscheidplatz and along Ku'damm. There is a legendary mime artist, dressed as a clown, who mimics passers-by outside the cafés on the eastern side of Ku'damm. In summer, in Charlottenburg and Prenzlauer Berg, you can often listen to street musicians and singers directly at your table or outside the restaurant or café.

Day of the Open Door
Since Berlin is Germany's political and cultural capital, many public and private institutions regularly offer the chance to take a look behind the scenes, free of charge. A

visit to one of the federal ministries is particularly interesting. Daily newspapers will list these events. Every year in summer, "Schaustelle Berlin" (a pun on "Baustelle", meaning building site) conducts guided tours to Berlin's major building sites and other projects *(see also www. berlin.de)*.

Free Concerts
Churches and smaller concert halls in the outer districts often put on classical concerts for a low admission fee or even free of charge. The city magazines and daily newspapers list such events in the appropriate columns. All Berlin daily newspapers also give away free tickets for current exhibitions and events. Look at the Berlin pages in the papers for what is currently on offer.

Markets
Berlin's weekly flea markets always have a vast range of special offers for sale, besides which they'll offer you the opportunity to try out your haggling skills *(see also pp60–1)*.

Parks
Admission to all of Berlin's parks and green spaces is free. You can enjoy their sports facilities, and often also open-air-concerts, without having to form out for a ticket *(see also pp68–9)*.

Left **Hotel Charlot** Centre **Reception in the Econtel** Right **Hotel Künstlerheim Luise**

Modest Hotels & Hostels

1 die fabrik
This hotel, its name meaning "the factory", is a guesthouse cum youth hostel. An alternative youth and arts centre in the middle of deepest Kreuzberg, it attracts backpackers from around the world, hoping to meet locals and others. ⚑ Schlesische Str. 18 • (030) 611 7116 • www. diefabrik.com • no credit cards • €

2 Hotel Künstlerheim Luise
The 30 rooms in this small, pleasant hotel were all individually and imaginatively designed by different local artists, with themes ranging from loud pop art to classic Modernism. The hotel is in a central location, close to lively Scheunenviertel and Unter den Linden. ⚑ Luisenstr. 19 • Map J/K3 • (030) 28 44 80 • www. luise-berlin.com • €€

3 Myer's Hotel
A family-run hotel in the centre of Prenzlauer Berg, ideal for families or young couples. The rooms are simply decorated yet modern, and the hotel is located in an historic part of town. The service is attentive and the atmosphere relaxed. ⚑ Metzer Str. 26 • Map H2 • (030) 44 01 40 • €€

4 Econtel
This small hotel, near Schloss Charlottenburg, is well suited to families, as some of its rooms have been specially designed for children's play. A buffet breakfast is included in the price. ⚑ Sömmeringstr. 24–26 • Map B3 • (030) 34 68 10 • €

5 Pension Niebuhr
A typical Berlin guesthouse, with a great atmosphere, situated in the most attractive part of Charlottenburg. Breakfast can be served in the rooms. ⚑ Niebuhrstr. 74 • Map P2 • (030) 324 95 95 • www.pension-niebuhr.de • €

6 Hotel–Pension Funk
Slightly antiquated, venerable guesthouse close to Ku'damm, based in the apartment of the silent-film star Asta Nielsen. The rates are unbeatable, while furnishings and service are personal and friendly. There are only 15 rooms however, so it is advisable to book in advance. ⚑ Fasanenstr. 69 • Map N/P4 • (030) 882 71 93 • www.hotel-pensionfunk.de • €

7 Pension Kreuzberg
Clean and friendly, this hotel-guesthouse in Kreuzberg boasts an excellent atmosphere – but unfortunately no en-suite bathrooms. The landlady takes great care of her guests and is happy to pass on her personal tips for nightlife and culture in Berlin. ⚑ Großbeerenstr. 64 • Map F5/6 • (030) 251 13 62 • no credit cards • €

8 Hotel Transit
Housed on two floors of a former industrial building, this international youth hostel is located in a lively area close to the town centre. It has large rooms, sleeping up to six people. ⚑ Hagelberger Str. 53–4 • Map F6 • (030) 789 04 70 • www.hotel-transit.de • €€

9 Hotel Charlot
A small hotel, popular with student and school groups, and therefore a little noisy at times. It is situated in a quiet square close to Ku'damm, where you will find several pubs and the UFA-Arthouse-Kino, which screens English-language films currently on release. ⚑ Giesebrechtstr. 17 • Map P2 • (030) 327 96 60 • www.hotel-charlot.de • €€

10 mitArt Pension
Tucked away opposite the Tacheles art centre is this small guesthouse, based in an old building dating from the 19th century. The rooms are plain, with modern furnishings, and the walls are decorated with avant-garde paintings. There are only nine rooms, which get booked up quickly, so you need to reserve early. ⚑ Linienstr. 139–140 • Map G2 • (030) 28 39 04 30 • €

Note: Unless otherwise stated, all hotels accept credit cards, and have en-suite bathrooms.

Price Categories

Price for a standard double room per night, with breakfast, taxes and other charges included

€ under €60
€€ €60–100
€€€ €100–150
€€€€ €150–200
€€€€€ over €200

Left **A small room in Bleibtreu-Hotel** Right **Courtyard of Hackescher Markt**

10 Medium-Priced Hotels

Bleibtreu-Hotel
Here, you'll fancy yourself in Tuscany – the hotel's stylish interior courtyard and bright, tastefully furnished rooms are an oasis of tranquillity in the bustle of the western half of the city. The international clientele is equally stylish. The hotel has its own restaurant, pool, sauna, massage and much more on offer, and there are shops right outside. ⊗ *Bleibtreustr. 31* • *Map P3* • *(030) 88 47 40* • *www.bleibtreu.com* • *€€€*

Hackescher Markt
A charming hotel in an unbeatable location right opposite Hackesche Höfe – few places in this price range can compete. Large, bright rooms with elegant furnishings, friendly service, an excellent restaurant and many pleasant extras, such as an attractive patio, guarantee a pleasant stay. ⊗ *Große Präsidentenstr. 8* • *Map J5* • *(030) 28 00 30* • *www.hotel-hackeschermarkt.de* • *€€€*

Alsterhof
A quiet classic, this hotel boasts attentive staff, rustic rooms and its own small beer garden in summer, all in an excellent location near the KaDeWe. Ask about special weekend rates. Non-smoking rooms available. ⊗ *Augsburger Str. 5* • *Map P5* • *(030) 21 24 20* • *www.alsterhof.de* • *€€€*

Hotel am Scheunenviertel
Well-run establishment with an intimate atmosphere (there are only 18 rooms), popular with tourists on cultural visits. Rooms and lobby have been kept deliberately plain, which creates a slightly spartan impression, but all needs are catered for. ⊗ *Oranienburger Str. 38* • *Map J4/5* • *(030) 282 21 25* • *€€*

Hotel-Pension Augusta
This small hotel is a little old-fashioned, and some rooms could do with refurbishing, but that's more than made up for by its surplus of old Berlin charm, central location and low prices. ⊗ *Fasanenstr. 22* • *Map P4* • *(030) 883 50 28* • *www.hotel-augusta.de* • *€€*

Hotel am Zoo
A trendy hotel in a uniquely central location, on Ku'damm. The rooms are all surprisingly large, and the windows have been sound-proofed. ⊗ *Kurfürstendamm 25* • *Map P4* • *(030) 88 43 70* • *www.hotelzoo.de* • *€€*

Hotel-Pension Kastanienhof
A charming hotel in a building dating back to the turn of the 20th century. The rooms are basic but well equipped (with safe, minibar and hairdryer). An ideal base for exploring Prenzlauer Berg. ⊗ *Kastanienallee 65* • *Map G2* • *(030) 44 30 50* • *www.kastanienhof.biz* • *€€*

Riehmers Hofgarten
In Riehmers Hofgarten you can live the life of a Prussian officer. Old Kreuzberg apartments, with sombre rooms and elegant bathrooms, are the perfect setting for a 19th-century lifestyle. The hotel, part of a large complex of 19th-century Gothic red-brick buildings, is certainly remarkable. ⊗ *Yorckstr. 83* • *Map F6* • *(030) 78 09 88 00* • *www.riehmers hofgarten.de* • *€€*

Hotel Berliner Hof
You can find a more attractive room in other hotels, but you'll be hard pushed to find one at such a low price and in such a central location, on Tauentzienstraße, opposite the KaDeWe department store. ⊗ *Tauentzienstr. 8* • *Map P5* • *(030) 25 49 50* • *www. berliner-hof.com* • *€€*

Hotel Ambassador Berlin
A medium priced hotel near KaDeWe, offering a full office service with quiet rooms, a lovely pool with good views and an excellent buffet dinner. ⊗ *Bayreuther Str. 42–43* • *Map P5* • *(030) 21 90 20* • *www.sorat-hotels.de* • *€€€*

 Online hotel bookings: **www.berlin.de/home/English/** *or:* **www.berlin.nethotels.com/english/**

Left **In the art'otel berlin** Centre **Lobby and bar in Hecker's Hotel** Right **Soral Hotel Spreebogen**

Designer Hotels

1 art'otel berlin-mitte

Berlin's best designer hotel emphasizes every detail, and everything here has been styled, from the furniture to the soap in your bathroom. The walls of the historic building are decorated with paintings by Georg Baselitz. The hotel is centrally located, close to Nikolaiviertel. ⊗ *Wallstr. 70–73* • *Map L6* • *(030) 24 06 20* • *www.artotel.de* • *€€€*

2 Dorint Schweizerhof Berlin

The newest of Berlin's luxury hotels, Schweizerhof features beautifully clean lines, precious woods and a large, well-designed fitness area – all in the centre of the western city. Art plays a major part in the hotel – the brightly furnished, Scandinavian-style rooms are decorated with paintings by the artist Ter Hell. ⊗ *Budapester Str. 25* • *Map N5* • *(030) 269 60* • *www.schweizerhof.com* • *€€€–€€€€*

3 Brandenburger Hof

One of the only hotels in Berlin to be influenced by the Bauhaus, the Brandenburger Hof has free-swinging leather seats and ball-shaped lamps, forming an exciting contrast to the historic building. ⊗ *Eislebener Str. 14* • *Map P4* • *(030) 21 40 50* • *www. brandenburger-hof.com* • *€€€–€€€€*

4 DeragHotel Großer Kurfürst

If you prefer modern designs, this hotel is not for you – the rooms here are all classically styled. The Großer Kurfürst has successfully incorporated modern facilities into an historic building. It also features many useful extras, such as free public transport and bicycle hire. ⊗ *Neue Roßstr. 11–12* • *Map L6* • *(030) 24 60 00* • *www.deraghotels.de* • *€€€–€€€€*

5 Hecker's Hotel

The plain façade of this modern business hotel, centrally situated in a side street just off Ku'damm, belies the much more sophisticated interior – you'll be greeted by modern art, cool minimalism, clever lighting and first-class service. ⊗ *Grolmanstr. 35* • *Map N3* • *(030) 889 00* • *www.heckers-hotel.com* • *€€€*

6 Sorat Hotel Spree-Bogen

Architect Wolfang Borchardt has succeeded in turning the old Bolle Dairy into a modern hotel with friendly rooms and a restaurant, both overlooking the Spree River. Next door are the semi-circular modern glass buildings of the Ministry of the Interior. ⊗ *Alt-Moabit 99* • *Map J1* • *(030) 39 92 00* • *www. hotel-spreebogen.de* • *€€€€*

7 artemisia

Art and women rule at this small guesthouse – the hotel is run by and for women and all the rooms are beautifully colour-coordinated. Regular exhibitions by women artists from Berlin are held. ⊗ *Brandenburgische Str. 18* • *Map B5/6* • *(030) 873 89 05* • *€€*

8 Maritim proArte Hotel Berlin

Predominantly styled in tones of green and blue, this modern business hotel boasts almost 300 modern paintings, which decorate the rooms. Every piece of furniture has been carefully styled. ⊗ *Friedrichstr. 151* • *Map K/L4* • *(030) 203 35* • *www. maritim.de* • *€€€–€€€€*

9 art'otel Kurfürstendamm

Works of art hang, stand and lie everywhere inside and outside this hotel, especially works by Wolf Vostell, and the interior is boldly designed in ultra-modern vibrant colours. ⊗ *Joachimsthaler Str. 29* • *Map P4* • *(030) 88 44 70* • *www.sorat.de* • *€€€–€€€€*

10 INN SIDE Residence Hotel

This small hotel is full of modern works of art – even the showers are art installations. The rooms also have kitchens. ⊗ *Lange Str. 31* • *Map H3/4* • *(030) 29 30 30* • *www.innside.de* • *€€*

Note: *Unless otherwise stated, all hotels accept credit cards, and have en-suite bathrooms.*

Price Categories

Price for a standard	**€** under €60
double room per	**€€** €60–100
night, with breakfast,	**€€€** €100–150
taxes and other	**€€€€** €150–200
charges included	**€€€€€** over €200

Left **Dining at the Hilton Berlin** Right **The lobby of Estrel Residence Congress Hotel**

⓾ Hotels for Business Travellers

Hilton Berlin
Top executives favour this luxury hotel because of its central location, the views across Gendarmenmarkt, an excellent breakfast and specially designed executive rooms. A full secretarial service is included. ⓢ *Mohrenstr. 30 • Map L4 • (030) 20230 • www.hilton.de • €€€–€€€€*

Heinrich-Heine City Suites
This hotel is the best choice if your business requires a longer stay in town. Close to Nikolaiviertel, the apartments are equipped with desks and kitchens; and staff are specially trained to cater for the needs of business travellers. ⓢ *Heinrich-Heine-Platz 11 • Map H4 • (030) 27 80 40 80 • www.nh-hotels.com • €€–€€€*

Estrel Residence Congress Hotel
With over 1,000 rooms, this hotel is Europe's largest, offering a three- to four-star service at moderate prices. Its numerous conference rooms and the latest technological equipment make it the perfect venue for conferences or international business meetings. Yet the hotel is equally ready to cater for the needs of the individual business traveller. ⓢ *Sonnenallee 225 • (030) 683 122 522 • www.estrel.com • €€–€€€*

Crowne Plaza Berlin City Centre
Part of an American hotel chain, the Crowne Plaza offers attentive service, tasteful rooms and all the creature comforts that business travellers expect, plus a central location, in the western part of the city. ⓢ *Nürnberger Str. 65 • Map P5 • (030) 21 00 70 • www.cp-berlin.com • €€€*

Holiday Inn Garden Court
It may seem a little impersonal, but the Holiday Inn's excellent location makes it popular with business travellers from the US. It doesn't have a restaurant. ⓢ *Bleibtreustr. 25 • Map P3 • (030) 88 09 30 • www.hi-berlin.de • €€€*

Mandala Suites
A central boarding house with suites of 40–100 square metres (430–1,076 square feet), elegantly equipped as offices and offering a secretarial service. ⓢ *Friedrichstr. 185–190 • Map K/L4 • (030) 20 29 20 • www.themandala.de • €€€*

Mercure Hotel Berlin Tegel Airport Ost
Conveniently situated near the airport, this hotel is ideal for brief business trips. A good night's rest is guaranteed, and the service is efficient and friendly.

ⓢ *Gotthardstr. 96 • (030) 49 88 40 • www.mercure.com • €€*

Berlin Excelsior
Prestigious member of Berlin's Blue-Band-Hotels, the Excelsior is characterized more by sober efficiency than by friendliness but hits the mark with moderate prices, excellent location and a vast range of business services. ⓢ *Hardenbergstr. 14 • Map N4 • (030) 315 50 • www.hotel-excelsior.de • €€€*

Jolly Hotel Vivaldi
This very Italian luxury hotel is in a brand new building on Friedrichstrasse that opened in 2002. Apart from its East Berlin location, the hotel's main attractions are the spacious rooms, large lobby and inviting bar, all furnished with only the best materials. ⓢ *Friedrichstr. 96 • Map F3/K4 • (030) 206 26 60 • www.jollyhotels.de • €€*

Ku'damm 101
This very stylish hotel is in a central yet quiet downtown location on Ku'damm. It offers a luxurious, international ambience with a retro-Bauhaus look. All rooms have state-of-the-art communications equipment in them. ⓢ *Kurfürstendamm 101 • Map B5 • (030) 520 05 50 • www.kudamm101.com • €€€*

See also pp72–3.

Left **Schlossparkhotel** Centre **Pool in Hotel zur Bleiche** Right **Relexa Schlosshotel Cecilienhof**

Hotels in Green Surroundings

1 Relexa Schloss-hotel Cecilienhof
Potsdam's best hotel, the Relexa is based in an historic building in the middle of Neuer Garten (see p154). At night, peace descends as the day trippers leave. ⊗ Am Neuen Garten Potsdam • (0331) 370 50 • www.relaxa-hotels.de • €€€€

2 Landhaus Schlachtensee
This villa, near Schlachtensee and Krumme Lanke, now a small boarding house, oozes the charm of bygone days in rural Berlin. The furnishings in its 20 rooms are a little old-fashioned, but the service is very person-able. ⊗ Bogotastr. 9 • (030) 809 94 70 • www.hotel-landhaus-schlachtensee.de • €€

3 Schlossparkhotel
Only a few minutes from the western part of the city, this is the only hotel near Schloss Charlottenburg, right next to Schlosspark. Attached to it is a health and fitness centre – the facilities and the service are surprisingly good for such a small place: the hotel has only 40 rooms. ⊗ Heubnerweg 2a • Map A/B3 • (030) 326 90 30 • www.schlossparkhotel.de • €€

4 Hotel Seehof am Lietzensee
A well-run hotel, centrally located in Charlottenburg, not far from Messegelände (exhibition grounds), in a picturesque spot on Lietzensee. Apart from a beautiful indoor pool, the hotel also has a delightful sun terrace. ⊗ Lietzenseeufer 11 • Map A4 • (030) 32 00 20 • www. hotel-seehof-berlin.de • €€€

5 Dolce Hotel Berlin-Müggelsee
A luxury hotel on Müggelsee, combining Mediterranean and Asian features. There is a skittle alley, a fitness club, tennis courts, sauna and billiards as well as boat and bicycle hire and an extensive programme of leisure events. ⊗ Müggelheimer Damm 145 • (030) 65 88 20 • www.dolce.com • €€€

6 Haus La Garde
This tiny guesthouse with only four rooms is hidden in a romantic, non-smoking villa on the Schlachtensee. If lakes aren't your thing, you can chill out in the villa's gardens. ⊗ Bergengrünstr. 16 • (030) 801 30 09 • www.haus-la-garde.de • €

7 Spreeidyll-Hotel am Yachthafen
A small family-run house on the Müggelspree, not far from a bathing beach and a boat-hire booth – the ideal place to relax and forget all about the hustle and bustle of the big city, which is, how-ever, only a few kilo-metres to the northwest. Come here to chill out. ⊗ Müggelseedamm 70 • (030) 645 38 52 • www.spree-idyll.de • €

8 Hotel Rheinsberg am See
You are guaranteed a relaxing stay at this rustic hotel in the north of Berlin, which offers a huge breakfast buffet. The hotel pool help you forget the stresses of life and improve your fitness. ⊗ Finsterwalder Str. 64 • (030) 402 10 02 • www.hotel-rheinsberg.com • €€

9 Courtyard Berlin-Köpenick
The slightly sterile and impersonal atmosphere of the Marriott is more than made up for by its perfect location. It is right in the centre of the southeastern district of Köpenick, on the banks of the Dahme River – and both Müggelsee and Schönefeld Airport are only a few minutes' drive away by car or S-Bahn. ⊗ Grünauer Str. 1 • (030) 65 47 90 • www.courtyard.com • €€

10 Hotel zur Bleiche
This country-house hotel, located in the middle of the Spreewald lake district, has great facilities including pool, steam rooms, saunas and a great restaurant – a veritable paradise for health and fitness fans. ⊗ Bleichestr. 16, Burg • (035603) 620 • www.hotel-zur-bleiche.de • €€

Note: Unless otherwise stated, all hotels accept credit cards, and have en-suite bathrooms.

Price Categories

Price for a standard double room per night, with breakfast, taxes and other charges included	**€** under €60
	€€ €60–100
	€€€ €100–150
	€€€€ €150–200
	€€€€€ over €200

Left **The Backpacker Hostel** Right **At BaxPax, you'll sleep in a VW Beetle**

🔟 Budget Hotels & Hostels

BaxPax
Much better than a youth hostel yet much cheaper than a guesthouse, BaxPax offers an unusual place to rest your head. You'll be sleeping in beds in decommissioned VW beetles, at under €20 per night. Plus you'll meet young, friendly people from around the world (great for making friends). This dive is in deepest Kreuzberg, and not suitable for those over 30. ✆ *Skalitzerstr. 104 • Map H5 • (030) 69 51 83 22 • www.baxpax.de • €*

Jugendgästehaus der DSJ
This vast youth guesthouse is situated in an excellent spot, in the heart of Kreuzberg, and close to the Jüdisches Museum. The showers are shared, but a bed in a multi-bedded room is not expensive. The hostel is favoured by a young and international crowd. ✆ *Franz-Künstler-Str. 10 • Map G5 • (030) 615 10 07 • no credit cards • €*

Jugendgästehaus Kluckstraße
One of Berlin's largest youth hostels offers slightly antiquated but comfortable multi-bedded rooms. The staff are very friendly for a hostel in a large city, but the hostel is often overrun by noisy hordes of school kids. ✆ *Kluckstr. 3 • Map E5 • (030) 261 10 98 • €*

acksel Haus
Basic apartment rooms in a small, slightly alternative guesthouse, based on an old tenement block. The "acksel haus" is near Kollwitzplatz, a popular area with young people. ✆ *Belforter Str. 21 • Map H2 • (030) 44 33 76 33 • www.ackselhaus.de • no credit cards • €*

Jugendherberge am Wannsee
One of Berlin's oldest youth hostels, popular with groups of students and pupils and not the best place for visitors seeking peace and quiet. The picturesque location on Wannsee makes up for communal showers and dormitories, particularly in summer. ✆ *Badeweg 1 • (030) 803 20 34 • €*

Bed & Breakfast
Berliner Mitwohnzentrale, an agency, arranges shared accommodation in private homes all over town, at low prices. You'll normally have your own room with one or two beds. Quality varies considerably but the rooms are mostly priced at under €25 per night. ✆ *(030) 746 14 46 • no credit cards • €*

Timmy's Bed and Breakfast
A private gay-and-lesbian-friendly guesthouse, offering basic rooms and many insider tips on culture and nightlife. The only disadvantage is its location in Moabit – not one of Berlin's most attractive areas. ✆ *Perlebergerstr. • Map D/E2 • (030) 81 85 19 88 • www.gaybed.de • €*

Backpacker Hostel Berlin
A typically charming Berlin guesthouse, in the most attractive part of Mitte. You can even have your breakfast served in the room. ✆ *Chausseestr. 102 • Map F2 • (030) 28 39 09 65 • www.backpacker.de • €*

Hotel-Pension Korfu II
The name of this small hotel with only 19 rooms may seem over the top, but this venue is ideally suited for young people and families. The rooms are basic but well cared for, and the service is efficient. The house is in a central spot, opposite Kaiser-Wilhelm-Gedächtnis-Kirche. ✆ *Rankestr. 35 • Map P4 • (030) 212 47 90 • www.hp-korfu.de • €*

Hotel Christopherus-Haus
This hotel is a little more expensive than others in the same category, but the accommodation in green surroundings is perfect for families. The hotel is run by the Protestant church. ✆ *Johannesstift, Schönwalder Allee 26 • (030) 33 60 60 • www.vch.de • €€*

Left **In Villa Kastania** Centre **The pool in Alexander Plaza** Right **Propeller Island City**

⑩ Hotels & Guesthouses with Charm

1 Golden Tulip Residenz Hotel

Although this hotel is part of a US chain, it is based in one of the most beautiful old-Berlin town houses near Ku'damm, and guests enjoy the intimate, characterful atmosphere. The late 19th century rooms are tastefully furnished, and the restaurant has outdoor seating in summer.
Ⓢ *Meinekestr. 9 • Map P4 • (030) 88 44 30 • www. hotel-residenz.com • €€€*

2 Hotel-Pension Dittberner

Berlin's best guesthouse, close to Ku'damm, consists of several rooms in an old building, connected by endless corridors with lots of nooks and crannies. Some of the furniture has seen better days, but breakfast and atmosphere are perfect.
Ⓢ *Wielandstr. 26 • Map P2 • (030) 881 64 85 • www. hotel-dittberner.de • €€*

3 Alexander-Plaza

Based in an historic building from the late 19th century, this hotel perfectly combines old and new features. The elegant rooms are decorated with plaster ceiling mouldings and equipped with timelessly sophisticated furnishings. This is a very pleasant hotel, both to look at and to stay in. Ⓢ *Rosenstr. 1 • Map J5 • (030) 24 00 10 • www.hotel-alexander-plaza. de • €€*

4 DeragResidenz-hotel Henriette

A stylish hotel with classic decoration – oak-panelled walls and thick carpets and curtains adorn the rooms, which are arranged around an inner courtyard. Few hotels in town are better than this, and the service is very friendly.
Ⓢ *Neue Roßstr. 13 • Map L6 • (030) 24 60 09 00 • www.deraghotels.de • €€*

5 Hotel Gendarm

This small hotel on Gendarmenmarkt is based in a venerable town residence. The rooms, too, with their design and furnishings, seem to hark back to the 19th century, but in fact everything is brand-new. The hotel also boasts a sauna, pool and fitness facilities. Ⓢ *Charlottenstr. 61 • Map L4 • (030) 206 06 60 • www.hotel-gendarm-berlin.de • €€*

6 Hotel-Pension Wittelsbach

The furnishings in this medium-sized hotel-guesthouse are stuck in the 1970s – and this is what makes it so charming. The service is very friendly, children and pets are both welcome, and the breakfast buffet is so generous that you won't need to eat anything else for the rest of the day.
Ⓢ *Wittelsbacherstr. 22 • Map B5 • (030) 864 98 40 • www.hotel-pension-wittelsbach.de • €–€€*

7 Art Nouveau Hotel

An old-fashioned but well-run guesthouse, based in a beautiful Art-Nouveau building. The rooms are furnished in a discreet modern style, and the hotel is typical of Berlin's older buildings.
Ⓢ *Leibnitzstr. 59 • Map P2 • (030) 327 74 40 • www. hotelartnouveau.de • €€*

8 Artist Riverside Hotel Berlin-Mitte

A small hotel promising big things, and in terms of its furnishings at least it keeps these promises. The stylish 19th-century house, with sophisticated interior and excellent service, is popular with American visitors.
Ⓢ *Friedrichstr. 106 • Map K/L4 • (030) 28 49 00 • www.great-hotel.com • €€*

9 Villa Kastania

Service of a high standard, and beautiful rooms with kitchen and bathroom – well suited for self-catering and situated in the middle of Prenzlauer Berg.
Ⓢ *Kastantienallee 20 • (030) 300 00 20 • €€*

10 Propeller Island City Lodge

If you're staying at this lodge, you will share it with the artist Lars Stroschen, who designed the rooms himself. Ⓢ *Albrecht-Achilles Str. 58 • (030) 891 90 16 • www.propeller-island.com • no credit cards • €*

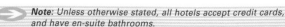

Note: *Unless otherwise stated, all hotels accept credit cards, and have en-suite bathrooms.*

Price Categories

Price for a standard	€	under €60
double room per	€€	€60–100
night, with breakfast,	€€€	€100–150
taxes and other	€€€€	€150–200
charges included	€€€€€	over €200

Left **The Dorint am Gendarmenmarkt** Right **A suite in Hotel Palace**

Top 10 Luxury Hotels

Hotel Palace
The expensively restored hotel on the second floor of the Europa-Center is a real find – all the rooms are exquisitely designed, two of the suites (Zackenbarsch and Panda) were styled by the director himself. The hotel staff are unobtrusive and very helpful. 🕙 Budapester. Str. 45 • Map N/P5 • (030) 250 20 • www.palace.de • €€€€

Dorint am Gendarmenmarkt
Relatively inexpensive and the smallest of the first-class hotels (70 rooms, 21 suites), the Dorint is probably also one of the most attractive, with excellent views of Gendarmenmarkt. 🕙 Charlottenstr. 50– 52 • Map L4 • (030) 203 750 • www.dorint.de • €€€€

Hotel Intercontinental Berlin
Luxury hotel in Tiergarten, renovated two years ago, with great views over the central park, this hotel is popular with business travellers. Although the building itself is not particularly attractive, the rooms are furnished in a timelessly elegant style. Its three restaurants offer first-class food, and the bars, pool and fitness area are also excellent. 🕙 Budapester Str. 2 • Map N5/6 • (030) 260 20 • www.berlin.interconti.com • €€€€€

Westin Grand Hotel
Luxury accommodation in an historic spot, at the corner of Friedrichstraße and Unter den Linden, offering large, elegant rooms and US-style service. The lobby and the grand stairs are breathtaking. There's also a café and a bar. 🕙 Friedrichstr. 158–164 • Map K4 • (030) 202 70 • www.westin-grand.com • €€€€

Grand Hotel Esplanade
Glitzy, modern, recently renovated hotel, with furnishings somewhere between functional sobriety and Bauhaus-style. Service and facilities are first-class and Harry's New York Bar is very popular. 🕙 Lützowufer 15 • Map N6 • (030) 25 47 80 • www. esplanade.de • €€€€€

Swissôtel Berlin
One of Berlin's new luxury hotels, the Swissôtel is located at the busy corner of Ku'damm and Joachimsthaler Straße. Great views of the city, especially at night. 🕙 Augsburger Str. 44 • Map P4 • (030) 22 01 00 • www.berlin.swissotel.com • €€€€

The Mandala Hotel Potsdamer Platz
This apartment hotel, in a great spot in Potsdamer Platz, has suites of 35– 100 sq m (375–1,100 sq ft) with kitchen, stereo, fitness area, sauna, daily papers and anything else you could possibly wish for. 🕙 Potsdamer Str. 3 • Map K3 • (030) 590 05 00 00 • www.themandala.com • €€€€

Kempinski Hotel Bristol Berlin
A magnificent, cosmopolitan blend of elegance and modern amenities – this hotel, one of Berlin's most famous – has it all. Its international reputation has attracted many famous guests, from Castro to Tina Turner. 🕙 Kurfürstendamm 27 • Map P4 • (030) 88 43 40 • www.kempinskiberlin.de • €€€€

Dorint Novotel Sanssouci Berlin-Potsdam
This new four-star hotel is located near Alexandrovka, the historic Russian colony, within walking distance of Schlosspark Sanssouci. Offering great facilities, it is particularly well suited as a base for excursions into Brandenburg province. 🕙 Jägerallee 20 • (0331) 27 40 • www.novotel.de • €€€€

SAS Radisson Berlin
A modern luxury hotel with a huge aquarium in the lobby. It has stylish, bright rooms with great views of Berliner Dom and Alexanderplatz. It has Asian and fusion cuisine restaurants. 🕙 Karl-Liebknecht-Str. 3 • Map K5 • (030) 238 280 • €€€€

www.btm.de/deutsch/unterkunft
See also pp72–3.

General Index

General Index

General Index

Acknowledgements

The Author

Historian Jürgen Scheunemann has published several documentary and photographic books on Berlin and other destinations. His award-winning articles are published in travel magazines and daily newspapers in Germany and the US, and have appeared in the Berlin daily *Tagesspiegel*, among others.

For Dorling Kindersley Verlag, Munich:

Publishing Director
Dr. Jörg Theilacker

Editors
Brigitte Maier, Gerhard Bruschke

Design & Layout
Ulrike Meyer

Proofreader
Linde Wiesner

Editorial Assistants
Jasmin Jouhar, Robert Kocon

Photography
Jürgen Scheunemann

Additional Photography
Dorota and Mariusz Jarymowicz, Günter Schneider

Artwork
www.chrisorr.com

Cartography
Dominic Beddow, Simonetta Siori (Draughtsman Ltd)

For Dorling Kindersley, London:

Translation & Editing
Sylvia Goulding/Silva Editions

Senior Publishing Manager
Louise Lang

Publishing Manager
Kate Poole

Senior Art Editor
Marisa Renzullo

Director of Publishing
Gillian Allan

Publisher
Douglas Amrine

Cartography Co-ordinator
Casper Morris

DTP
Jason Little, Conrad van Dyk

Production
Sarah Dodd

Picture Credits

t-top; tc-top centre; tr-top right; cla-centre left above; ca-centre above; cra-centre right above; cl-centre left; c-centre; cr-centre right; clb-centre right below; cb-centre below; crb-centre right below; bl-below left; bc-below centre; br below right.

The publishers would like to thank the following individuals, companies and picture libraries for permission to reproduce their photographs:

Alexander Plaza: 178tc; Ars vitalis: 69br; Art'otel Berlin: 174tl; Back-packer Hostel/Axbax: 177tl, 177tr; Bar jeder Vernunft: 57cla; Berliner Bäder-Betriebe: 69tl; Berliner Film-festspiele: 62cl; Bleibtreu-Hotel: 173tl; Deutsche Guggenheim: 113clb; Dorint am Gendarmenmarkt: 179tl; Econtel Hotel: 172tc; Estrel Residence Congress Hotel: 175tr; Funpool: 68tr; Galeries Lafayette: 119clc; Heckers Hotel: 174tc; Hertha BSC: 68bl; Hotel Adlon: 8crb, 116cb; Hotel Hackescher Markt: 173tr; Hotel Künstlerheim Luise: 172tr; Hotel zur Bleiche: 176tc; Jüdisches Museum: 102tr; Margaux: 74b; Kempinski Hotel Bristol Berlin: 86c; Museum für Kommunikation: Herbert Schlemmer: 117b; Propeller City Island: 178tc; Quartier 206 Department Store: 60tl, 115tl; Relaxa Hotel Cecilienhof: 176tr; Rocco Forte Hotel de Rome: 120tc; Schlossparkhotel: 176tl; Sorat Hotel Spreebogen: 174tl; Siegessäule: 58b; Tourismusverband Spreewald e.V.: Rainer Weisflog 167tr; Trabrennbahn Mariendorf: 68tc; Trenta sei: Benjamin Hüter 120tc; Jens Gläser 121tr; Zoologischer Garten: 36-7c.

ASPRIA: 69tr; BILDARCHIV PREUSSISCHER KULTURBESITZ, Berlin: 20tl, 31tr, 35c; Ägyptisches Museum/ Margarete Büsing 4c; Antikensammlung 7tl, 21tl, 21clb, 21br, 21–2c, 22b, 22t, 46tl, 114c; Antikensammlung/Ingrid Geske-Heiden 114b; Ethnologisches Museum 30br; Gemäldegalerie, *Madonna in Church* by Jan van Eyck (c1425) 32t, *Portrait of the*

Merchant Georg Gisze by Hans Holbein (1532) 34tr, *Venus and the Organ Player* by Titian (1550–2) 34tc, *Portrait of Hieronymus Holzschuher* by Albrecht Dürer (1529) 34tr, *Madonna with the Child and Singing Angels* by Botticelli (c1477) 34c, *Victorious Eros* by Caravaggio (1602) 34bl, 48tc, *Adoration of the Shepherds* by Hugo van der Goes (1470) 48tl, *The Glass of Wine* by Jan Vermeer (c1658–61) 48bu; Kunstgewerbemuseum 7cb, 33t, 46tr, 47c; Kupferstichkabinett, *Portrait of Dürer's Mother* by Albrecht Dürer 114c; Museum für Vor- und Frühgeschichte 29br; Nationalgalerie, *Farm in Daugart* by Karl Schmidt-Rottluff (1910) © DACS, London 2006 32b, *Mao* by Andy Warhol (1973) © Licensed by The Andy Warhol Foundation for the Visual Arts Inc. / ARS, NY & DACS, London 2006 48cra; Nationalgalerie, Berggruen Collection, *Head of a Faun* by Pablo Picasso (1937) © Succession Picasso / DACS, London 2006 49tl; Vorderasiatisches Museum 20c, 20cbr, 20b, 21cbr, 23c, 23b, 23t; BRECHT-WEIGEL-GEDENKSTÄTTE Berlin: 50cr; BRIDGEMAN ART LIBRARY: National-galerie, Berlin, *Portrait of Georg Wilhelm Friedrich Hegel* (1770–1831) by Jacob Schlesinger (1792–1855) 50tl; BROEHAN MUSEUM: 49c; DEUTSCHE PRESSEAGENTUR: 9b, 42tr, 50tc, 50tr, 50bl, 51tl, 51b, 62tc, 62tr, 62c, 63tl, 63tr, 63cr; DEUTSCHES HISTORISCHES MUSEUM: 15t, 18cl, 42cr; *Gloria Victis* by Antonin Mercie 14c; *Pieta Sculpture at the Neue Wache*, Kathe Kollwitz © DACS, London 2006 51c; *Martin Luther* by Lucas Cranach the Elder (1529) 14b; *Opening of the German Reichstag* (1871) 15b; DEUTSCHES TECHNIKMUSEUM: 103bl; FIT OT PRINT, Berlin: 166tc; HENRY MOORE FOUNDATION: *Three Way Piece Nr.*

2. (The) Archer (1964–5) 35t; HOTEL VILLA KASTANIA: 178tl.; INTERCONTINENTAL, BERLIN: 74bc; KÄTHE-KOLLWITZ-MUSEUM: *Mother and Child* by Käthe Kollwitz © DACS, London 2006 83bl; KOMISCHE OPER BERLIN: Arwid Lagenpusch 112tr.; MUSEUM FÜR NATURKUNDE: 47tr; PRESSE- UND INFORMATIONSAMT DES LANDES Berlin: BTM/Drewes 17bl; BTM/Koch 17cra; LOLA LOUNGE: Nela Koenig 54tl; POPKOMM: 62tl; KARSTEN SCHIRMER: 56cl; GÜNTER SCHNEIDER: 42tl, 95–6; JÜRGEN SCHEUNEMANN: 121tc, 128tl; STAATLICH MUSEEN ZU BERLIN, PREUSSISCHER KULTUR-BESITZ KUNSTGEWERBE-MUSEUM: Hans Joachim Bartsch 47c; STIFTUNG STADTMUSEUM BERLIN: 14t; Peter Straube 130tr; STIFTUNG PREUSSISCHE SCHLÖSSER UND GÄRTEN BERLIN-BRANDENBURG: 152tr, 153br, *Frederick's Watteau Paintings* by Antoine Watteau (1720) 30tc; *Frederick the Great* by Antoine Pesne 31tl, *Frederick Playing the Flute* by Adolf von Menzel 42b, 152cl; STRANDBAR MITTE: 52tc; ANDREAS TAUBER: 101tc; TEEGSCHWENDNER: 85tr; HAUS DER WANNSEE-KONFERENZ: 89cb; WERNER OTTO BILDARCHIV, OBERHAUSEN: 76–7; www.csd-berlin.de: 160tr.

All other images © Dorling Kindersley London. For further information see: www.dkimages.com

Phrase Book

In an Emergency

Where is the telephone?	Wo ist das Telefon?	voh ist duss tel-e-fone?
Help!	Hilfe!	hilf-uh
Please call a doctor	Bitte rufen Sie einen Arzt	bitt-uh roof'n zee ine-en artst
Please call the police	Bitte rufen Sie die Polizei	bitt-uh roof'n zee dee poli-tsy
Please call the fire brigade	Bitte rufen Sie die Feuerwehr	bitt-uh roof'n zee dee foyer-vayr
Stop!	Halt!	hult

Communication Essentials

Yes	Ja	yah
No	Nein	nine
Please	Bitte	bitt-uh
Thank you	Danke	dunk-uh
Excuse me	Verzeihung	fair-tsy-hoong
Hello (good day)	Guten Tag	goot-en tahk
Goodbye	Auf Wiedersehen	owf-veed-er-zay-ern
Good evening	Guten Abend	goot'n ahb'nt
Good night	Gute Nacht	goot-uh nukht
Until tomorrow	Bis morgen	biss morg'n
See you	Tschüss	chooss
What is that?	Was ist das?	voss ist duss
Why?	Warum?	var-room
Where?	Wo?	voh
When?	Wann?	vunn
today	heute	hoyt-uh
tomorrow	morgen	morg'n
month	Monat	mohn-aht
night	Nacht	nukht
afternoon	Nachmittag	nahkh-mit-tahk
morning	Morgen	morg'n
year	Jahr	yar
there	dort	dort
here	hier	hear
week	Woche	vokh-uh
yesterday	gestern	gest'n
evening	Abend	ahb'nt

Useful Phrases

How are you? (informal)	Wie geht's?	vee gayts
Fine, thanks	Danke, es geht mir gut	dunk-uh, es gayt meer goot
Where is/are?	Wo ist/sind…?	voh ist/sind
How far is it to…?	Wie weit ist es…?	vee vite ist ess
Do you speak English?	Sprechen Sie Englisch?	shpresh'n zee eng-glish
I don't understand	Ich verstehe nicht	ish fair-shtay-uh nisht
Could you speak more slowly?	Könnten Sie langsamer sprechen?	kurnt-en zee lung-zam-er shpresh'n

Useful Words

large	gross	grohss
small	klein	kline
hot	heiss	hyce
cold	kalt	kult
good	gut	goot
bad	böse/schlecht	burss-uh/shlesht
open	geöffnet	g'urff-nett
closed	geschlossen	g'shloss'n
left	links	links
right	rechts	reshts
straight ahead	geradeaus	g'rah-der-owss

Making a Telephone Call

I would like to make a phone call	Ich möchte telefonieren	ish mer-shtuh tel-e-fon-eer'n
I'll try again later	Ich versuche noch ein mal später	ish fair-zookh-uh nokh ine-mull shpay-ter
Can I leave a message?	Kann ich eine Nachricht hinterlassen?	kan ish ine-uh nakh-risht hint-er-lahss-en
answer phone	Anrufbeantworter	an-roof-be-ahnt-vort-er
telephone card	Telefonkarte	tel-e-fohn-kart-uh
receiver	Hörer	hur-er
mobile	Handi	han-dee
engaged (busy)	besetzt	b'zetst
wrong number	Falsche Verbindung	falsh-uh fair-bin-doong

Sight-Seeing

library	Bibliothek	bib-leo-tek
entrance ticket	Eintrittskarte	ine-tritz-kart-uh
cemetery	Friedhof	freed-hofe
train station	Bahnhof	barn-hofe
gallery	Galerie	gall-er-ree
information	Auskunft	owss-koonft
church	Kirche	keersh-uh
garden	Garten	gart'n
palace/castle	Palast/Schloss	pallast/shloss
place (square)	Platz	plats
bus stop	Haltestelle	hal-te-shtel-uh
national holiday	Nationalfeiertag	nats-yon-ahl-fire-tahk
theatre	Theater	tay-aht-er
free admission	Eintritt frei	ine-tritt fry

Shopping

Do you have/ Is there…?	Gibt es…?	geept ess
How much does it cost?	Was kostet das?	voss kost't duss?
When do you open/ close?	Wann öffnen Sie? schliessen Sie?	vunn off'n zee shlees'n zee
this	das	duss
expensive	teuer	toy-er
cheap	preiswert	price-vurt
size	Grösse	gruhs-uh
number	Nummer	noom-er
colour	Farbe	farb-uh
brown	braun	brown
black	schwarz	shvarts
red	rot	roht
blue	blau	blau
green	grün	groon
yellow	gelb	gelp

Types of Shop

antique shop	Antiquariat	antik-var-yat
chemist (pharmacy)	Apotheke	appo-tay-kuh
bank	Bank	bunk
market	Markt	markt
travel agency	Reisebüro	rye-zer-boo-roe
department store	Warenhaus	vahr'n-hows
chemist's, drugstore	Drogerie	droog-er-ree
hairdresser	Friseur	freezz-er
newspaper kiosk	Zeitungskiosk	tsytoongs-kee-osk

bookshop	Buchhandlung	**bookh**-hant-loong
bakery	Bäckerei	beck-er-**eye**
post office	Post	posst
shop/store	Geschäft/Laden	gush-**eft/lard**'n
film processing shop	Photogeschäft	**fo**-to-gush-eft
self-service shop	Selbstbedienungsladen	selpst-bed-**ee**-nungs-lard'n
shoe shop	Schuhladen	shoo-lard'n
clothes shop	Kleiderladen, Boutique	klyder-lard'n boo-**teek**-uh
food shop	Lebensmittelgeschäft	**lay**-bens-mittel-gush-eft
glass, porcelain	Glas, Porzellan	**glars, Port**-sellahn

Staying in a Hotel

Do you have any vacancies?	Haben Sie noch Zimmer frei?	harb'n zee nokh **tsimm**-er-fry
with twin beds?	mit zwei Betten?	mitt tsvy bett'n
with a double bed?	mit einem Doppelbett?	mitt ine'm **dopp**'lbet
with a bath?	mit Bad?	mitt **bart**
with a shower?	mit Dusche?	mitt **doosh**-uh
I have a reservation	Ich habe eine Reservierung	ish **harb**-uh ine-uh rèz-er-**veer**-oong
key	Schlüssel	shlooss'l
porter	Pförtner	**pfert**-ner

Eating Out

Do you have a table for…?	Haben Sie einen Tisch für…?	harb'n zee **ine**-uh tish foor
I would like to reserve a table	Ich möchte eine Reservierung machen	ish **mer**-shtuh ine-uh rezer-**veer**-oong makh'n
I'm a vegetarian	Ich bin Vegetarier	ish bin vegg-e-**tah**-ree-er
Waiter!	Herr Ober!	hair **oh**-bare!
The bill (check), please	Die Rechnung, bitte	dee **resh**-noong bitt-uh
breakfast	Frühstück	**froo**-shtock
lunch	Mittagessen	**mitt**-targ-ess'n
dinner	Abendessen	**arb**'nt-ess'n
bottle	Flasche	**flush**-uh
dish of the day	Tagesgericht	**tahg**-es-gur-isht
main dish	Hauptgericht	**howpt**-gur-isht
dessert	Nachtisch	**nahkh**-tish
cup	Tasse	**tass**-uh
wine list	Weinkarte	vine-kart-uh
tankard	Krug	khroog
glass	Glas	**glars**
spoon	Löffel	**lerff**'l
teaspoon	Teelöffel	tay-lerff'l
tip	Trinkgeld	**trink**-gelt
knife	Messer	**mess**-er
starter (appetizer)	Vorspeise	**for**-shpize-uh
the bill	Rechnung	**resh** noong
plate	Teller	**tell**-er
fork	Gabel	**gahb'l**

Menu Decoder

Aa	**arl**	eel
Apfel	**upf**'l	apple
Apfelschorle	**upf**'l-shoorl-uh	apple juice with sparkling mineral water
Apfelsine	**upf**'l-seen-uh	orange
Aprikose	upri-**kawz**-uh	apricot

Artischocke	arti-**shokh**-uh-or-ber-jeen-uh (eggplant)	artichoke
Aubergine		aubergine
Banane	bar-**nam**-uh	banana
Beefsteack	**beef**-stayk	steak
Bier	beer	beer
Bockwurst	**bokh**-voorst	a type of sausage
Bohnensuppe	burn-en-zoop-uh	bean soup
Branntwein	brant-vine	spirits
Bratkartoffeln	brat-kar-toff'ln	fried potatoes
Bratwurst	brat-voorst	fried sausage
Brötchen	bret-tchen	bread roll
Brot	brot	bread
Brühe	bruh-uh	broth
Butter	**boot**-ter	butter
Champignon	**shum**-pin-yong	mushroom
Currywurst	**kha**-ree-voorst	sausage with curry sauce
Dill	**dill**	dill
Ei	**eye**	egg
Eis	**ice**	ice/ ice cream
Ente	**ent**-uh	duck
Erdbeeren	ayrt-**beer**'n	strawberries
Fisch	**fish**	fish
Forelle	for-**ell**-uh	trout
Frikadelle	Frika-dayl-uh	rissole/ hamburger
Gans	ganns	goose
Garnele	**gar**-nayl-uh	prawn/shrimp
gebraten	g'**braat**'n	fried
gegrillt	g'**grilt**	grilled
gekocht	g'**kokht**	boiled
geräuchert	g'**rowk**-ert	smoked
Geflügel	g'**floog**'l	poultry
Gemüse	g'**mooz**-uh	vegetables
Grütze	**grurt**-ser	groats, gruel
Gulasch	**goo**-lush	goulash
Gurke	**goork**-uh	gherkin
Hammelbraten	hamm'l-**braat**'n	roast mutton
Hähnchen	haynsh'n	chicken
Hering	**hair**-ing	herring
Himbeeren	him-beer'n	raspberries
Honig	**hoe**-nikh	honey
Kaffee	kaf-**fay**	coffee
Kalbfleisch	kalp-flysh	veal
Kaninchen	ka-**neensh**'n	rabbit
Karpfen	**karpf**-sei	carp
Kartoffelpüree	kar-toff'l-poor-ay	mashed potatoes
Käse	**kayz**-uh	cheese
Kaviar	**kar**-vee-ar	caviar
Knoblauch	k'**nob**-lowkh	garlic
Knödel	k'**nerd**'l	noodle
Kohl	**koal**	cabbage
Kopfsalat	**kopf**-zal-aat	lettuce
Krebs	**krayps**	crab
Kuchen	**kookh**'n	cake
Lachs	**lahkhs**	salmon
Leber	**lay**-ber	liver
mariniert	mari-neert	marinated
Marmelade	marmer-**lard**-uh	marmalade, jam
Meerrettich	may-re-tish	horseradish
Milch	**milsh**	milk
Mineralwasser	minn-er-**arl**-vuss-er	mineral water
Möhre	**mer**-uh	carrot
Nuss	**nooss**	nut
Öl	**erl**	oil
Olive	o-**leev**-uh	olive

191

Petersilie	payt-er-**zee**-li-uh	parsley
Pfeffer	**pfeff**-er	pepper
Pfirsich	**pfir**-zish	peach
Pflaumen	**pflow**-men	plum
Pommes frites	pomm-**fritt**	chips/ French fries
Quark	kvark	soft cheese
Radieschen	ra-**deesh**'n	radish
Rinderbraten	**rind**-er-brat'n	joint of beef
Rinderroulade	**rind**-er-roo-lard-uh	beef olive
Rindfleisch	**rint**-flysh	beef
Rippchen	**rip**-sh'n	cured pork rib
Rotkohl	roht-koal	red cabbage
Rüben	rhoob'n	turnip
Rührei	**rhoo**-er-eye	scrambled eggs
Saft	**zuft**	juice
Salat	zal-aat	salad
Salz	**zults**	salt
Salzkartoffeln	zults-kar-toff'l	boiled potatoes
Sauerkirschen	zow-er-**keersh**'n	cherries
Sauerkraut	zow-er-krowt	sauerkraut
Sekt	**zekt**	sparkling wine
Senf	**zenf**	mustard
scharf	sharf	spicy
Schaschlik	shash-lik	kebab
Schlagsahne	shlahgg-zarn-uh	whipped cream
Schnittlauch	shnit-lowhkh	chives
Schnitzel	**shnitz**'l	veal or pork cutlet
Schweinefleisch	**shvine**-flysh	pork
Spargel	**sparg**'l	asparagus
Spiegelei	shpeeg'l-eye	fried egg
Spinat	shpin-art	spinach
Tee	**tay**	tea
Tomate	tom-art-uh	tomato
Wassermelone	vuss-er-me-lohn-uh	watermelon
Wein	**vine**	wine
Weintrauben	**vine**-trowb'n	grapes
Wiener Würstchen	**veen**-er voorst-sh'n	frankfurter
Zander	**tsan**-der	pike-perch
Zitrone	tsi-trohn-uh	lemon
Zucker	**tsook**-er	sugar
Zwieback	tsvee-bak	rusk
Zwiebel	**tsveeb**'l	onion

Numbers

0	null	**nool**
1	eins	**eye'ns**
2	zwei	**tsvy**
3	drei	**dry**
4	vier	**feer**
5	fünf	**foonf**
6	sechs	**zex**
7	sieben	**zeeb**'n
8	acht	**uhkht**
9	neun	**noyn**
10	zehn	**tsayn**
11	elf	**elf**
12	zwölf	**tserlf**
13	dreizehn	**dry**-tsayn
14	vierzehn	**feer**-tsayn
15	fünfzehn	**foonf**-tsayn
16	sechzehn	**zex**-tsayn
17	siebzehn	**zeep**-tsayn
18	achtzehn	**uhkht**-tsayn
19	neunzehn	**noyn**-tsayn
20	zwanzig	**tsvunn**-tsig
21	einundzwanzig	**ine**-oont-tsvunn-tsig
30	dreissig	**dry**-sig
40	vierzig	**feer**-sig
50	fünfzig	**foonf**-tsig
60	sechzig	**zex**-tsig
70	siebzig	**zeep**-tsig
80	achtzig	**uhkht**-tsig
90	neunzig	**noyn**-tsig
100	hundert	**hoond't**
1000	tausend	**towz**'nt
1,000,000	eine Million	**ine**-uh **mill**-yon

Time

English	German	Pronunciation
one minute	eine Minute	**ine**-uh min-**oot**-uh
one hour	eine Stunde	**ine**-uh **shtoond**-uh
half an hour	eine halbe Stunde	**ine**-uh hullb-uh **shtoond**-uh
Monday	Montag	**mohn**-targ
Tuesday	Dienstag	**deens**-targ
Wednesday	Mittwoch	**mitt**-vokh
Thursday	Donnerstag	**donn**-ers-targ
Friday	Freitag	**fry**-targ
Saturday	Samstag/ Sonnabend	**zums**-targ zonn-ah-bent
Sunday	Sonntag	**zon**-targ
January	Januar	**yan**-ooar
February	Februar	**fay**-brooar
March	März	**mairts**
April	April	april
May	Mai	my
June	Juni	**yoo**-ni
July	Juli	**yoo**-lee
August	August	ow-**goost**
September	September	zep-**tem**-ber
October	Oktober	ok-toh-ber
November	November	no-**vem**-ber
December	Dezember	day-**tsem**-ber
spring	Frühling	**froo**-ling
summer	Sommer	**zomm**-er
autumn (fall)	Herbst	**hairpst**
winter	Winter	**vint**-er